Spirit's Path

Spirit's Path

A story of three women

Lisi Mayer

authorHOUSE®

AuthorHouse™
1663 Liberty Drive
Bloomington, IN 47403
www.authorhouse.com
Phone: 1-800-839-8640

Published by AuthorHouse   10/27/2012

ISBN: 978-1-4634-4291-0 (sc)
ISBN: 978-1-4634-4289-7 (hc)
ISBN: 978-1-4634-4467-9 (e)

Library of Congress Control Number: 2011913184

Preface

In writing this memoir, I have used the third person in order to present my story from the viewpoint of an observing ego. The use of "I" and "me" can become tiresome for the reader. I have also changed the protagonist's first name to Karla, as it was easier to give myself some distance from my story. Additionally, some living persons have fictitious first names.

I relate major events in this book—events that have shaped my character, emphasizing the importance of family relationships during my life, in a painful background of childhood sexual abuse and rape. The spiritual guidance I have received, and been aware of receiving, is also chronicled. Because I have been a practicing psychiatrist for the greater part of my life, I also tried to focus on the practice of medicine, including alternative medicine such as acupuncture and meditation. I have practiced eclectic psychiatry, combining physical approaches and meditation with psychotherapy, herbs, and medications.

Stressed in this writing is Karla's intuitive nature, which causes her to embark on a journey that is both stressful and fulfilling. Her cognitive self, her rational self, is often in the background.

Elizabeth Reynolds, M.D.
A.K.A Lisi Mayer,
Child and Adolescent Psychiatrist

Chapter 1

*K*arla was eight years old when the direction of her life changed forever. She could pinpoint the exact day: November 29, 1949. A Saturday. She also knew the place: a dairy farm located in a mountain valley in southern Austria.

That day, her mother Johanna was to marry Karla's future stepfather. Karla was waiting for her to return. Her mother, a milkmaid, had left the farm and taken a train for the hour's journey to Spittal, a city to the north. That was where her future husband had moved into a displaced person's camp while he applied for emigration from Austria. Johanna had met Dimitri, a Ukrainian refugee, after World War II ended, at the dairy farm; he had been employed as a horse team driver.

Many former soldiers had been forced into service by Germany when she invaded Ukraine and Russia. When the war ended, these conscripted men knew, from hearsay, that Stalin had ordered all such forced soldiers to be killed should they try to return to their homeland. Despite their innocence, they were seen as traitors. Dimitri had been forced to serve in the German army at the age of seventeen. When the war ended, he found himself as part of the retreating forces in Germany. He fled from the advancing Russians until he reached Austria; the dairy farm quickly employed him, as there was a great shortage of manpower. However, the Russians and Allies occupied Austria; Dimitri did not feel safe remaining there.

The decision to marry meant that Johanna would join Dimitri and live in the camp, and she would go with him to a new country away from Europe when he was relocated. After a civil ceremony, Johanna would return alone to the dairy farm to make her own final arrangements.

The dairy farm was surrounded by pastured fields around the main house. The front of the house faced a lumber yard, which went up to the river. The main building sat up against the steep hill, one that Karla climbed twice a day on her way to and from the school, two miles away in the forest. A very large, imposing barn, typical of the southern Austrian countryside, built of stone and wood, had windows as large as doors on all sides, latticed with bricks for aeration. It sat off to the right of the front entrance of the two-storied farmhouse, an extension of which jutted out on the right and housed the workers. They numbered about fifteen to twenty, many of them refugees with nowhere to go.

Karla's mother had only one room in the worker's quarters, a room in which she slept with her three children. Karla was the youngest; her brother and sister, Franz and Fritzi, often stayed at their father's family farm during the school week and with Johanna on the weekends. Karla usually stayed with Johanna, even though the dairy farm was not a particularly comfortable place. The food was post World-War II rationing, with worms in the soup from decaying ham bones and the like. Karla often refused to eat it, standing in the corner as punishment. Her taste buds were exquisitely sensitive and she loathed the slimy scum in her morning milk; she went to school hungry instead of drinking it. Her mother often became very frustrated with Karla's truculence.

In fact, Karla's happy memories of the time on the dairy farm were few and far between, but they did exist. She enjoyed the magic of words and drawing, and spent many hours reading and decorating her homework assignments with colorful borders. She also loved the outdoors; adventurous and free-spirited, she was known around the farm as a tomboy, completing daring stunts in her outdoor playground. One day, people came running to Johanna to alert her that her daughter was riding a young horse in the pasture. Karla loved horses passionately, and often went up to them where they grazed, stroking them and talking to them. She had a big scar between her big and second toe from a horse stepping on her when she got too close. Another time her penchant for climbing any tree that had low branches ended with a fall onto a barbed-wire fence, resulting in lifelong scars on her right leg. In the spring she picked daisies and buttercups, weaving a garland to grace her long braids. She would lie on the ground and listen to the gurgling of the brook as it trickled from the mountains above; she thought she could understand spirits in its rushing sound. Hearing something more than just the rushing and gurgling water was

Karla's first experience with sensing beyond the ordinary. In that sound she heard essence, an awareness of the energy of the universe.

During her jaunts in the woods she had befriended the beekeeper, an Austrian man about forty-five years old, with a balding head and an imposingly tall figure. He would encourage her to sit on his neck as he strode back to the farm and would reward her with a piece of honeycomb. She relished his kindness and thought of him as a friend, for she had none. Karla did not understand why she did not have any friends among her peers at school, not cognizant of the fact that as a child of divorce and shame she was not sought out and was often ridiculed. She would often share her honeycomb in order to be included in their play. The other children bullied her on her way down the mountain after school—usually a group of boys threatened to beat her up. She ran scared every day, but one day she suddenly turned around and kicked one of the boys in the shin, hard. He followed her to the barn where her mother was milking cows and complained to Johanna that Karla had beaten him up. Johanna ignored his complaints but said nothing to Karla. After that, the boys stopped chasing her.

On that November morning, Karla did not know her mother was going away to be married, only that she would return by early evening. Karla was alone. She first went into the woods and explored, picking up a pinecone here and there, sitting under a canopy of trees pretending it was her house, and generally amusing herself. The forest had a fresh pine smell and the air was crisp and cold and damp, the grayness of the sky promising imminent snow. Karla was enjoying her freedom, thinking herself alone in the woods, when the beekeeper approached her. This time, he picked her up and carried her, not on his neck but in his arms. With long strides he walked up to the workers' rooms, lay her down on his bed, and then pulled down her panties. Without a word he thrust sharply into her; a searing pain shot through Karla's body, her eyes opened wide in surprise and stupefaction, and she cried out. She began to feel numb as she felt a fluid heat in her lower abdomen. She did not have any idea of the passage of time; a veil dropped over her, shielding her from the outside world.

Eventually the beekeeper left her there. She did not know how long she lay on the bed. Sometime later, Karla got up and walked in a trance to the common toilet at the end of the hall. Something was running down her legs. She sat down, but she could not urinate. When she got up, she saw the toilet seat covered in blood, but she had no idea where it came from. She made her way back to her mother's room and slept.

When her mother returned that same evening, Karla did not remember what had happened. Her underwear was bloody and she was in a daze, but Johanna was preoccupied, for she had a hard task at hand, and had very little time to prepare herself to leave. Karla dimly recalled being taken that evening to her aunt Mitzi and uncle Willie's house down the road. Her mother said a brief goodbye, then left her there and disappeared. Karla was too numb to understand why she was to stay with her aunt and uncle, or when her mother would return.

Chapter 2

Aunt Mitzi, her father's sister, and Uncle Willie lived about five miles down the road from the dairy farm. Uncle Willie was a contractor who also ran his own lumber yard. As far as Karla could remember, she had not seen Aunt Mitzi since her father kicked them off the family farm when he returned from the war in early summer 1945. He had served as an Austrian soldier in the German army, and had been a prisoner of war in France.

Unbeknownst to Karla, her mother had made an arrangement with Karla's father. Johanna had wanted to take Karla with her to live at the camp after she remarried, but her father had not given permission. In Austria, the father had the final say; even though Johanna had raised the children so far, she had no rights to them unless he agreed. She could appeal to the courts, but she was fearful of doing so because of the way in which she had been forced to leave Anton, Karla's father. So it was decided: Karla was to remain with Mitzi and Willie; they were going to adopt her.

That night, Karla was put to bed in the master bedroom, since Aunt Mitzi had not had time to prepare a bed for her. She slept beside Aunt Mitzi with Uncle Willie on Aunt Mitzi's other side. Karla had not asked any questions; she responded to all directions given by her mother and aunt as if in a dream. The next morning, her aunt was shocked to see a big bloody area where Karla had slept. She questioned Karla, who told her about the events of the day before. Aunt Mitzi immediately put her in the truck and drove about three miles up the road to a small town where a doctor examined Karla and treated her for a vaginal tear. The bleeding stopped then.

Aunt Mitzi was outraged at what happened to Karla and pressed charges against Rudel, the beekeeper. Karla did not go to court, but was told later by her aunt that witnesses said Karla seduced the older man. The case was dropped; Rudel was not punished. Karla later learned that the beekeper had actually gotten married the same morning that he raped her.

The outcome was certainly not typical of the way the rape of a child would usually be handled by the Austrian courts, but it was reflective of how the community felt about Johanna and her children. They resented her for being divorced, unheard of at the time in that community, and for running off with a foreigner, especially one considered an enemy.

Chapter 3

Karla came out of her fog slowly, realizing day by day that her mother was gone.

"When is my mother coming to get me?" she asked.

"Your mother has remarried and lives in Spittal, far away from here. She is never coming back," Aunt Mitzi replied.

Hot, salty tears ran down Karla's face, but Mitzi ignored her and did not discuss it further. There was no way to reach Johanna except by letter, and Aunt Mitzi was not interested in fostering any communication. She was furious about what happened to Karla and how Johanna had ignored such a grievous injury.

Karla loved animals. She was given a kitten by her aunt. Left alone one afternoon, she began to stroke the kitten, and then she began to throw the kitten repeatedly against the wall. After the third throw, she caught herself, her bitterness rising up in her throat. She realized the kitten was as helpless as she was. She stopped and from then on treated the kitten well.

One day, she was given a white rabbit. She dearly loved coming home from school and holding the rabbit and tending to its needs. As they ate the big midday meal a few days later, she was chewing on some meat and asked what it was.

"Your rabbit," Aunt Mitzi said with a smile on her face.

Karla's eyes widened in disbelief. She ran from the table, huddled in the corner underneath the stairs, and sobbed. No one came to comfort her.

Each day Karla sat at the window seat off the kitchen and cried quietly for her mother. She knew now that Aunt Mitzi was not sympathetic to her tears, so she hid them. She was kept busy at all times with crocheting, knitting and helping out in the kitchen after doing her schoolwork.

She went to a different school now, located in the same community as the doctor's office she had recently visited. There was a market square with a stone bench around a central fountain where she ate her lunch. One day, as she was sitting on that bench, her older brother Franz joined her; he was also attending that school since he lived on his father's family farm. Karla hadn't seen him at school before now because he had attended the school near his father's farm; also, he was two years ahead of her in class. Franz started to look after Karla, protecting her from bullies, and she felt very comforted by his presence.

She did not really understand their situation. Johanna had not explained any changes to her or her brother, who now lived permanently on the family farm. Fritzi, a year older than Franz, now lived in Friesach, the largest town in the area and about ten miles from Aunt Mitzi. Again unbeknownst to Karla, Johanna had arranged for Fritzi to live with the owner of the dairy farm. Somewhat ironically, Johanna had been concerned that Fritzi was approaching preadolescence and she feared her being in the presence of so many men at the dairy farm, worrying that she might be approached and harmed by the sex-starved men.

Karla did remember the day Fritzi sat on the horse-drawn carriage next to Mr. Greiler, and he drove off with her. Apparently their father had no objection to Fritzi's move to Friesach. After that Karla saw Fritzi a couple of times when Aunt Mitzi brought her to the house for a visit. Her memories of time with her sister were faint, but the bond she felt was very strong.

Karla was happy and content when learning in school. Her first-grade teacher, a young lady, was very kind and taught the children well. In second grade she had a man teacher in his thirties who played his violin for the children out in the woods during lunch breaks. From her first exposure to school, Karla loved the environment of learning, which continued the rest of her life.

In Austrian schools at the time, the borders around all written work were to be decorated with colored pencils in whatever designs the children wanted. Karla was enthralled with colors and designs. She drew flowers and fruits, her favorites. She also was fond of free-style drawing. Karla was amazed thirty years later to find that her brother had saved a couple of her drawings.

Karla began attending her new school during the third grade. Here the experience was quite different: the principal, a stern man in his forties, had focused his sternness on Karla. One day, after accusing her of talking, he slapped her hard across the face. She was shocked! She had not been talking out of turn, and physical violence seemed extreme. She feared angering him again.

Sadly, as before in the old school, the boys in the class made fun of her, calling her names and bullying her. Karla did not understand at the time why her peers disrespected her so. Only later did she realize that her parents being divorced and the shameful history in her mother's recent past might have given the community a reason to mistreat her. Because she didn't understand these forces at work, Karla began to protect her fragile self by distancing herself emotionally, not only from her peers but from the adults she should have been able to trust.

As the year with Aunt Mitzi and Uncle Willie progressed, Karla came to appreciate some nicer parts of her existence. She was well fed, Aunt Mitzi being an excellent cook; she had a nice room fixed especially for her, which smelled of fresh pine and had a veranda looking out on the garden and the road beyond; Aunt Mitzi was very social, so there were lots of visitors; Uncle Willie was a very nice man, full of humor and enjoying himself sharing it with everyone; and most of all, Aunt Mitzi was an entrepreneur who loved learning new things and dove into everything with avid interest. When she learned how to drive, she acquainted herself with the engine of the truck, learning how everything functioned, relishing attaining knowledge of new and modern gadgets. Although Karla never recalled being hugged by either adult, she began to feel relaxed and very peaceful at times, especially when her hands were busy with needlework or crocheting.

Karla never forgot her mother and still pined for her secretly. And then, a whole year after she had left, Johanna reappeared. Karla was so happy she thought her aching heart had burst within her chest. Johanna told Aunt Mitzi she was taking Karla to see her mother who lived up the valley. It was summer now, so Karla was out of school. Flowers ran rampant over the hills and fields, fulfilling Karla's nose with the sweet, fragrant smell. They sat amid the flowers on a hill, and she leaned against her mother's chest. Both felt blissful. Karla looked her mother in the eyes and began to beg her, "Please take me with you. I will be good."

Her mother's eyes glistened with tears as she hugged Karla tighter. "Let's go," she said. They headed down the hill to the bus stop. When they stopped at the station near Mitzi's house, however, Karla was surprised to see her aunt board the bus. She and Johanna both felt fear rising in their throats.

"Where are you taking her?" Aunt Mitzi asked, her face tight. "With me. I am taking her with me," was Johanna's firm reply.

"We shall see about that in court." Aunt Mitzi's face settled into a stern expression as she got off the bus again.

Karla and her mother continued on their bus ride, and then took the next train to Spittal. Karla had no baggage, only the dress she was wearing and worn-out shoes. She held on tightly to her mother's hand, an excitement in her chest she could barely contain: at last she was with her mother again.

Johanna lived with her new husband Dimitri in the displaced persons camp. The camp had been quickly erected under the direction of Dag Hammerskjold after World War II ended. Europe was overrun with emigrants, forced or otherwise, from the Balkan countries, Ukraine, and Soviet Russia. The buildings resembled those in trailer parks in the United States: wooden one-story rectangles, where four families each got a bedroom and a kitchen. A common water spout provided water for cooking and communal showers, and outhouses were located near the railroad at the rear of the camp, about a three to four minute walk away. There was electricity, but heating came from wood-burning stoves.

Johanna had wanted to take all three children to the camp, but Karla's father blocked her, and she settled for having just one of her children. Karla, the baby, was the most likely to want to be with her. At age nine, she was just entering fourth grade, which Johanna assured her she could do in Spittal.

Karla's stepfather was gone during the week, working in Magdalensburg at an archeological excavation site. He returned each Saturday and left again on Sunday. Austria at that time was uncovering buried Roman settlements, later opening them up for tourists. Since Dimitri was so rarely there, Karla was able to snuggle with her mother and sleep in her bed most of the time. She felt very secure and loved in that bed with her mother, but that wonderful feeling of contentment was short-lived.

Soon they heard more on Mitzi's court appeal. Part of the process in Catholic Austria, where the father had more rights than the mother, was to have the living quarters inspected by nuns who then reported to the court. Two nuns came to Johanna's unit and recommended that a curtain be placed around Karla's bed, shielding her from the parents' sexual activities. This was done. At that point, Karla's father did give permission for Karla to remain with her mother. Now Karla could relax: she was with her mother for good.

Because Karla had only one dress, Johanna took her to a used clothing store, but could not even afford the used dress found there. So she borrowed a friend's sewing machine and made a dress. Karla did receive a pair of shoes from her father—the first he had ever paid for. They were handsome if ill-fitting, but she had no choice; they were her only shoes.

Johanna worked as a laundress during the week, going to the well-established upper-middle class homes in the city. She spent a whole day in each house, washing the laundry by hand, wringing it manually, and hanging it to dry, then ironing the whole load the next day—even the bed sheets and towels. She was given a good lunch but paid a pittance for her work.

During the rest of the summer, Karla joined her mother at work, as there was no one else to stay with. There she was exposed to the refined living of the city people. The furniture was fine and old, there were Persian rugs on the parquet floors, there was a bathroom in the house, and the food was fresh and nourishing. Karla often visited the *molkerei*, the dairy store, for the lady of the house. The store was sparkling clean, smelling of cheese and butter and fresh milk—a smell Karla remembered always and never experienced anywhere else. She let them fill her metal canisters with fresh whole milk, straight from the dairy farm, with cream and froth at the top. The milk tasted of the flowery meadows in which the herd grazed, a fresh, clean, herbal bouquet.

Karla loved accompanying her mother as they crossed fields ablaze with red poppies. Each time, they stopped to say a prayer at the roadside crucifix in a covered station. She felt all was right with the world then.

Chapter 5

One weekend day a few months after Karla had joined Johanna and Dimitri, her mother went out on an errand while her stepfather stayed home. It was early morning on a Sunday, so she was still in bed. Dimitri came over, spread her legs, and proceeded to put his mouth and tongue all over her private parts. Karla lay still, shocked to the very core. Then came a wonderful rushing feeling that enveloped her body and coursed through every cell—followed by guilt, shame, and embarrassment.

Dimitri committed this crime against Karla knowing she had been raped, fully aware how vulnerable she was. The lovely peace of her new environment was shattered: Karla knew that what Dimitri had done was wrong and that her mother was being wronged as well. He never said anything, but she knew she should not say anything to her mother. Her mother would be very unhappy and maybe even send her away again. Karla had expressed many times her fear of losing her mother again. She was subdued and obedient, her exploratory spirit and self-confidence almost gone. From that day on, Karla faced her mother with a nagging guilt in her chest, an oppressive feeling that never left her but for brief moments.

It was a criminal act not only against Karla's body, but also, and much more, against her spirit and her emotional self. That these acts are criminal apparently meant nothing to Dimitri; he had experienced only criminality his entire life, first in the Soviet Ukraine, then in the German army, and finally in the way he was treated by Austrians who still saw in him the former enemy.

Karla suppressed the memory, but her relationship with her mother changed in subtle ways. Still, Karla loved her mother passionately and saw no faults in her despite the recent event. When she looked at Johanna, sadness blurred her eyes.

Karla's rape, having gotten more negative support than positive (the court trial, the support for Rudel, and her own mother's refusal to acknowledge what had happened), ended up being stored in Karla's memory as a shameful reflection of herself. The only mitigating factor was her aunt's appropriate urgency in getting her medically treated and suing Rudel in court. But even her aunt never discussed the matter with Karla afterwards; it was all buried. But it would rear its ugly head in a deeply disturbing manner throughout Karla's life, affecting all her relationships which were now formed atop a wound not healed. Her ability to love herself, and any feeling of worthiness as a human being, had been compromised.

Karla's ability to draw had changed dramatically; she was no longer able to sit, carefree and lost in her art. She became conscious of every line she drew; the light, the shadow, the colors disappeared. She felt rigid. Her fourth-grade class held a drawing contest, which she entered, but she felt at a loss sitting in front of her paper, colored pencils in hand. Nothing came to her mind; she felt blunted and blocked. In desperation she asked a friend of her mother, a Hungarian refugee who was known to be an artist, to draw a picture. Wordlessly, he sat down and drew a church. Only later, on reflection, did Karla realize the man was telling her not to cheat.

All of a sudden one day, her mother was taken to the hospital, on the brink of death from severe blood loss. Karla only knew that her mother had an emergency delivery of a baby girl, two months premature. It represented yet another big change in Karla's life; while her mother was hospitalized, Karla stayed with a married couple her mother had befriended. The girl was in a state of shock, realizing her mother was in danger of dying. She recalled a classmate whose father had died. The class went to pay their respects at the morgue, a room whose walls were a stark white around the wooden coffin. Karla remembered the grief and mourning, remembered feeling how final the loss seemed for her classmate. She now had fearsome thoughts of her mother lying in a coffin at the morgue.

Her mother survived the blood loss and came back with a small, very frail infant. Karla heard the adults saying the child might not survive. This was how her younger half-sister Olga arrived in the world.

The closeness Karla had so yearned for with her mother was taken up by this needy infant who nursed and cuddled with her mother in a warm bed. Karla had, for the first time, experienced a new addition to her family. She was used to being the only child; she had lost contact with her older brother and sister. This lent caution to her approach to Olga; Karla held herself back from becoming too closely attached, even to a baby.

Chapter 6

*K*arla slowly became aware of her parents' plans for the future. They often spoke of the International Refugee Organization, or IRO, which helped displaced people find a home in other lands. In order to be placed, the family took monthly train trips to Villach, a town about forty-five minutes to the south. There they waited in a large hall with other desperate applicants for their name to be called; if that happened, they would hear about available possibilities, offer their documents for review, and put their names on a list. The wait was tedious, usually lasting all day usually. Karla did what her mother requested of her—small errands, holding the baby—again devoid of emotions, actually apathetic. She felt she had signed on for this when her mother took her; now it was a matter of accepting whatever came her way, as long as her mother was with her.

Just after Karla finished the fourth grade in Spittal, they got the news: they had been accepted by the United States of America and would make a series of moves through different centers over the next several months to get there. Her parents were happy about receiving their first choice. The family was transported to Salzburg, Austria, in the back of an old army truck, to await further processing.

The summer in Salzburg was a break filled with beauty; although they were housed in a camp again, they visited the city and enjoyed its beautiful landscape, a city nestled against the mountains with clear streams running through the center, draining the water from the snowy mountains. The houses, pink and yellow and blue and white, were well preserved and very lovely. Interesting shops lined the streets and the air felt fresh and invigorating. *Schloss Mirabell* (Castle Mirabelle) had a lovely park in which Karla spent some afternoons enjoying the glorious sunshine. This

Austrian glow feels special, enveloping one in a mantle of benevolence and warmth.

That summer, Karla babysat a few times for the friends with whom she had stayed during her mother's hospitalization. Their small infant, Marianne, was ill; Karla had to feed her tea from a bottle. After two weeks she had succumbed to a gastrointestinal virus. Karla again felt a twinge of guilt—since she had watched her recently was she responsible? No one said any such thing, but Karla felt bad.

After the rape, Karla had developed an exaggerated feeling of responsibility. After all, she was made to feel she was the guilty one by what people had said and by how her mother handled it by not speaking with Karla about what had happened to her and not offering support at the time after the rape. So she felt extremely responsible about the baby, fearing it was some of her doing that the child had died.

In mid-September, the family went by night train from Salzburg to the seaport of Bremen, Germany. They would stay there until a ship was available for transport to America. On the night train, her mother was immersed in caring for sickly Olga, who was now about nine months old. Karla perched in a berth alone, listening to the rumbling, shaking, and belching of the steam locomotive as it hurtled toward Bremen. Again, they were housed in a displaced persons' camp, but this time they lived in tall, rectangular "Bauhaus" buildings with numbers printed on their sides. The buildings all looked the same and Karla felt lost among them, feeling lucky to remember numbers and find the right one. She was not enrolled in any school, although she should have been in fifth grade now.

In late October 1951, the family were getting ready for the sea voyage. Dimitri and Johann explained nothing to Karla; she was to obey and be quiet regardless. It didn't really matter, for she was too afraid to ask questions. She was still suffering from anxiety, fearing her mother might decide she should not accompany the family. She rejoiced inwardly the night she heard her parents saying they would board a big ship the following day, the *General Hahn*, a former troop ship.

Chapter 7

On the huge ship, the berths below were all occupied by women and children; men were housed separately. It was fun the first day when the ocean was smooth, and Karla enjoyed a heavenly dinner served in the dining hall. That was her last full meal for about seven days, for she began to feel very seasick; hunger was staved off by her stomach's inability to anchor itself. Now the berths began to smell of vomit and sickness and rancid body odors. Karla escaped by going up on deck to inhale the fresh air there. She looked out on the endless expanse of churning water as the ship rolled into the waves. The ocean was gray, menacing, and pictures of drowning toyed with Karla's fearful mind.

Suddenly one afternoon, the waves were calmer again, the ship stopped rolling, and Karla was able to eat her last dinner on board, particularly enjoying the fruit cocktail.

Up on deck, everyone was pointing and talking. Karla followed their gestures with her eyes and saw the Statue of Liberty in New York Harbor. The ship approached Ellis Island, where the passengers disembarked, lined up, and dusted with some white powder, supposedly for pests they might be harboring on their unwashed bodies. It was November 7, 1951, Olga's first birthday. Karla was ten-and-a-half years old.

That evening, they were taken to a hotel. On the elevator a finely dressed woman smiled at Karla. No one had noticed Karla before. She smiled back, carrying her case down the hall to the room they had been assigned.

A little while later, Karla sat on the bed in the room, trying to pry loose a wobbly molar with her tongue, when there was a knock at the door. A young man came in, telling them, "Pack. You are going to another hotel." It seems the responsible agency had mistakenly booked them into a fairly high-end hotel; they had to transfer to a lower-class lodging. The family packed and, some hours and another cab ride later, they checked into the second hotel. All were so exhausted that they immediately fell into a deep sleep.

Early the next day, they met their hosts. Mr. and Mrs. Hartley were dairy farmers from Westfield, Massachusetts, who came to retrieve them in their large 1940s-era car. The ride fascinated Karla, who watched the scenery pass for hours until they arrived at the farm outside Westfield, off a country road.

Karla and her family spent that night in the attic room of the Hartley's farmhouse. In the morning, Johanna tried to make Mrs. Hartley understand that she needed some cereal for Olga's bottle. Mrs. Hartley tried her best to understand the word *farina* but was not successful, nor did Johanna comprehend Cream of Wheat. Finally, going through the cupboards, Johanna found a box she thought might be farina and it was. Such instances of failing to communicate would become all too common.

That afternoon the family moved to a small, abandoned house across the road. It had a basement and two bedrooms; the kitchen had running water, electricity, and gas. Johanna and Dimitri took the large bedroom/sitting room, while Karla got a small bedroom off to the side. There was an indoor bathroom with a tub and sink and toilet. To the immigrant family, it was heaven.

Compared to the houses in Austria, the little cottage was light and airy, if flimsily constructed of wooden boards. Karla's father's farmhouse in Austria was built of stone, had small windows, and was dark inside. It was sturdily built, her father's family having lived there continuously for three hundred fifty years. The house in Massachusetts looked like it would not last another twenty. The house was surrounded on three sides by woods. Again, Karla felt at home exploring in the woods—it gave her comfort— but she dared not go far; her previous adventuresome nature had disappeared.

The family had not a dollar to their name. Neighbors began to donate things they no longer needed, including a washing machine and wringer, a sewing machine, bedding, and dishes. At one point Karla was given a white rabbit by the Hartleys—just like the one she had been given by

Aunt Mitzi. Karla made her parents promise they would not kill her rabbit and eat it.

The school in the town of Westfield was about twenty-five minutes by bus. Karla received language tutoring during the week in the basement of the school. She picked up the language rapidly, particularly thanks to one family that lived down the road a bit had a daughter, Mary, who was Karla's age. Karla began to pick up English through play more than anything, so Mary's friendship was important. For the first time, Karla really had a friend she could romp and play with.

Unfortunately, social customs were harder to fathom. One day she accidentally bumped a girl during a game on the blacktop. She did not think anything of it, but suddenly everyone stopped, waiting for Karla to say she was sorry. Karla understood what they meant but did not agree it was necessary since the bump was not an intentional act. Finally, she gave in and said, "Exkiss me." Everyone broke into laughter and repeated her version of "Excuse me."

Karla loved living in Massachusetts. That Christmas she was asked to sing *Silent Night* for the church in the community. Karla's voice was high and pure as she sang in German. She was presented a gift, a beautifully-wrapped oblong box. Karla's heart was pounding; she just knew they were giving her a violin, which she had always wanted to play. Alas, the box contained a doll—a gorgeous one, to be sure, but still just a doll. Karla hoped she hid her disappointment as she gushed her thanks. She had very little interest in dolls; she was a tomboy and delighted instead in playing outdoors with her friend Mary. The doll was put aside, but four or five years later, her sister Olga discovered it and quickly made it her favorite toy.

When she couldn't play outside, Karla did enjoy movies and reading. She saw her first Western, which it both thrilled and scared her. She loved the horses and the nature and adventures, but the killing struck a very sad tone in her core; she feared death, especially the separation it entailed. Reading was rich and rewarding in Westfield as her mother befriended a German college teacher who had all the classics in her German book collection. She would loan the books to Karla, who would sit of an afternoon in the warmth of the sun on the couch and relish Goethe and Schiller and other famous authors whose stories stirred her heart and mind.

Chapter 8

One day when Karla was almost eleven, Johanna was still at the farm across the road tending to the dairy herd while Dimitri was at home with the girls. Karla was reading in the living room when her stepfather beckoned her to her room to "show her something." He told her to lie down; then, spreading her legs, he again molested her by performing cunnilingus. Something shattered inside Karla; her idyll was broken as the guilt feelings and shame rose up in her chest and oppressed her even as she had an involuntary orgasm. Again she felt she had to keep a sinful, bad secret inside her, blotting out all the brightness she had experienced, as if a curtain had fallen.

Karla saw Dimitri's behavior as her sole responsibility, a shameful one that must be hidden at all costs. She did not have any thoughts at the time that she was not his only victim. After all, she was the "seductive" bad girl, as they'd said back in Austria . . . but she really had no idea what that meant, either.

Soon, the family was moving again. Karla was not told anything except that they were leaving to take a train to Omaha, Nebraska, to join Marianne's parents. They had assured Karla's parents that there were plenty of jobs out there and they would not have to work as farmhands.

Since it was June, Karla's year in fifth grade had just ended. Her English was very passable. She hated leaving her house and her friends and the Hartleys, who had been so kind. Her parents returned all the items that had been given them and were still useful. They again left, this time with a few dollars in their pockets after paying for the train fare. The Hartleys were loath to see them go as well; her parents had been good, honest workers. The family had only stayed seven months.

Karla had no idea where Omaha was and what was in store. The train trip took two days, it seemed, but she was not sure. When they arrived, Else and Georg Krijan picked them up at the station and took them by taxi to their house in South Omaha, on U Street, just off 36th. There Karla slept on the couch in the living room while her parents and Olga had a bedroom.

That summer of 1952 was a dusty one, the brown powdery silt coming off the plains, covering everything. It was hot in Omaha, and it was not pretty. South Omaha was home to the stockyards where the cattle came in off their grazing grounds, being confined in pens before they were slaughtered. There were three major packing houses, and some smaller ones as well. The sticky, sweet smell of blood hung in the air.

The houses in the neighborhood were ranch style, with basements where the washing was usually done. There was always a front porch where people sat in the evenings to cool off; air-conditioning was not yet a household word. They would all talk to one another, neighbors swapping news and discussing their daily events.

Karla had immersed herself in jungle tales at this time. She would sit with the next-door neighbor, a kindly lady, and relate her imaginary adventures in Africa. The neighbor encouraged her and was amused by the stories. And she discovered comics, depicting good and evil and horrors that reverberated with her.

She was cramped and uncomfortable on the couch; she always had to be on her best behavior while sharing the living space with their benefactors; and she always feared being alone with Dimitri.

School was not any better. She was enrolled at Corrigan School for the sixth grade. Every day other students followed her on her way home from school, running after her and shouting, "DP, DP!" They teased the displaced persons mercilessly. Karla's heart pounded in her chest and she ran, holding her books tightly to her chest, memories of the boys in the Austrian forest returning. She was living the whole nightmare again.

Despite these handicaps, she made two wonderful friends, Genevieve and Louise. Genevieve invited Karla to her birthday party, which was Karla's first. She loved playing pin the tail on the donkey and eating cake and ice cream. Genevieve had a Collie, a wonderful, friendly animal who enjoyed Karla's attentions. She was settling in, enjoying the comics on Sunday and meeting kids in the neighborhood who came calling at the gate, "Karla, Karla, come out and play with us."

Chapter 9

Then it began again; Dimitri came at night to Karla's couch. Her mother had taken a night job, working until 10 P.M. cleaning offices in downtown Omaha. Karla's stepfather had not yet found employment and took odd jobs helping Georg who had work at a contracting firm. He was home in the evenings, and Karla found herself at his mercies.

Trying to avoid him, Karla went every night to await her mother on the bus. She was trying desperately to keep away from the couch until her mother was home. Then one night, the pharmacist on the corner at the bus stop came out and said to her mother, "You should not let your child stand out here in the dark by herself waiting for you." Johanna nodded, and that put an end to it. Karla had to stay home, and her stepfather continued to accost her with his unwelcome attentions.

Six months after coming to live with the Krijans, her mother and father found employment at the Polish Home on 24th Street, even closer to the stockyards. The Polish had two large halls, a central bar and dance floor, and a large kitchen used by people renting the halls to serve food. Next to the bar was a small room where the family of four slept. Olga, now three, slept in a bed with Karla. Unfortunately, this meant Karla now awakened every night to wet sheets, because Olga was a chronic bed-wetter. She also had a spastic gastrocnemius muscle in her left leg due residual damage from the polio virus. To lengthen the muscle, she wore a metal brace on her leg at night, which made sleeping in the same bed with her very uncomfortable.

The foot of Karla's parents' bed faced the door. In the narrow space from the door to the windows were a small dresser and a small table with chairs.

It was November 1952. This time Karla had to go out looking for a nearby school. She found one about six blocks from the Polish Home, but the principal informed her that she needed to attend Hawthorne School in her district. To get there, she had to cross a major street, and walk about two miles to get to the school. Karla registered at Hawthorne and began the sixth grade there in the middle of the year.

Mrs. Haas, her 6th grade teacher, was a woman in her early sixties with glasses, who wore her gray hair pulled back in a bun. She had a kind, encouraging smile, and Karla enjoyed being in her class. In fact, Karla rather liked her new school. Although it was far, attending Hawthorne made Karla feel truly independent; her mother and stepfather actually never went to the school and did not know where it was.

Karla was intrigued by Ghenghis Khan, whom they studied in her world history class. She felt an attraction to all things of the Far East, especially Mongolian facts and stories. At home she avidly watched *Flash Gordon* fighting a Mongolian race in outer space. Karla felt drawn in a mysterious way to the Mongolians in the series, even though they were the enemy. She had been betrayed by heroes in her life, so the underdog always interested her more—and why not? Had that not been her role in her life so far?

Chapter 10

Karla felt that the new world the Polish Home and Hawthorne School opened to her was a haven from her insecurities of the Her stepfather dared not touch her, because there were always too many people around, even though her mother took another nighttime job at an established hamburger place up on 24th Street. Karla felt free at last, and allowed herself more interest in her world. She was enchanted by all the activities that took place at the Polish Home. There were music and dance recitals, all of which she watched from the back of the room. The Polish wedding celebrations that usually occurred on Saturdays were thrilling: there was wonderful Polish sausage which she was allowed to eat, lots of soft drinks, and brilliant, festive dances. The bands played polkas and waltzes; Karla ached to get on the floor and dance. She was good at it, and cajoled her friend Sally (who was usually there with her) to join. The music in Karla's ears catapulted her into another dimension, one of expansion and wholeness and joy. Dancing was a huge part of Austrian culture, and the Polish music was not all that different songs played at Austrian gatherings. Although she had been too young to personally attend those gatherings, Karla had heard the music from a distance and remembered it.

When seventh grade started, Karla began flirting with the boys from her back seat. Her teacher, Ms. Mabel Spraktes, immediately called her to step into the coat room behind the classroom. There she was given a talk about proper classroom behavior and consequences if she did not obey. From then on, Karla kept her eyes on Ms. Spraktes and did her work, but still she never turned in homework and brought home an F the first quarter. Her mother looked at the report card and handed it back to her without a word. That impressed Karla; she expected a reprimand. When her mother said nothing, she took on the responsibility herself; after all, they were *her* grades. Ms. Spraktes observed Karla keenly and appeared to understand the situation much better than Karla herself. She told Karla, "You are not leaving the classroom after school until all your homework is done."

Ms. Spraktes stayed there with Karla, grading papers, and when Karla could show her she had done the homework, the teacher released her. This went on for about a month, after which Ms. Spraktes told Karla to look for a quiet place to study at the Polish Home. Karla found such a place, a room in the back off the corridor that was seldom used during the week. She brought her homework there and began working diligently, surprised to find she felt a sense of accomplishment with her finished work. Her grades now went up to all A's.

Ms. Spraktes took over a general caretaker role for Karla. She noted Karla's mouth full of rotten teeth and arranged with Creighton University Dental School to do gratis work to repair Karla's teeth. Every week for a while, Karla caught the bus after school to go to the dental clinic. There she learned how she must take proper care of her teeth, following their guidelines diligently the rest of her life.

Ms. Spraktes also gently encouraged Karla to take a weekly bath at least. There was only a make-shift shower at the Polish Home, in the basement. Karla had avoided it because of the bugs that lived among the moist boards that served as the place to stand. But she began to shower regularly. Unfortunately, since her young sister Olga still wet the bed every night, Karla apparently smelled of urine anyway.

Karla lived at the Polish Home from the time she was twelve until she was fourteen, a time of a lot of physical change. She was in the seventh grade when her female peers began to get their first menstrual periods. One day, when she was almost thirteen, Karla saw blood in her panties and thought somehow she had damaged herself. She told her mother, who did not explain but gave her some clean sanitary napkins. Karla learned this event was to be repeated monthly, but she still had no idea of its connection to pregnancy and childbirth. She imagined that children came out of the belly button which would open to release them. Sexual education was not part of the curriculum at the time, and her mother did not enlighten her.

Karla was becoming quite a beautiful young teenager. Her hazel eyes fooled many: some thought her eyes were brown, others thought they were blue or green, it depended on what kind of light shone on them. She also had beautiful, thick, naturally wavy auburn hair, but she paid very little mind to it. It hung loosely around her shoulders. Her mother Johanna was bothered by the loose tresses, so she sent Karla to the beauty shop next to the movie theater on 24th Street, just around the corner from the Polish Home. There her hair was thinned and was subjected to the chemicals and heat of the permanent wave. It was really torture for Karla. She was amazed her mother paid for this. After a few more appointments about two months apart, Johanna suggested Karla ask the beauty operator if she could clean her house to pay for the hair styling and cutting. So, she went to work, cleaning the upstairs apartment on a weekly basis. The living quarters of this busy beauty operator were messy and dirty; Karla was not up to the task, not being compulsive enough for her boss. Karla was not disappointed when the woman dismissed her after a month; it had never been her idea to go to the beauty shop nor to clean. Her hair appointments ended then too.

There was another gift for Karla at the Polish Home: her friend Sally. Sally was the daughter of the bartender and was one year older than Karla. The bartender's wife, Rose, often came to keep her husband company as he tended the bar every afternoon and evening until 10 P.M. on weekdays and midnight on Saturdays, and usually Sally came with her. Karla would rush to do her homework so that when Sally came after dinner with her mother, they could spend time playing jacks and pick-up-sticks, or just walk around and talk. They promised each other to stand up at the other's wedding, a promise they both kept, Karla being Sally's bridesmaid when she married at eighteen and Sally being Karla's matron of honor when she married at twenty-five.

Karla had been helping Sally, who attended Catholic school, memorize the catechism. It may have been an influence on Karla, who had not attended church since her first grade communion in Austria. She had been baptized at age five and had her first communion, but felt nothing in her heart that could be called devotion at the time. In fact, she had been irreverent, running from pew to pew at the church as if she were on a playground. But in Spittal she had read much about the teachings of Jesus and began to feel a deep veneration, saying daily prayers when she went to bed. In Westfield, the family attended a Protestant church; because the community was so small, that church had been very socially oriented, running many suppers and special celebrations. Now, at the Polish Home,

Karla began to look for a church to attend. She found one on the other side of the stockyards. Crossing the bridge over the pens, hearing the cattle lowing as they were wedged into their small enclosures, Karla felt empathy for these unfortunate creatures calling out their own misery and their lost freedom.

The Catholic church had a large brick edifice; its solid structure and sureness drew Karla to it. She went alone, as her parents were not churchgoers. Karla was responding to a deep-felt loneliness that had spurred her search. She wondered why was she always alone, why she felt uncared for by her parents.

Chapter 11

When Karla was fourteen, her parents announced in April that they had bought a house and were moving a week later. Karla, for whom these sudden changes in her life with no advance warnings had become commonplace, informed Ms. Spraktes she would be leaving Hawthorne. But to her surprise, her teacher contacted the superintendent of schools and got permission for Karla to remain with her class until graduation in June. Karla then took a bus twice a day to and from school; Ms. Spraktes asked for volunteers in the classroom to take Karla home at lunchtime. Thanks to the support of her teacher and peers, Karla graduated from eighth grade with her class.

Karla was in Ms. Spraktes' class for both seventh and eighth grades, and really grew to admire her. She incorporated many of her teacher's traits: her seriousness about work, her honesty and integrity, and her charity.

The house Karla's parents had bought was on U Street again, this time at 39th and U. It was a one-story wooden frame structure painted white with big windows, a front porch, and a basement. There was an ample backyard which was closed in on one side by a stone wall, and by fences on the other two sides.

The house had a bathroom with a tub, and Karla had no fears about taking baths there; there were no bugs like in the shower at the Polish Home. Karla still shared her bedroom with her sister who was now five years old and still wetting the bed every night. Still, Karla was thrilled with having her own room and new bedroom furniture, a blonde bedroom set. She also had a closet. Karla cherished that room as her own. Her sister only shared it by night and played in a spare bedroom during the day.

For the first time since leaving Massachusetts, she had a space of her own again.

Karla began to notice her own features with some adolescent narcissism. She had a curvaceous body, full breasts and wide hips with very graceful arms and legs. She admired her bow-shaped eyebrows, light brown in color. Her eyes were somewhat hooded and almond shaped. They were mellow eyes, concealing much hurt, radiating hope. She noted her aquiline nose, thinking it was unattractive, wondering how she could diminish its presence. She had a lower lip that protruded. Her skin was very fair, with a slight rosy tinge in her cheeks. Luckily, any acne was limited always to a few spots right between her breasts, never on her face. Her hair shone with a reddish glow that framed her face. If she let it grow long, it would shimmer when she looked at her back in the mirror.

Although Karla noted her individual features with the curiosity of the young adult, she never saw herself as beautiful because she focused on each particular feature, forgetting to take in the whole except when she saw a picture of herself. Then she noted a soft spiritual calmness and grace, a lovely, innocent smile sometimes changing to craftiness with the laugh that crinkled her eyes and made her glow. She still disliked the roundness of her face, but at those moments, she could see her own beauty.

Chapter 12

Karla felt something missing in her life: her older brother and sister were still in Austria and she was very homesick for her country. It was beginning to settle in that she was not going back there. She may never see her brother and sister and father again. America was an ocean away from Austria.

Praying gave her solace; she had learned the Lord's Prayer in Spittal and would recite it as she went to sleep. On her dresser she placed an album open to a large picture of Jesus praying at Gethsemane, asking that the cup be removed if it were God's will. She identified with that, feeling that the sexual abuse and the secrecy in her life was like a bitter cup she had to drink. Her helplessness and fear that the adults were not really there for her became more prominent as she entered adolescence. Since she had begun menstruating, her breasts had fully developed and her hips had widened, and as she began to feel attracted toward boys her age and older, she felt more confused. Were these feelings sinful? Was she tempting her stepfather? These questions were an uncomfortable presence always.

She put up the proverb of St. Theresa of Avila, "Patience attains all it strives for." She needed much patience, for she was helpless.

Karla found a church again; this time it was St. Mary's on 36th and Q Street. She started taking Olga with her, helping the younger girl through her first communion. At St. Mary's, Karla would go up into the choir loft and join in the singing of Mozart's music, which she found hauntingly beautiful. There was no choir practice; people could just come up there and sing, and the organist, a woman, never said a word or asked any questions.

She sought to resolve her inner conflict. How could she reconcile her strong belief in God, in Jesus, with what was going on at home with her stepfather? He had started his abuse again, and Karla hated how she had to deceive her mother and hold this awful evil secret in her heart. She tried talking to the priest once, but he was not a particularly empathetic person. Instead of telling him what was really in her heart, she asked him if there was a devil. He told her there was a devil but was not astute enough to question Karla regarding her situation.

Her stepfather's attentions now took on more urgency. He would get into her bed on the side not touching Olga, who always slept very soundly. Her mother had taken another nighttime job, this time as a cook at a bowling alley from 6 P.M. until 1 A.M. Dimitri would stay in Karla's bed until then, nestling against her, prodding his erect penis against her. It felt so good and so awful. Soon he started entering her, very quietly without moving a lot, pushing his penis ever more deeply. Karla became very quiet. She knew it was so wrong and yet it felt so good. He would pull out to ejaculate into a handkerchief he had with him; he had no condom.

Soon Karla began to fear getting pregnant. Her mother would hate her; moreover, she was too young and did not want a child. Each month she wondered, would she menstruate and be safe? It preyed on her mind day and night. When her period finally arrived, it was so painful that she had to come home from school sometimes and put a hot water bottle on her tummy. Her anxiety distracted her from her schoolwork; she felt exposed and vulnerable.

Karla started to harbor vengeful feelings toward her stepfather. Knives in the kitchen began to look more and more like weapons she could use to defend herself. She had seen the movie *Psycho* and the images of the murder in the shower, the victim being slashed repeatedly, replayed in her mind, holding an eerie attraction for her. She began sleepwalking: her stepfather would discover her trying to open the door to get outside. She became anxious, a free-floating anxiety that never really left.

As she matured, Karla was attracted to boys her own age, enjoying their companionship, but when sexual thoughts entered her mind, she drew back in shame. She avoided dating, having succeeded in making herself pretty invisible by retreating from any interaction that might lead to being asked. She did accept an invitation to a double date from a clerk who worked in the produce department of the Phillips department store, a serious young man with deep blue eyes and a gentle look that allayed her fears. He kissed her at the end of the night, and as his mouth met hers, she felt a thrill all the way to her toes and responded wholeheartedly. He smiled and said, "You are true blue, aren't you?" But then she began to avoid him. He picked up on her reticence and pursued no further.

One night, after her mother had come home and was in bed, Karla approached and awakened her. Her mother asked what was going on, but Karla could not get the words out. She did not really trust her mother; her fears of abandonment surfaced and she panicked. Johanna sent her back to sleep, unaware and unable or unwilling to pick up the signs of her daughter's distress. Karla had trained her mother well; Johanna never expected her daughter to be in need. Passivity and obedience were Karla's ways of relating to her family.

Chapter 13

*O*nce Karla was a teenager, Johanna did not like to see her idle. One day early in the summer she turned fourteen, Karla was reclining in the backyard, reading a book. Her mother came up to her and said, "You have to get a job." A colleague at the hamburger place where Johanna cooked needed a babysitter for her two children, a three-year-old girl and a boy aged six months. Karla was transported back and forth by the husband of the waitress, a burly man who was stationed in the military. Karla noticed the man staring at her legs as she sat next to him in the hot car.

One day, the father of the children came home earlier than usual. She stared in alarm as he lurched to the front door, obviously drunk. She tried to close the door but he was stronger and pushed it open. He dragged her to the bedroom, pushed her on to the bed, and pulled off her shorts, and demanded she perform fellatio. Karla was crying so hard she could hardly understand what he was saying. Finally the man stopped and took her home.

Unsure what to do, Karla told her stepfather about the incident. Oddly enough, he did the right thing, taking her to the police. Karla was sent to the clinic and examined; no semen was found, as she had succeeded in preventing penetration with her tears and pleas. Later Karla realized Dimitri had only done it to protect himself in case she got pregnant, so he would escape detection himself.

Karla had now been raped by three people. From that point on she found it very hard to trust any man, always fearing the worst.

After the incident, Johanna decided that Karla would work at the restaurant as a waitress. Karla liked the work and the uniform she got to wear; she felt very responsible for her customers. But once the summer of her fifteenth year was over, Marlowe's no longer needed her and gave her notice. By now Karla knew deep inside that she was always expected to work as long as she lived at home. She bought all her own clothes and would buy clothes as well for her sister and her parents. She began saving her money at the bank. When she wanted to learn to play the accordion, she bought one out of her own money and paid for her lessons. Her stepfather grudgingly drove her to lessons, but soon he complained about the inconvenience and Karla had to stop the classes.

When she was let go by Marlowe's, she filled out a job application at Philips on 24th and O. Philips was the most fashionable store in that borough. She was hired to help operate the switchboard and to write down the billing statements when customers paid their utility bills at the store. She assisted the switchboard operator, Margaret, and served as her replacement when she got off work at 5:30. Karla worked weekdays after school until 8:30, and all day Saturday. She walked the six blocks from school to the store, stored her books in the women's lounge, and went to work. She loved the work and was very happy she had a real job—it even paid her health insurance, although the wages were meager, typical of the time.

Karla learned to do all kinds of office odd jobs and formed friendships with the other workers. One woman in particular took Karla under her wing. Sue was middle aged, had awful wrinkles for her age from smoking, and coughed constantly. Karla soon began to have a cough of her own, an involuntary soft cough. She noticed that her lungs hurt and she felt very tired a lot. Only a few years later, Sue died of tuberculosis; some years after that, when Karla had her X-ray taken for entrance to medical school, there was a calcified tubercle in her lung. Her own TB test came back positive.

Waiting for the high-school bus at 6:30 A.M. in the cold of winter, the rains of spring, and the winds of the Midwest autumn meant Karla often got sick. She was particularly prone to strep infections. Her mother would call Dr. Rance, their family physician, and he would come to the house, boil the syringe in the kitchen, and administer a shot of penicillin into her hip. She would recover after a few days.

Karla loved high school even though she worked so much she could not do any extracurricular activities. Academics were like entertainment for her, so she was so happy in her classes and took part enthusiastically. She also found time to sing in the choir, having a beautiful soprano voice. Otherwise, she obediently did whatever her parents requested of her. She experienced no teenage rebellion, her fear of abandonment not allowing that.

One day in the spring of her senior year, she was called to see the guidance counselor, a blonde, heavy-set woman whom Karla respected for her directness and businesslike demeanor. She went over Karla's file, saying, "You are at the top of your class; only one peer is your better. I think we could get a very handsome scholarship for you." As she continued looking through the file, she asked, "You are a citizen of this country, right?"

"No, I'm not. We have not gotten our citizenship yet."

"That's really too bad. You need to be an American citizen to be considered for this particular scholarship."

Karla went home and told her parents they must study for the citizenship exam; she offered to coach them. Even so, it was a year before they actually sat for the exam. In 1961, ten years after arriving in the United States, the family became citizens.

Karla unwittingly deprived herself of some good opportunities as high school came to an end. She got a scholarship to the University of Nebraska, but her fears made her too insecure to explore the possibility of moving to Lincoln. Despite her independence, she feared leaving home. She found it impossible to do what was in her own best interests, to advance herself, to assert herself. Instead she attended the University of Omaha, continuing to work at Philips. Without even asking them, Karla knew her parents were not going to support her college expenses; she could live at home and work, and that was the extent of it. She paid all of her college expenses out of her earnings at the store.

Chapter 14

Kalra loved college. The University of Omaha in 1959, her first year there, was still a small institution situated in a very pretty park. Across busy Dodge Street was another park dedicated to veterans; it had a rose garden where Karla went in the spring and summer to view the beautiful reds and pinks and yellows and whites of the petals. There were also flagpoles that rattled musically in the wind, a sound that kept time for her and was reassuring, although she knew not why.

Karla loved math and pursued many courses in the field. One of teachers had told her she should go further in math and into computer science, a thing of the future. She also loved English, and in creative writing found herself writing animal stories similar to Aesop's fables. In political science she found herself intrigued by Hegel's thesis and antithesis and by Freud's studies in religion. Her professor wanted her to go into a graduate program for philosophy and political science. The university also required foreign language study. Monsieur Hazard, a French Canadian, was a small, pudgy man wearing glasses, sporting an encouraging smile always. He spoke only French in his classes and Karla thought she understood what he was saying. She studied the French classic writers and felt at home with this language. Science remained a favorite; she adored the study of nature. She tried an anatomy class as a test to determine whether the study of the human body was of interest, and it was. Every day for Karla was filled with expanding knowledge of her world and its jewels, the accumulation of hard-won information.

While she was in college, her parents badgered her about her future plans for herself, what was she focusing on and what did she want to be. One good trait of her stepfather that stood her in good stead was his insistence that she not limit her aspirations because of her gender. He said women could do everything men could. This was one of the few positive statements in regards to herself she ever heard from this man. However, it was such hypocrisy, as he had made Karla feel that her body was not her own but his, for pleasure. The sexual offender truly suffers no guilt, nor any concept of responsibility, she realized.

At the end of her sophomore year, she woke up one morning knowing with certainty that she would study medicine and become a physician. Karla did not know where the message came from on that morning, but it was so certain and final she never doubted it. It was an unusual choice: she feared blood, hated going to the doctor, and had always been very afraid of needles. But she followed what had been so clear to her and stayed firm in her resolve. That morning, she went to her counselor and signed herself into pre-med. She graduated with a degree in French as she had the most hours in that study. The year was 1963.

Karla had taken another job on graduating from college, having quit her seven year stint at Philips. She signed up for one year with a research lab testing the Papanicolau cervical smear's accuracy in picking up cancer cells. She learned to stain the smears that arrived at the lab from the physicians' offices across the street, and also was taught how to read them under a microscope. Her teachers were two African-Americans, Alice and Nathan. The lab was part of the pathology department at the University of Nebraska Medical School. There was a lot of spare time between staining and reading, and often they were finished for the day by two in the afternoon. She learned to play chess with LeAnn, the other research student. Everyone joined in the chess games, which was so exciting for Karla. She had enough time to take two courses at the University of Omaha during that year, and would take her books upstairs to the medical library and study on some of those afternoons at the lab. Meanwhile she had taken the Medical School Entrance Exam and had given her application to the staff at the dean's office at the medical school, down the hall from the lab.

Strange to say, Karla had no doubt she would be accepted. The secretary came down one day and said she had been tentatively accepted; a few days later, "You've been accepted."

Chapter 15

$\mathcal{K}$arla lived in her family home through her first year of medical school. Her forty-three-year-old mother had given birth two years earlier to a premature boy, born after only six months in the womb. Karla named him because her parents were too nervous about how tiny (two pounds, four ounces) the infant was even to give him a name. Karla named her half-brother Michael Alexander. Only many years later did she realize he was born on St. Michael's Day, September twenty-ninth.

Karla was disappointed that her mother did not stop her night job to take care of her son. It became Karla's job to take over and feed him and prepare him for bed. Dimitri didn't care for the baby, but luckily, he had also stopped taking a sexual interest in Karla some time ago. One day, Johanna said to Karla, "Don't you think you should leave him alone?" She meant the sexual activity. Karla was shocked: her stepfather had actually convinced her mother that Karla was pursuing him sexually! Karla was outraged but said nothing, for now she realized that Johanna would not believe her if she told her the truth. This behavior is actually very typical of the sexual offender, to assign blame to others and not themselves. It hurt Karla deeply, for she felt she had sacrificed so much for her mother and now she was the bad person on top of it.

Many times Karla had thought about registering a complaint to the police. She felt Dimitri should be in prison for his abusive activity, but she was not going to disrupt this fragmented family further. Also, in Karla's mind, her mother's need for Dimitri superseded her own need for justice. The family would collapse without Dimitri's paycheck. In other words, it came down to economic survival of the vulnerable younger family members, Olga and Michael, and Johanna as well.

Karla loved taking care of Michael and also tending to Olga. Each evening she served a meal her mother had prepared, cleaning up and making sure Olga did her homework before putting Michael to bed early. She realized she could stay with the family all her life, tending to them, but she would have no time for herself. Although she loved it, she decided that, despite her fears and trepidations about the world out there, she must move out. She felt enslaved in her family. Her parents never considered her needs, only what she could do for them.

She began looking for a small efficiency apartment, but she knew she would have to pay for her apartment as well. Her family was not going to help her. They were peeved and hurt that she was moving out. She looked at a few places, but they were small and dirty, yet surprisingly expensive. Growing discouraged, Karla suddenly recalled that Mrs. Shores, a widow who ran the household goods department at Philips, had approached her one time a few years before and said, "If you ever need a place to live, come see me." So she looked up Mrs. Shores and reminded her of her promise, telling her she needed a room to rent while attending medical school.

Mrs. Shores looked surprised—possibly she could not remember having made the invitation some years earlier—but said, "Come inside and look at the rooms I have."

There was a nicely decorated bedroom adjacent to a bath she would have to share with Mrs. Shores. There was also a loft room with a toilet but no bathtub or shower. The upstairs loft was quite roomy but dark, while the downstairs room was very bright although small. Karla opted for the downstairs room and moved in one Sunday with one suitcase; she had left most of her stuff at home as space was limited.

Mrs. Shores' house was walking distance from the medical school, but soon, Karla needed a new car. Her 1955 Chevrolet was losing oil a lot and each time she took it in to the garage to be fixed, the mechanic told her, "Get rid of this car." Finally she decided to listen to him.

At the time she was attending a Baptist church with fellow students from the medical school. At church a man was offering his Volkswagen for sale, cherry red and about a year old. Karla sold her car and bought the Volkswagen. She got her first loan at the bank for the balance. It was a great little car and gave her no problems at all.

Karla felt like she was starting life on her own, pulling herself up by her bootstraps. It was all a big effort financially. She was working now at Bishop Clarkson Hospital just across the street from the medical school.

She left school and went to work from 5:30 to 9:30 every night, and afternoons on Saturday, reading pap smears. It paid just enough that she could make her car payments and cover her tuition, books, and rent, with very little left over for food. She ate very sparingly, planning her meals carefully, and actually lost about forty pounds her first year away from home. On Wednesdays she would bring her laundry to her mother's house and her mother would give her five dollars, saying, "Don't tell your dad." Still, her parents never paid Karla a compliment on how she was managing without asking them for help; in fact, they were resentful that she had escaped her responsibilities at home.

Chapter 16

The first year of medical school entailed studying the basic sciences. The most challenging thing for Karla was dissecting the cadaver. She worked with five other people at her station; they met for four hours every afternoon. The corpse had a greasy feel and reeked of formaldehyde which got into their skin and clothing. Names and functions of muscles and organs—everything had to be memorized; the professor would stop by and quiz the students on the name, the attachments and functions of different muscles.

Neal and Karla first met in anatomy class. He was one of the hundred people in her class (there were only eight women). Neal was very attracted to Karla and she to him; the almost electrical connection between them filled the table with tension. Unfortunately, Neal was having difficulty adjusting to the rigors of medical school. His father was a physician and a professor (although not at that university) and demanded Neal study medicine. He had great difficulty remembering the facts and was often not able to answer questions put to him, so Karla jumped in, hoping to save him from embarrassment. When chance permitted, they would step over to the window and talk. He gave her a book to read, *The Prince*, and recommended she listen to *Bolero*.

Karla wanted him to ask her out, but he never did. The most he did was ask her to meet him at their dissection table in her spare time to go over things with him. In the end he flunked anatomy and had to repeat the year. Karla felt sad for him. She loved him and did not care that he was flunking. He was living at the fraternity dorm; gossip had it that those men drank a lot and took recreational drugs. They also got exam papers from previous years for a heads-up on the weekly tests. However,

41

Neal was so introverted that Karla had difficulty imagining him in that raucous setting at the fraternity house. She worried about him and wished he would invite her to give him more support. He did confide in her that he was very chagrined at disappointing his scholarly and successful father. Karla knew enough psychology to realize that deep down Neal was trying to tell his father something, and this was his way of doing it.

One day Sally, a fellow student, told Karla that Neal had bought a convertible. The women knew Karla liked Neal and were trying to tell her they expected Neal to take her out in that car, but it never happened. Eventually she began to feel very lonely and forlorn. She was not dating, whereas the single girls in the class were all dating and going to parties and having fun. She was going to school, working and studying until she could no longer keep her eyes open.

Karla never got a phone call from her parents asking how it was going. As time passed, depression set in: the hard work and grueling hours began to take their toll on her. She felt alone and forgotten. Marilyn, a class member who had taken the loft at Mrs. Shores' house, always studied with one of the other women, but by the time Karla came home from work, they were finished with their studies and Marilyn was turning in.

Karla was very hungry most of the time also. One day she bought a steak and cooked it on the stove at the house. Mrs. Shores smelled it when she got home and told Karla it was strictly forbidden to use the stove except to heat water for tea or coffee. So Karla would buy a loaf of French bread and eat the whole loaf to assuage the hunger pains. She was losing weight so rapidly that Marilyn was concerned she had diabetes, but it was just unintentional calorie restriction.

Marilyn would come downstairs in the evening to take a bath; she had to go through Karla's room to get to the bathroom. She always knocked on the door so Karla was aware she was coming in. One day, she asked, "Do you have a hearing problem, Karla? I have to knock often before you hear me."

"I don't think so," Karla said.

Marilyn shrugged. "Maybe you should get checked out."

Karla went to the clinic next day. The nurse didn't administer a hearing test, but she did find a large nugget of wax in one of her ears.

"There is your culprit," she said, showing it to Karla. "I think your hearing will be fine now."

Not until Karla was practicing psychiatry in Napa did she become acutely aware how difficult it was to hear the patient if they had a soft voice or low tone. She got her hearing checked, this time with a test. The audiologist told her she had a "cookie bite" congenital hearing loss with actually no hearing in the normal range. She could hear high frequencies better than low-frequency sounds. It turned out that there was a family history: her mother had progressive hearing loss and her maternal grandmother was deaf during all the time Karla knew her. She never thought she had a problem, but once she began wearing bilateral hearing aids, she found she was much less stressed and tired from straining to hear.

Chapter 17

*I*n Karla's second year of med school, the exams came one after another, up to six or seven a week, requiring serious study and memory skills. Two bright spots in her grueling life came unexpectedly at the laboratory at Bishop Clarkson Memorial Hospital. First, she enjoyed the daily service at the chapel there in late afternoon, just before she went up to the lab to work. Second, she joined the receptionist at the lab, Lynnae, for a break in the cafeteria. Lynnae was a former beauty queen and enjoyed a life of dating and fun outside of work. She regaled Karla with her romantic escapades, and for a moment Karla imagined herself participating in the parties and happy events Lynnae described.

Lynnae told Karla about her good times with a group of officers form Offutt Air Force Base and the parties they threw. She described one officer who was a riot, very entertaining and charming. Karla did not drink alcohol at all and had not been to a dance since high school; she had nothing to laugh about in her bleak life.

One day, Lynnae suggested to Karla she might enjoy a blind date with one of the officers. He had studied divinity at college, she said. Karla thought, *That seems pretty safe; someone studying divinity could be serious.* She felt could be herself.

The day before, Karla got off work and drove out to the big mall to the west of the city. She went to a dress shop and tried on some dresses for her date. She started with a size sixteen, but it was much too big; finally she ended up with a size ten black dress, simple in design, which fit very well.

The date was set for the twelfth of March, 1966, a Saturday. She felt hopeful and excited all day, but had no idea why. She expected nothing more than a nice evening out from her blind date. But she intuited much more than that, the feeling rising up from her chest one of brightness and hope.

Promptly at six, Mrs. Shores knocked at her door. "Your escort is here," she piped.

Karla followed Mrs. Shores out to the living room. On the couch sat a tall, slender young man, about her age, twenty-four or so. He had blond hair and handsome features with very kind blue eyes. When he stood up, he towered above her at six foot four. His name was Malcolm.

Something passed between them on first sight. Karla felt like her prince had arrived; just like the fairy tales, he had come to rescue her from her impoverished life. She was not conscious of this thought at all, but it was instantaneous knowledge, an intuition on both their parts—for she could see in his pleased look that he felt something as well.

Malcolm drove a white Volkswagen bug. They went to the Officer's Club at Offutt; a band was playing ballroom dance music. As they ate, they talked about their lives. He respected her for going to medical school, he said. He recited his own history, how he had volunteered for the Air Force after Kennedy was assassinated; before that, he had been studying linguistics at the University of Pennsylvania. He had not been doing well, could not keep up the average which his four-year scholarship required, and when Kennedy was shot, he felt a desire to serve his country. He had hoped for so much more from the Air Force: traveling, seeing the world, further developing his language skills and returning to his studies after the service. He had wanted to learn to fly. Instead he was trained as an intelligence officer, relegated to the basement of Offutt Air Force Base where he never saw the light of day for four long years. The Vietnam War was heating up and his job was in photo intelligence.

He asked her to dance. He held her close and both felt this warm feeling that permeated their very souls and a very strong attraction. He kissed her on the dance floor, and she was amazed how thrilling it was.

Chapter 18

From that first date, they were inseparable. They wrote letters every day. Malcolm came to the cafeteria at Bishop Clarkson and waited for Karla to get off work so that they could enjoy a cup of coffee before they parted for the night. Although he was the same age as the men in her class, Malcolm was so mature and intellectual—no boyish pranks or petty behavior. He wrote her poetry, and he could draw her exactly. He was thoughtful and considerate of her, always a gentleman.

The summer after her second year was the last summer she still had free and could work full-time. She got a job preparing the chemical fluids they needed in the laboratory, and in addition she continued reading Pap smears as well.

By the end of May, both Malcolm and Karla knew they never wanted to be apart. He asked her to marry him and they set a date for August sixth, that summer. Then he received news he would be assigned to the CIA training center on the East Coast, and after that he would do a tour in Viet Nam.

"I hate the job I have now and I want nothing to do with the CIA. They told me if I were married, I would not have to go and could continue at Offutt but would have to do extra hours every day," he related to her over a cup of coffee. "I'm also sure I would be killed or maimed if I went to Vietnam. Let's get married in June instead of August, and then I can remain here," he added in a serious voice.

So they set the date: June 25, 1966,.

She did not have much time to prepare. She told her parents, who really said nothing and were not enthusiastic.

She went with her mother to buy her dress, a bargain at $100. Karla was surprised that her parents were going to pay for the dress and a reception after the service at the bowling alley where her mother still worked. Actually, it had a nice hall.

She invited few people, just her medical school female friends, and a few other friends from her past. Sally, her old friend from the Polish Home, was her maid of honor and her only attendant. Malcolm had a friend, a photographer for the pictures, and his roommates were ushers; his younger brother served as best man.

Malcolm suggested the reading from Kahlil Gibran, *Marriage*. Instead of the wedding march, he instructed the organist to play the *Fugue in D* by Bach. Knowing about Karla's abuse by her stepfather, Malcolm deleted the traditional giving away of the bride by her father; instead, Karla came from behind the altar to join Malcolm who walked in from the other side. They were a handsome couple, Karla stunning in her simple wedding dress. Malcolm had chosen a white tuxedo, looking dashing and handsome.

The reception was well attended; Johanna and Dimitri had invited their friends. They enjoyed sumptuous wedding feast prepared at Johanna's place of work.

Again, Malcolm whisked Karla off soon and took her to a friend's house. The friend was on a two-week vacation and gave them the use of his home to give them time to find an apartment.

Malcolm carried her across the threshhold and took her to bed. As they made love, he told her, "We will have children later. Now we have much to finish; you have your studies and I my tour of duty. Both of us will get doctoral degrees, yours soon and mine later." Karla was relieved that they had a definite plan for their future.

They did not have a honeymoon, as Malcolm had to be on duty and Karla needed to work to pay for the next semester. They would take one later, he told her.

Karla ended up cleaning the messy house of their friend, being very appreciative of that space the first two weeks.

Chapter 19

Malcolm went out to search for an apartment to rent and found one off Highway 29, close to the turn-off for Offutt and also close to the medical school. It was a basement apartment but had windows looking out on the house next door. The apartment had a separate entrance from the main house and was simply furnished, with a small kitchen and a bathroom that reminded Karla of the shower stall at the Polish Home.

Malcolm smoked heavily at the time. Karla objected for she knew it was bad for the heart. That led to their first fight; he blew up at her and she in turn took off her wedding ring and threw it across the room and left. She did not know where to go; she was shaking and very scared, wondering, would he leave her over this?

She ended up at her parents' house, fearful of complaining to them lest they say, "You made a mistake in marrying him." So she kept quiet. They sensed she was upset but also said nothing, and soon she left again to return home.

From that day, Malcolm stopped smoking. Karla put her wedding ring back on, relieved that the subject did not come up again.

Malcolm respected Karla's need to study and devote herself fully to her two clinical years; she likewise never commented on his long stays at the base, often coming home around seven when he had left at five that morning. He told her he had to sacrifice for not being shipped off to CIA training and Vietnam. Both put their best energies into their commitments.

Sex was a great pleasure for both of them. Malcolm never asked her to do anything that had been part of her abuse. They were well suited for each other in bed; he was considerate and gentle and she overcame her fear of sex. She also started on the birth control pill, new in the 1960s.

Karla had no expectations of Malcolm other than that he love her and be happy with her. She did not think about the future, too concerned about getting through each day's demands. It was Malcolm who planned and mapped their future.

She began her third year of medical school in the fall of that year, starting with anesthesiology training at the Omaha Veteran's Hospital. There she came face to face with the terrible injuries of servicemen during the Vietnam War. There were sad stories of soldiers coming back injured physically and mentally and their loved ones abandoning them.

One day as she walked up the stairs to her floor, Neal was coming down. They both stopped, she, looking up at him. He asked her, "Did you get married?"

"Yes," was her only reply.

He said nothing more but his eyes showed everything: disbelief, sadness, and hurt.

When her third year came to an end at school, Karla received a surprising offer: a scholarship to do a simultaneous Ph.D. in pharmacology. It would mean maybe one or two extra years of study. Malcolm stepped back, telling her it was strictly her decision. She gave it more thought, and went to talk to the medical school office secretary one day. "What do you think?" she asked.

"Just graduate with your class," said the secretary.

Karla decided to turn down the offer, to the surprise of the Dean. Karla was always open to these chance answers that came from unexpected sources; she always saw them as more than just a person talking—it was destiny.

Malcolm, meanwhile, had definite plans for them upon her graduation and the end of his four-year term with the service, which happened to coincide exactly. But first, he told her one day, they must have a real honeymoon. So in November of her third year of medical school, they drove out to California. Malcolm loved northern California, so they headed for San Francisco.

The weather in Omaha had been cold and icy, but in San Francisco it was warm and pleasant, everything green and leafy and bathed in sunshine. The magnificent rolling hills of California, decorated with the sprawling oak trees native to that area, cradled Karla among them as if they were reaching out to her, wrapping her in an enveloping warmth that was new in her life.

They visited San Francisco briefly and then headed up north to Napa Valley; Malcolm had read about the emerging wine-growing area there. Karla felt attracted to the surroundings, hills of verdant green, the valley (that at the time still was dominated by plum trees) . . . it was paradise in her eyes. They stayed at a motel in Napa, at that time a small town of about 50,000 souls—a very simple, lower middle class kind of a place with no industry to speak of. Many workers from the Mare Island nuclear ship building site, located in Vallejo, had their homes in Napa. Other than that it was mostly the infrastructure support that gave people their jobs.

The biggest employer was Napa State Hospital, a large, spread-out hospital of many buildings spread over almost fifty acres, most of which was open, rocky and hilly land. There were about 6,000 severely mentally ill patients housed at the hospital: chronically ill schizophrenics, the criminally insane, and a large cohort of autistic children; additionally, there was a comprehensive children's and adolescents' center serving those who were too ill for the mental health clinic treatment or private practice of psychiatry.

Malcolm and Karla continued north visiting the wineries already established at that time. They toured Mondavi and Beaulieu. When they came to Heitz, the lady there was very accommodating, asking them about their lives and plans.

Karla told her she was in medical school and interested in psychiatry. The lady suggested, "Why don't you train at Napa State Hospital?" Karla heard that as destiny speaking and kept it in her heart.

Karla definitely saw the Napa area as a place she would choose to live her life. She did not know exactly what it was that endeared the place to her; it had something to do with being small and uncomplicated and rustic. Coming from rural Austria herself, it felt similar . . . it felt like home.

The two years until she graduated and Malcolm finished his stint with the Air Force passed quickly. Johanna invited Malcolm and Karla to come to dinner with the family every Wednesday. She told Karla to bring her laundry, but Karla soon felt better just doing the laundry at the nearby laundromat, reading her medical journals while she waited for the washer or dryer to finish.

Malcolm soon objected to the heavy meals at Karla's parents' house; he much preferred the light, simple meals they ate at home. Johanna had a habit of pushing food; to her it was the duty of a hostess to do so.

Malcolm wrote a play about the interaction of Johanna, Dimitri, Olga and Michael, and Karla, a satire implicating they were all crazy. Reading the play opened Karla's eyes. For the first time she could see the craziness of the enmeshed relationships; she had not picked up on while being a part of it. At the time, Karla was still very concerned about the survival of her family in a complex society. She focused more on what allowed them to stay together than on what should have pulled them apart. Still, she had no doubt that all the craziness in her family influenced her interest in psychiatry, where these aberrations are studied in an educated manner.

For her senior medical school thesis, Karla reviewed the literature on the biological aspects of schizophrenia. The review staff offered to get it published but Karla declined. She was still hiding herself, avoiding attention.

Karla graduated, amazed herself that the day had actually arrived. That day in June, 1968, marked the beginning of her life as an M.D. She was twenty-seven years old.

Chapter 20

*M*alcolm had promised Karla that when she finished medical school, they would fulfill her yearning to visit her family in Austria, especially Franz and Fritzi and her father, Anton.

For two years now, they increased their physical stamina by hiking with backpacks every Sunday in Hancock Park near their apartment. Karla applied to the University of Zurich, Burgholzli, a famous psychiatric clinic, to work as a volunteer resident with Dr. Manfred Bleuler, son of the renowned Dr. Eugen Bleuler who had written extensively about his work with schizophrenic patients. His son carried on that work as director of the inpatient hospital. A doctor from their institute had done a semester working with a psychiatrist, Dr. Muffly, at the Nebraska Psychiatric Institute, and Dr. Muffly gave Karla a referral. She was immediately accepted.

Meanwhile, Malcolm had requested admissions information to pursue German studies in either Austria and Switzerland; the excessive documentation Austria required put him off, but the paperwork to study in Switzerland was relatively simple. He was accepted at the University of Zurich. He also enrolled at the Goethe Institute located in Schaffhausen to restart his German studies before the start of the university term in the fall.

Karla did not fully realize the immensity of Malcolm's plan: they were to stay in Europe a whole year, to study and travel. He had saved up a sum of $2,000, which he felt could last the whole year with careful planning and very simple living. He had also bought a Volkswagen Beetle to be picked up in Hamburg, Germany the following March; it would be shipped back with them when they returned to the United States. They put both their Volkswagens up for sale.

Karla was a very willing partner in Malcolm's scheme, letting him chart their course without any editing, willing to be happily surprised, trusting his judgment completely. But her tendency to live only in the moment, and her relative passivity in regards to planning their lives, made her a rather poor partner for Malcolm, who planned everything with great detail. He had to nudge her along and baby her because she never knew what was coming next. The positive aspect of this was that she was so willing to follow along, enjoying the small things in life, never expecting more than what she got, that she was never disappointed.

Malcolm broke their lease, and they packed their belongings to be shipped by the armed services to Switzerland. They left a few things at Johanna's house, such as the music system and some pots and pans. Everything fit into a steamer trunk and two rucksacks weighing thirty-five pounds each. The rucksacks each contained a sleeping bag, light clothing that could easily be washed and dried overnight, a canteen, and even a small cooking set with cutlery. The cold water available in the cheap pensions they stayed in would suffice for sponge baths.

A week after graduation and Malcolm's honorable discharge, they departed from the Omaha airport on Icelandic Air. Karla was so excited but also on edge for her first time on an airplane. Actually, they spent four hours waiting on the tarmac because there was a lightning storm. The propeller plane was very noisy and uncomfortable. They had a brief stop in Iceland, and then went on to Luxembourg. It was nighttime when they arrived the next day. It was raining in Luxembourg, too.

Getting off the plane, Malcolm told her to shoulder her backpack so they could walk. Karla, not having asked any questions about this plan, felt scared and uncomfortable, but made no comment. It turned out they were spending the night in the woods! Karla said nothing, but she had expected to spend that first night in a comfortable bed—especially because of the rain. Instead they set out along the road with signs pointing the direction to Germany.

There was a forest along the highway that they soon entered. Malcolm spread some plastic on the ground and covered some branches above them to make a shelter. They were both very tired and, although it was uncomfortable, slept surprisingly well.

In the morning it was no longer raining. They gathered their sleeping bags and began to walk. That is when Karla realized they were going to walk to Germany! Both of them hoped someone might stop and shorten their course with a ride, but no one did, and they trudged on. After about twenty-five miles, Karla began to complain; her legs were hurting, she was hot, hungry, and thirsty, and smelled of sweat.

They arrived at Trier, in Germany, around 4 P.M. on that mid-June afternoon in 1968. Karla was now hoping for a bath, but the pension room Malcolm had taken only had a sink with cold running water; more amenities were not in their budget. But the meal and the wonderful white wine from the region soothed Karla. They slept in a bed that night, this time Malcolm being the more uncomfortable because he was too tall for the short bed, so he had to sleep curled up. The uncomfortable beds in Germany and Austria at the time consisted of two single beds pushed together, the two boards in the middle making cuddling uncomfortable.

This was the beginning of their year in Europe and Karla was duly initiated: no baths, uncomfortable beds, and hitchhiking from place to place. But she was happy, even inspired. She loved seeing her birthplace again, and the culture had not altered much from when she left seventeen years earlier. Europe was on the road to recovery from the impoverishing effects of World War II.

They arrived in Zurich at the beginning of July. Now Malcolm informed Karla that finding a place for them would be up to her while he studied in Germany until September. He gave her an approximate monthly figure for the rent and let her know they were on a shoestring. Meanwhile they rented a medium-sized bedroom with kitchen privileges in a house that was shared by some workers from Italy. Their room had only one twin bed and just cold running water in the sink; Malcolm and Karla slept uncomfortably in the cramped space.

Malcolm left the next day for the Goethe Institute just across the border; Karla accompanied him to the train station. Once he left, her anxiety took over. How was she going to find a space for them? Walking by the city rental department, she was struck by signs that said, "No Italians." Karla shared the kitchen with the Italians in her current spot; she conversed in German with them, learning a few Italian words in the process. They were very nice, and she felt comfortable there.

She was now really aware of how little money they had at their disposal. She was afraid to eat much and her meal often consisted of *Wehen*, a fruit tart-type dessert the size of a large pizza. She would carry one home, put it on her dresser, and eat only this for three or four days. Once in a while she made some packaged soup in the kitchen, but for the most part she figured cutting back on food was the most frugal way to save their limited resources.

She began looking for a permanent place for the remainder of their stay in Zurich, a period of about eight months. The first place she looked at appeared to be perfect for their needs. It was a fairly large bedroom and sitting room with a cold-water sink. It was a basement apartment on Rehalpstrasse 71, facing dense woods to the back; she could hear a rushing brook running through the forest. She was told there was a walk through the woods which would end up a short distance from Burgholzli, the hospital, and a tram ran just down the street from the house.

The owner was actually a relative of Dr. Bleuler who was delighted to have Karla and Malcolm, for she liked to speak English. She offered the use of the kitchen on the second floor "once in a while" to cook pasta, and allowed Karla to procure a hot plate which was placed on the terra cotta floor in their room. Karla set about cooking one-pot meals, which she got quite good at. The bedroom had two long twin beds, side by side, with no board at the end, so Malcolm could lie flat with legs outstretched. It was set off from the sitting room by a curtain. The toilet was also on the second floor, and there was also a shower upstairs which had to be shared with the French couple renting the upstairs. The owner had a lovely attic apartment with a bathroom for herself.

Malcolm was very pleased with Karla's choice. On his first weekend home from school, they explored Zurich and lounged in bed on Saturday. Karla was sad when he left again Sunday afternoon by train, but he was able to come home on most weekends. One Saturday they went to a wine tasting; both were barely able to make it home on the tram, they were so drunk and sick—they had swallowed all the samples instead of spitting out the wine! As soon as Karla reached home, she vomited and was sick in bed with a terrific hangover. She learned her lesson from that!

Chapter 21

Karla walked to Burgholzli on the eighth of July to meet Dr. Bleuler. She had set the date of her arrival earlier, so she was expected.

The physicians at Burgholzli met in a large meeting room that had about ten desks in a U shape facing the desk of Dr. Bleuler. Dr. Angst had offered his desk to Karla since he was rarely at the morning rounds; he was most often in the research department. She sat opposite a physician from the Philippines who always had an open chocolate bar on her desk, nibbling during the rounds. The aroma wafting across her desk to Karla was excruciatingly delicious.

Dr. Bleuler himself was an elderly gentleman, probably in his sixties, with white hair, glasses, and a perpetual half-smile on his kind face. He was cordial and welcoming to Karla, who found herself easing back into speaking German. Karla had passed the national and state boards; although these were usually given after internship, at Nebraska they were administered after of the four years of medical school, so she was licensed and that was honored in Switzerland. She was given a patient load and shown the procedures they followed in treatment. The hospital admitted acute and chronic patients who needed inpatient treatment. Part of the work-up was a physical exam, followed by a history and mental functioning evaluation, including diverse psychological tests. The Rohrschach, which had originated at Burgholzli and was named after the psychiatrist who devised it, was one of the core tests.

The hospital building dated back to the turn of the century or earlier. The wooden floors creaked when Karla walked on them. The hallways were tastefully decorated with art, as were the patient rooms; all was very clean and invitingly warm. On the grounds were vegetable gardens and a dairy herd, tended to by the patients, and there was a cafeteria where healthy, appetizing food was served.

The clinic had excellent ancillary staff from the University of Zurich, psychoanalysts and psychologists. In place of payment, Karla was allowed free access to any class in the field offered at the hospital, out in the community, or at the university. She signed up for a few, learning much about psychosomatic medicine from the clinic presentations at the University of Zurich Medical Center outpatient clinic. She took courses in Jungian psychology and in psychoanalytic studies. She went for evening presentations in psychoanalysis. Happy, she felt stimulated and challenged.

Karla soon found herself very appreciated by staff and patients, as she took some of the load off the overworked psychiatrists and was able to give more time to the patients. She developed a psychotherapy relationship with some very ill patients. They improved under her care, and she often found flowers or a box of candy in her locker from appreciative family members and patients.

She continued a habit she had begun at the University of Nebraska clinics: assessing the medications a patient was on carefully, looking for interactions, and checking ongoing necessity for the medication. Hence it happened that in her exuberance she took a bipolar patient off his lithium, resulting in exacerbation of his condition. She realized that she had to be more cautious. Luckily the patient quickly remitted when the lithium was restarted, and Karla only received a mild reprimand.

Soon Karla realized she felt very at home doing psychotherapy. The unconscious/conscious energies that were demonstrated in the patients' symptoms fascinated her, and she delved more into the literature for better understanding. She encouraged patients to express themselves freely and took careful note in her mind about the progression from energy to symptom expression to effects on the lives of these people.

Karla's hours at the clinic were nine to six Monday through Friday and eight until noon on Saturday. She was not on the on-call roster. She enjoyed that, when meetings occurred to discuss admissions or discharges, tea or coffee was served in porcelain saucers and cups. One moment that remained vivid in her mind involved a comment from a staff member who said, "This person became ill when he left Switzerland. One must be crazy to leave this country."

Karla and Malcolm were invited by several of the clinic staff; additionally, Malcolm's German professor from the university developed a friendship with him and also invited them to dine with them. Considering how short their stay in Zurich was, they were surprised that they had an active social calendar.

Life in Switzerland was very predictable, the citizens being law abiding and hard workers. They tolerated strangers among their midst but did not mingle easily. Everything was neat and tidy. Karla became aware of the introverted nature of the Swiss. She herself had become introverted as a child after all her traumas. Sitting in the quiet tram as she traveled around Zurich, she often became dreamy and spaced out.

During the fall of 1968, Malcolm and Karla hitchhiked to Paris, having gotten an invitation from a friend for a free stay at his apartment in the city while he traveled. The French were kind, giving Malcolm and Karla rides in their comfortable Citroens, Karla speaking French but having a hard time understanding what was communicated. Malcolm had a very good ear for language and could understand the spoken French better than Karla, so between the two of them, they got along well, Karla talking and Malcolm translating back to her the responses. They both loved Paris, a bright city with broad avenues and classic scenery, full of history and grandeur. Being gourmands, they loved eating in France, the carefully prepared, delicious food served with a true appreciation for the art of dining. When they returned to Zurich, they were struck by its stodginess compared to France.

One Saturday morning, Karla was startled by loud noises coming from the forest; it sounded like gunfire, and it was. The Swiss Army reservists practiced marksmanship on the weekend, and the shooting range was in the forest. This brought on a morbid state of mind for Karla, this constant reminder of the murderous aspects of mankind, added to by the constant grey skies with very little sunshine. The malaise was compounded by a high dose of birth control pills which were not so refined in those early days, upsetting her hormonal regulation. She became depressed and developed headaches. She also developed chloasma, dark circles surrounding her eyes that were due to to liver disharmony from the pill. She resembled a raccoon.

Malcolm attended one semester at the University of Zurich and in January was applying to graduate schools in the United States to continue his German studies. First he got a letter from the University of Colorado tentatively accepting him, followed by denial two weeks later. They had chosen Colorado as the place for Karla's internship and his continuing school. He was downcast and now added his depression to hers, but after some deep thinking, he applied to the University of Denver, to get his master's at the School of Library Science. He was accepted; Karla, meanwhile, had been matched with St. Joseph Hospital in Denver for her internship, to begin in July 1969.

Now Malcolm's plan was to finish his semester at the end of January and for her to finish up at Burgholzli in March. They would pick up the Volkswagen in Hamburg and travel around Europe for three months.

Chapter 22

*T*hat Christmas of 1968, while on holidays from school, Malcolm and Karla took the train to Vienna. Her brother Franz met them at the station and drove them about forty-five minutes to the south on the freeway, to Wurflach, a village set against the piedmont, called *Die Hohe Wand*, or the high wall. Arriving at his house, they met his wife Poldi and their three little daughters. Susi was five, Heidi three, and Waltraud just eight months old.

Karla had not seen Franz since she was nine and he was eleven. She had never forgotten the day he was taken away on the back of Uncle Victor's motorcycle, Karla waving from the veranda at Aunt Mitzi's house. As the motorcycle receded into the distance down the road, Karla burst into uncontrollable sobs and deep inside her she felt certain she would never see him again. And now, here he was, a very handsome twenty-nine-year-old man with his own family. Their father was also living with Franz and Poldi, working at a nearby factory. Karla embraced him as well. It had been almost twenty years now since they last saw each other.

Franz and Malcolm were able to converse well in German and they hit it off. Wine was served and they sat around to talk about their lives. Poldi was very cordial and made Karla feel right at home. It was snowing and bitterly cold that winter, but inside the house, the *Kachelofen*, a tile oven that radiated heat very effectively, kept them warm. There was a potbellied stove in the living room where Karla and Malcolm were bedded, her father bringing wood and feeding the fire.

After spending time with Franz for a week, Karla and Malcolm took the train to the south of Austria, to Friesach, a medieval market center, where her Fritzi lived now, working in her mother-in-law's shop. Franz accompanied them as he also wanted to reconnect with Fritzi whom he had not seen in some years.

The meeting with Fritzi was quite emotional. All three siblings were just amazed at the adults they had become; the last pictures they had sent each other had been from adolescence. Karla had a photo of Fritzi at around age eighteen or nineteen, a slender girl with blonde hair and almond-shaped blue eyes. Now Fritzi was the mother of a five-year-old boy and had filled out; she looked more beautiful than all her pictures.

As they sat after dinner reminiscing about their past, Fritzi put on some tapes of the Karntner Singers, an a cappella group liked in the region. Soon, Karla and Fritzi had a very hard time keeping themselves from outright bawling. The music plucked the heartstrings of longings neither woman had ever fulfilled, a longing for parents, for a family home, for being loved and cared for.

Karla kept looking for tenderness in Fritzi but did not find it except in the food she made. She gave Malcolm and Karla her bed to sleep in. Horst, her husband, was friendly and humorous, trying to inject a less serious note into this meeting. He was discomfited by his wife's tears.

Then Aunt Mitzi called; she had heard that Karla and Malcolm were there and invited them to come by in the evening for tea. Karla had not seen Aunt Mitzi and Uncle Willie since the incident on the bus when her mother kidnapped her. She felt a tightness in her throat, felt somehow threatened while at the same time ashamed at the way she had left, without a proper goodbye. After all, she had wanted for nothing at Aunt Mitzi's—except empathy concerning her feelings for her mother. Later, Karla's mother had not any nice things to say about Aunt Mitzi and was still scarred by her own experience with that family. Karla, a staunch supporter of her mother, harbored some resentment toward her aunt on Johanna's behalf, so she expected a tense visit.

When they arrived, Mitzi and Willi greeted them joyously. Karla's adoptive parents still looked the same, as if she had left yesterday. Franz was very comfortable with them; in fact, he visited them regularly in the summer. Fritzi, however, had not had any contact with Aunt Mitzi except running into her in town on errands. Karla found herself surrounded by people happy to see her. Her aunt and uncle did not hold it against her for leaving them; they had been sad, as they loved her and missed her. They said they were proud of her accomplishments. Not long after Karla had left them on that fateful day, they adopted two more girls, one a half-sister to Karla from a relationship her father formed later, while the second girl was a cousin.

Karla, Franz, Fritzi, and Malcolm also paid a visit to Johanna's family. Aunt Fini, Johanna's younger sister, lived with her mother in a small, sparsely furnished hillside cottage. Karla's grandmother was in her eighties and very hard of hearing but very pleasant. Johanna had always described her mother as saintly, patiently enduring many hardships including Johanna's temperamental father and caring for eight children.

Karla posed a question to Aunt Fini. Gathering her courage, she asked, "Why did my parents divorce when father returned from the war?" Johanna had always told Karla that Anton and his family at the parental farm were mean to her, considering her unworthy of joining their family. This did not ring true for Karla. She knew her father's family had some very unkind members and that Franz and Fritzi were treated as second-class citizens, made to work on the farm on supposed visits with their dad; but she had never heard her father say an unkind word about her mother. Also, shortly after the divorce, her father often visited them at the dairy farm, urging Johanna to return to him. Karla was thus puzzled. First of all, divorce was practically unknown at the time in that valley, and a woman having to fend for herself with three children without any monetary support from her erstwhile husband was also never heard of. Families were very treasured there; men would not leave their families without support, but her dad had done so.

Aunt Fini, hesitation in her voice, told the three children that Johanna, had befriended a French prisoner of war who was sent to the farm to work during the labor shortage. Karla's father had been drafted even though he was already thirty-two, so only her grandfather Gottfried and the oldest son remained on the farm. Prisoners came to work. Johanna befriended the French prisoner, name unknown, and became pregnant by him and had an abortion. Much of the family found out, and since they already looked down on Johanna, this added fuel to the fire of their resentment toward her. She had overstepped her bounds in a shocking manner.

The matron of the farm, Karla's grandmother Hedwig, was a very kindly woman who treated Johanna well but died of ovarian cancer in 1943. This grandmother had a very benevolent attitude toward Johanna and her children, protecting them. Another kindly person at the time was Aunt Kundel, who was the same age as Johanna, but her voice was drowned out by the other family members. They wrote to Anton about

Johanna and the prisoner, telling him he must divorce her; she could even be imprisoned for her unpatriotic behavior.

Johanna and the three children met Anton after he was released from the French prisoner-of-war camp, in 1945. As he walked up the steep road that led to the farm, his young family met him halfway before he reached the farm. Then and there Anton told Johanna he was divorcing her, that she had shamed him and the whole family and she had to leave. Johanna got down on her knees, folded her hands in prayer, and begged him not to cast her and the children off, but to no avail.

Karla had very few memories of World War II as her family lived in a remote area, far from scenes of actual war activity. She heard stories when she was about six years old of a parachute jumper who had landed in a tree. She saw a tank moving along the road one day, apparently dismantled, but that is all. Unfortunately, Anton had been subjected to inhumane treatment by the French, so carried his own resentment that this had been a French prisoner who had taken advantage of his wife with her consent.

Now Karla understood the reason for the unusual divorce and how they were all cast out. She also realized how brave her mother had been to refuse to return to Anton and his family, and that marrying Dimitri seemed much the better choice for her.

Franz and Fritzi then had a confession of their own: they had always been very jealous of Karla, feeling that her being with her mother meant that her mother preferred her to them. They were not aware of the kidnapping of Karla at her own insistence. Not only that—they had suspected that she might not be their full sister.

Fritzi recounted how their mother had sent her at the age of ten to live with her boss, Mr. Greiler, as a house help and be allowed to attend school there. Before Karla was raped, Johanna had been concerned that the many men working on the Greiler farm might molest or abuse Fritzi. She also recognized Fritzi's intelligence; the teacher at the small mountain school told her that Fritzi needed a more challenging education. Mr. Greiler agreed to send Fritzi to the school run by the nuns in Friesach all the way through high school. Karla recalled watching Fritzi ride away; she had been too young to understand that it was for the sake of opportunity.

Fritzi related pining for Johanna to come one day and take her back. Her dad visited her only once when she was in her teens, asking the Greilers to hand Fritzi over to him. They told him if he paid for all the years she had been with them, he could have her. He declined and she remained.

Johanna did send for her once, when Fritzi was about seventeen, and invited her to come join the family. They talked about her going to college in America. At the time, Johanna had befriended an elderly gentleman, Mr. Block, a reporter for the German newspaper in Omaha. He often visited and relished the Austrian food Johanna doled out to him. He was a great lover of Austria, going there every summer and staying at a pension run by a woman who was also a great cook. Mr. Block heard Johanna's lament over having to leave her children behind. She asked him, as he was about to leave for his usual month abroad in Austria, if he could call on Fritzi in Friesach and ask her to accompany him back to the states. Johanna gave him money for the airfare for Fritzi, but Fritzi never came.

Fritzi related a slightly different story. Mr. Block came to see her, suggesting she travel to Italy with him and then come to the states to rejoin her mother. She was suspicious of Mr. Block's intentions in asking her to go with him to Italy, so she refused to go with him. He returned to Omaha telling Johanna that Fritzi's foster parents left the decision to Fritzi and she declined the invitation to come join her mother.

Franz had his story as well. Before Johanna left for the displaced persons camp in Spittal, she told Anton she wanted to take Franz with her. He refused, furious that she had married Dimitri instead of coming back to him. Both held on to one of Franz's hands and pulled on him. At that time Franz was living on the farm with Anton. He told his siblings how they made him work before and after school, and how their father never stood up to protect him, allowing him to be abused and treated as a servant. He, too, wanted nothing more than to be with his mother. After the heart-wrenching pulling of his hands by his parents, he found himself handed over a year later to Uncle Viktor, Aunt Kundel's husband, who took him to his farm in Lower Austria to work as a farmhand. Franz had to take the cows out to their pastures and spend the day with them in the summertime; in addition he did a lot of manual labor around the vineyard and farm. Kundel, however, was very loving and treated him much better than her relatives had done. He said that was the only things that saved him from despair—her kindness and her love. She did treat him as a son. Much later, after Franz had shown his ability as a man, Uncle Viktor also treated him as a son but never adopted him.

Franz did not hear from his mother until he was sixteen. A package arrived from Johanna: some clothes and a carton of cigarettes. He became a smoker. He recounted with sadness how he would sit and cry out in the cow pastures, wishing for his mother to come get him.

Karla told her siblings the sequence of events of her life for the first time. She also opened up about the extended sexual abuse she suffered. Her siblings were horrified. Karla later wondered if she should not have told them everything, but then she would not be letting them see her life as it had been, and they had been open about theirs.

To understand Johanna, Karla had to put herself in her place. Times had been very hard after World War I in Austria. Johanna's father came back from the Italian front with an injured stomach from eating frozen roots dug out of the ground during winter troop forays in the mountains. Back home, the failing economy and a country floundering after the loss of the emperor made supporting a family difficult. Johanna was born in 1920. Her father worked as a woodcutter for a paper manufacturer in the local community. Again, he was exposed to the environment as he spent all day in the forest, but he was also as very active in local politics. He was a free thinker and knew many wise sayings that he passed on to his eldest daughter.

Johanna had been fourteen when she went to the store in Grades asking the farmers if they needed any help. She had been sent to look for work after finishing the eighth grade; her parents sent her off on her own so they could continue to feed the seven other hungry mouths around their table. Anton's mother was in the store that day and took pity on the young girl. Frau Maier told Karla she could come home with her and serve as a water-bearer to the folks working in the fields.

Johanna developed a respect for the family, especially Frau Maier, an honest and loving woman who had borne twelve children herself. She soon considered the farm up on the hill her home, working from morning until evening bearing water, helping in the kitchen, and tending to the cows. Karla could close her eyes and envision the young girl with a big shoulders and breasts, wavy strawberry-blonde hair, green eyes, and full cheeks with high cheekbones.

Johanna was seventeen when she became pregnant with her first child by Anton. Just before her eighteenth birthday she gave birth to Fritzi, who resembled her father and was their so-called love child Her second child, Franz, was born only a year later. The boy bore no resemblance to Anton. Karla arrived eighteen months later with her father's aquiline nose, almond-shaped eyes, and arching eyebrows.

According to Johanna's sister, a little more forthcoming with the family secret, Johanna was kind to the French prisoner while Anton was off at war; they spent time together, and she fell in love with him. Aunt Fini said that she had aborted the child she'd conceived with him, but some of Anton's siblings doubted Karla's origin anyway. Even Franz and Frieda wondered, and Karla never understood why.

Years later Karla once talked with her mother and asked her about the Frenchman, her mother's short answer was, "I was only kind to him. Nothing more." That answer meant the case was closed, no further questions. As Karla thought about her mother as an innocent young girl, loyal to her family, not fearing work, and ambitious, she pictured her as being open to the world and not prepared for all the deceit in it. Her heart felt a thrill at what a wonderful young woman her mother had been.

Karla also thought about her maternal grandmother, staunchly raising eight children. Grandmother had been patience incarnate, bearing all the hardships of her daily life without complaints. In fact, the only complaint she ever made concerned Karla. One afternoon as Johanna attended to an errand in town, six-year-old Karla swallowed a penny, got into her grandmother's knitting, and proved herself a nuisance. "Don't ever leave her with me again," a shaken-up grandmother told Johanna when she came to retrieve her little daughter.

After that Karla visited her grandparents only when Johanna could stay with her. She remembered the wooden cottage with a second-floor veranda that was large enough to hang the clothes out to dry. After grandmother had scrubbed the kitchen floor, she would put down cardboard mats to keep it clean. The cottage faced a fork in the road, one leading up to the Greilers' farm, and the other to a wealthy manor where Johanna moonlighted when they were short of help. A stream ran on the left side of the road, and the area was surrounded by forests, dairy farms, and lumberyards.

Johanna would join her father on long walks and would discuss her sad fate, having been kicked out of her husband's family home. Her father, an ardent supporter of freedom, did not support the Nazi regime even though two of his sons were conscripted and sent to the Greek and Italian fronts. He abhorred how Johanna's husband's family had cowed under pressure, changing their name from Mayer to Maier so it would have a German spelling, having their sons conscripted as well into the service.

He appeared to despise Karla's father's family, but Karla was too young to pick up why.

Johanna's father did support her marriage to Dimitri even though he was an escaped war prisoner. When Olga was a baby and Johanna last visited her family before emigrating, he lovingly carried the baby as he and Johanna walked ahead of Karla, ignored by her grandfather as the child of that coward.

Karla loved her mother with an unspoken depth that would be sorely tested in the future to come. This love never changed, no matter the circumstances. Energized by this love, Karla observed her mother carefully, trying her best not to cause her any distress or ask for anything that might be beyond her means to give.

Karla remembered her mother as a morose person who she seldom saw smile. She was amazed on visiting her years later to find she was smiling at everyone, saying, "Thank you" and "I love you." Karla had never heard those words growing up. How did her mother become so friendly? She never found out, for those words were meant for others. When Karla visited, her mother invariably reverted to her morose and tearful self, reminding Karla of her deprived childhood and describing the time in Austria with Fritzi and Franz as miserable. Karla knew her mother cried out of love and regret, but it invariably made her sad, for the past could not be changed. Sadly, Johanna never lost her bitterness at how badly they were all treated by Anton's family. Karla saw then that that she was a reminder to her mother of a time best forgotten.

Chapter 23

Karla was thrilled to see the hills and valleys she had loved as a child and to enjoy the Austrian food, beers and wines, and delicious coffee and tea. She loved eating *Semmel* again, an Austrian breakfast shaped like a rotating wheel; it could be easily sliced in half and filled with farm-fresh butter tasting of the herbs in the fields, and preserves from the cellar. She adored the *Waza*, a regional yeast bread filled with rum-soaked raisins and cinnamon. Yes, she was home again.

Malcolm began to see Austria in a different way. His annoyance with the Austrian bureaucracy when he first applied for the German program led him to prefer Switzerland, but now he told Karla he was impressed with the culture and the friendliness of people they met. He said he regretted their stay in Switzerland and thought they could have progressed more in their studies in Austria. He was becoming quite fluent in the language as well.

It was snowing heavily as they went to the train station at the beginning of January, 1969, for the trip back to Zurich and their studies. Both began to feel ill before they reached home; they had picked up a nasty flu that kept them in bed almost a week. It was miserable; there was no one to fetch things, so they had to venture out while ill to get supplies.

Karla was looking forward to March, when they would pick up their car and do their own road trips. The plan was to travel through Austria, Germany, France, Luxembourg, and the Scandinavian countries. When the time came, Karla bade goodbye to the patients and staff at the Burgholzli; she received a letter of thanks from Dr. Bleuler. Her heart felt heavy upon leaving; she had cherished this experience and all it taught her.

Malcolm and Karla hitchhiked part of the way to Hamburg in the cold March rain. They stood out on the shoulder of the Autobahn, getting drenched as the cars spewed water as they sped by. The clouds were dark, saturated with moisture; it would be raining all day. After about two hours with thumbs up begging for mercy, they finally found refuge in the Mercedes of an elderly couple.

What a relief to have their own car again! Karla adored the green 1969 Volkswagen Bug, and despite Malcolm's towering height, it was comfortable for him as well. Now they could travel comfortably, stopping wherever they wanted without worrying about the next mode of transportation. They traveled up into Denmark, Norway, and Sweden, and then back into Germany before heading over to Holland, Belgium, and France. Traveling by car allowed them to see much more. The beds in France were queens or kings, even at the reasonable pensions they chose, and very comfortable, with no board in the middle. Even the sparsest pensions were tastefully furnished, although it often required a long walk down the corridors to find the single toilet, and there was usually just a washstand in the room.

Karla was disappointed at the lack of sunshine in the Scandinavian countries and how somber they appeared, even drab. Denmark was an exception; there they loved the *smorresbrod*, the open faced sandwiches decked with seafood of all kinds. They stayed with a friend Malcolm had made when he biked through the nation as a student; the friend had also married, and the two young couples had a wonderful time together.

Back in Germany Karla and Malcolm relished the food, the wine, the beer, and the coffee. Germany was recovering nicely from the aftermath of the devastating war; their natural inclination to industry made that happen fast. At last, the couple ended up back in Hamburg to ship the car home; it would be awaiting them when they returned in June.

In June of 1969 they arrived home in Omaha and stayed at Karla's parents' house to gather what belongings they could fit into the car for the trip to Denver. They had arranged to stay in the intern quarters at St. Joseph Hospital, which was a relief to Karla—they wouldn't have to struggle to find housing. Also, the intern quarters were connected to the hospital via a walkway so it was easy to get back and forth. In terms of safety, the hospital did not have good location; Karla saw cars stolen off the lot almost daily by teen gangs, the police too far behind to catch them. Another time an intern's wife was raped as she entered the building from the parking lot. Still, St. Joseph Hospital new and beautiful, comprising two round towers with connecting walkways. It had large windows from which one could see the sun rise and set against the backdrop of the Rockies. The staff was kind and helpful, and Karla's intern colleagues were all as happy to be there as she was.

Karla and Malcolm were very busy and content, she with the internship, he with his Master's program at the University of Denver. Their bright and airy apartment boasted a furnished kitchen, living room, bedroom, and bath—the largest place they had lived in so far, and downright luxurious compared to the Zurich living arrangements.

The internship was a wonderful experience medically for Karla, with supportive teachers who served as good role models. Somehow she ended up being on call most of the holidays of that year, as there were many interns begging her to take call for them once they discovered she was not a skier. She obliged them, but Denver General Emergency Room was abuzz with needy cases during holidays. She never had a second to herself, rushing from one patient to another. Malcolm, too, was busy with his master's program and part-time work in the business library. He learned a lot about business that helped them with investments later.

They spent most of their spare time taking drives in the mountains nearby and going for picnics as the weather allowed. Evenings were spent reading; Malcolm gave Karla *The Hobbit* for a Christmas present. He would also fix a delicious ice-cream floats for her (she did not have to worry about her weight anymore, since she was on her feet all day and many nights). She relished those cold, snowy evenings when they felt snug in their recliners.

Internship year was very intense, the hours long, many nights spent awake and on call. Karla found that she had another talent besides psychiatry; she was expert at surgical diagnoses, picking up embolisms of the lung, ovarian cysts, and numerous other conditions in her emergency work. At the end of the internship, the director of the hospital told her that she would be welcome as a surgical resident. However, Karla felt intuitively drawn to psychiatry, some inner longing pulling her in that direction. If she was asked why, she said, "I am amazed at how just talking helps me solve problems with patients. I want to know what is on their minds as well as what is happening physically."

By early spring, Malcolm was close to getting his masters in library science and Karla needed to find a residency program. The University of Colorado residency program was full when she applied at the beginning of the year, but then she remembered the Napa State Hospital training program for psychiatrists that the woman at Heitz Cellars had recommended. Malcolm had no objections to going to Napa, so she applied. Dr. Magno Ortega, director of the program there, encouraged her to visit for an interview and a tour.

Once again, Karla fell in love with the magnificent Napa Valley. The hospital's Spanish stucco buildings were spread over the large campus. There were also bungalows available for some residents who applied and wanted housing on the grounds, and Karla was eager to do so as she did not want to be burdened with house hunting. The program was eclectic; all fields of psychology were studied and applied as was suitable for the patient. At the time there were six thousand patients in residence.

Dr. Ortega himself was a Filippino man in his mid-forties, very attractive, with an engaging smile, piercingt eyes, and easy charm. He was also practical; he'd had experience with the mental health system in England and saw it coming to this country in the near future. In England they had separated medication therapy and psychotherapy, relegating medication to psychiatrists and psychotherapy to therapists of diverse educational backgrounds; whereas in the United States it was still usual for the psychiatrist to do both. Dr. Ortega aimed to train his residents for the future.

He told Karla they would accept her for residency, which would also involve traveling to San Francisco for psychoanalytic psychotherapy study and to the various mental health centers spread throughout northern California. He assigned her a bungalow for one year, after which she and Malcolm would need to find housing elsewhere. Karla was excited, feeling that the beauty of her surroundings and the gentle weather were an additional boon.

In the last week of June, Karla finished her year of internship. She received a very complementary letter from Dr. McDowell, lauding her for her dedication to patient care. Malcolm transferred to dormitory housing so he could finish his term, which ended in September. He accompanied Karla on the drive to Napa, leaving her the car and flying back to Denver himself. Malcolm was looking forward to living in Napa as well and would be busy applying for jobs in the area so he could start working once he arrived.

Chapter 24

Karla was alone in Napa for July and August. She set up residence in the small bungalow, which had three bedrooms, two baths, a large family-living room, a dining room, and a kitchen. She ordered some drapes for the curtains in the living room and the bedroom. There was also a fireplace, a first for Karla, as fireplaces were not usual in the lower-middle-class houses in Omaha when she was growing up.

Karla was very excited to start her program and to meet the other residents. All eight were eclectic thinkers who had chosen the program for that reason. They were friendly and easy to talk to; in addition, they were joined by residents from Langley Porter Psychiatric Institute in San Francisco, doing a six-month rotation working with chronic inpatients. Her mentors also came from the San Francisco once a week to train and advise.

She was surprised that the pay for residents was much better than for interns; she began saving, as she paid minimal rent. She was so excited about giving all of her time to the program that she did not cook for herself in the absence of Malcolm, only buying TV dinners and ready-made foods. She lost weight, which pleased her because she was again battling weight gain.

She was delighted to find a productive peach tree in the backyard, the peaches were luscious that year and she relished their sweet taste and smell, not like supermarket peaches that have no aroma. There was also a stone grill in the backyard and she invited her fellow residents to a hamburger cookout. It was a wonderful summer, that one of 1970.

She most enjoyed her walks back and forth to the hospital. There was a trail with giant eucalyptus trees on either side, the pungent odor penetrating her nostrils; the benevolent blue sky lifted her spirits. To Karla, this was paradise.

Malcolm arrived in mid-September after receiving his master's degree in Denver. He quickly found a job with the Vallejo Public Library as one of the reference librarians. It did not pay well. Vallejo, twenty-five miles to the south of Napa, was dominated by the naval shipyards building nuclear subs. There was a sizeable African-American population which Malcolm enthusiastically embraced in his aspiration to open up knowledge and possibilities to this underserved group.

On the weekends they explored the valley and its surroundings. There were luxurious Saturday and Sunday mornings in bed with the San Francisco Chronicle and cups of Peet's coffee. They continued enlarging their knowledge of Napa Valley wines with wine tasting, since they both enjoyed classical music, they started attending the San Francisco Opera and the symphony.

In October Malcolm received a call from his paternal uncle, Don, who had moved from Connecticut to Walnut Creek that year, inviting them to dinner at his newly built home. The fall was gentle and beautiful; the leaves were turning and the sun was at a slant. Karla found the drive to Walnut Creek pleasant and relaxing. Don introduced Malcolm and Karla to Yumiko, his Japanese wife, and their three children. All were happy to have family close by; Don and Yumiko invited Malcolm and Karla back for Thanksgiving dinner.

A few days before Thanksgiving, Karla began to feel queasy and nauseated, especially near food. She figured she had a virus, and Malcolm called to cancel dinner with Don. But the virus didn't go away; it got worse, and soon Karla was vomiting after eating. At the same time, she felt ravenously hungry in between meals. Soon she realized she was pregnant. She had gone off the birth control pill because of increasing migraines, switching to the rhythm method of birth control. The pregnancy was unexpected and the timing wasn't wonderful, but Malcolm was very happy and gave her a dozen roses.

Secretly, Karla was scared. The fears she always had about pregnancy during the years of her abuse came out of the depths of her memory. Malcolm was taking it all in stride while she was almost in shock. Even the safety of her relationship with Malcolm, as much as she trusted him and loved him, at first offered little respite from unknown fears. It was as if Karla had never ever considered that she might get pregnant and have children. As a young girl, she heard women in post-war Austria say, "How awful!" on finding out they were pregnant. Having a child after the war brought fears of hunger and want. Karla had never heard someone say they were happy when finding out they were pregnant. And now here she was, pregnant herself.

Karla began to feel the effects of the early months of her pregnancy when at the office counseling patients; she felt weak after a session and retched into the sink in her office. She had a new awareness that counseling took energy; she had never felt drained doing her work before now. Her patients were really happy for her and often told her so. That is when she actually began to relax and recognize her pregnancy as a positive development in her life.

After the first three months, she no longer felt queasy, and her fatigue lessened. She felt the first movement around the fifth month and began to have maternal feelings for the growing child within her. By the time she was in her eighth month, she was dreaming of playing with her baby. She bought pretty baby clothes, pink and blue. Sonograms were not yet done in 1971 so she wasn't sure if it was a boy or girl, but she thought it was a girl.

Her labor pains began early in the morning, waking her up. Malcolm took her to Vallejo, where Kaiser had their hospital. The pains were very bearable and at 11:22 on July 22, 1971, Thais entered the world, without a complaint. She was lovely, weighing in at seven pounds, fifteen ounces, and made eye contact from the start. There was a reddish tint to the skin between her eyes and another red spot at the base of the spine that later disappeared. Her eyes were a beautiful blue. She was a joy to her parents from the start, sleeping and eating well.

Karla was home on six weeks of maternity leave. As she held Thais in her arms in the rocking chair, she felt sad and tearful, not knowing why. This child was her greatest gift. Maternal feelings overpowered every ambition she had for herself; her happiness now was being with her daughter. However, Karla felt she was in crisis; she had just finished her first year of residency. When she returned to work, who was going to care for the child? It seemed so cold to be looking for a complete stranger to take care of a vulnerable baby. She could not quit the residency, for Malcolm's income was not enough. Also they had to find a place to live, as they had been in the bungalow a little over the allowed one year.

Karla was so attached to this little house in which her daughter was conceived and brought home to. She asked Malcolm to find them a place; she felt emotionally too drained with the concerns about babysitters to be involved. Malcolm located a house out in the western suburbs of Napa, off Trower Street. It was very similar in size to the bungalow and was fairly new, maybe five years old, and clean. Karla put the baby's crib next to her bed so she could always be close at night. Also she wanted Thais always to see them on awakening, to feel secure and loved. The joy this little girl brought Karla and Malcolm was something they relished deeply and daily.

That joy was matched by the pain they both felt handing Thais to a babysitter while they worked. The first sitter Karla found, Joyce, was a woman in her mid-thirties who had three daughters of her own, from kindergarten to preteen. Karla took the baby to Joyce's house in the morning; Thais would smile at her mother in her car seat. Karla came every noon to breastfeed her daughter, which was fine with Joyce. Unfortunately, Thais ate well when Joyce fed her, but was not so interested when Karla fed her. There seemed to be many tricks to making eating fun for a baby.

One day Joyce told Karla that she had a doctor's appointment that afternoon and that her husband would be home to watch Thais until Karla picked her up. Karla had never met the husband and was surprised at how distant he seemed. She picked Thais up from her crib, she felt oddly light; somehow Karla had a feeling something went wrong, but on inspection she could not find anything. Thais did not seem as happy as she always was to be greeted by her mother that day; maybe she missed Joyce and did not like a strange face.

Karla did not discuss anything with Joyce as it was a solitary incident, but two weeks after that, Joyce called her on the phone, saying she needed surgery and prolonged convalescence and would no longer be able to babysit. Karla was shocked. Joyce also advised her, "In your ad, be sure you ask for a loving person."

Karla had learned how important it was for the child to be happy with the sitter. She had some pangs of jealousy on seeing how much Thais enjoyed Joyce, but on reflection, Karla realized that the child's happiness was much more important than her own feeling of importance. So Karla did advertise for a loving person and she asked that the person come to the house to babysit; she no longer wanted unknown persons to be near her infant daughter when she was not aware of it. Anna, a Columbian woman in her late sixties, was very appreciative of the opportunity to work and have someone pay her Social Security. Her daughter would bring her in the morning and Karla would take Anna home in the evening.

Anna was very loving and Thais called her "Ya-Ya." They were a happy pair. In addition to babysitting, Anna did the laundry and made healthy food from scratch for Thais, giving her carrot juice to drink and other nutritious, tasty snacks.

Anna reported one day to Karla that Thais loved picking up all the smooth rocks when she took her for walks outside, and would scream and cry when Anna tried to take them away from her before entering the house. This interest in smooth rocks continued all of her life; when they made trips to the ocean on their vacations, even when she was an adolescent, she would collect the smooth rocks.

Thais had begun talking early; she had said "elephant" at about seven or eight months and had voiced several other words then too. She liked to say "Mama" and "Dada" the most. She walked at ten months and was always interested in studying the alphabet in the books she played with. She was very good-natured and loving.

When she turned one, Thais got her own room with Scandinavian furniture. Malcolm's mother donated a maple rocking chair in which Karla and Malcolm took turns rocking with Thais to read her stories.

Chapter 25

Thais had turned two and there were problems surfacing with Anna. Her young adult daughter was very dependent still and would come to the house to discuss her problems, wanting to avoid her older sister with whom Anna lived. It looked like she was hitting her mother up for money. Then Anna would be upset over issues her daughter could not resolve; she began to be sad and distracted. It was becoming unsafe to leave Thais in her care, as Thais was very mobile and Anna was overweight and not so mobile; she had the usual arthritis and weak limbs so common with aging.

Malcolm and Karla again put an ad in the paper for a loving person to babysit in their home, this time asking that the sitter have his or her own transportation. Anna was distraught at losing her job because it was apparent she was giving the younger daughter money she earned. It was a difficult step for Karla and Malcolm, but they gave her an extra month's pay. Also, since they had been paying her Social Security, she could apply for that to have an income.

The parting was very sad for the little family and Anna. Thais would keep asking for Ya-Ya for some months after Anna left. In Karla's heart she was always grateful to Anna for her service.

Malcolm and Karla hired Mabel, another woman in her sixties. She had a strict appearance that belied how warm and tender she was. Malcolm instructed her to teach Thais American customs. The little girl learned manners and appropriate behavior. Mabel helped get her through the terrible twos with less vexation than she had exhibited with Anna. Quickly she learned to ask for permission and to obey.

When Thais turned three, Mabel insisted that she attend preschool in order to learn to get along with kids her own age. She was now three years old. Mabel also told Karla, "Stop carrying her around all the time. She is no longer a baby." Indeed, Karla was carrying her toddler whenever she could. Thais had entered a stage of exploration that included forays, though short, away from her mother and back to her. Was she encouraging or discouraging this by carrying her so much?

Karla listened to Mabel and off Thais went to the local preschool. At first she was put into Montessori and drop off was not difficult, but pick-up was: she screamed and did not want to leave whatever she was doing. Karla and Malcolm were confused; was the screaming a sign of unhappiness? They changed her to a regular preschool not far from home, and she went there five mornings a week. One day, she came home with a bite mark on her left cheek and after that she cried when she was dropped off. Karla and Malcolm both spoke to the teachers to make sure this event did not recur, and it did not.

Thais made friends at the school, in particular one boy she nicknamed Freddie the Frog because he liked to imitate the Sesame Street characters. Then, one day, she was told Freddie was killed. He was on his tricycle and a person backing out a car from their driveway did not see him behind the car. It was Thais' first experience of death. She was sad and Karla went with her to the funeral so she could say good-bye. Karla always wondered later if it was the right thing to do, to let Thais experience what death is.

When Thais was seven or eight, she made up stories and drew pictures to accompany them. Karla was struck by the stories: her little girl always wrote about death. She was quite a good artist for her age and drew haunting pictures of a little girl who died.

Chapter 26

*K*arla graduated from the general psychiatry residency program in 1973 and decided to extend her training another year as a fellow to become a child psychiatrist, which she did, graduating in 1974. Malcolm encouraged her to work only part-time, twenty hours, so she could enjoy Thais more, and she agreed. She began work as one of the physicians of a forty-bed autistic children's unit, sharing the work with another female physician, Elsa, who was in her mid-sixties. They got along well; the staff were kind, supportive, and knowledgeable people. Karla enjoyed working with the team, volunteering to help them with particularly difficult problems.

That summer Karla again realized she was pregnant, but just as she realized it, she had a miscarriage. She and Malcolm were sad; luckily, just a few months later, she became pregnant again, the child was due in early June, 1975. They were happy as her pregnancy progressed well. Karla was much more at ease with the changes in her body and actually enjoyed all the stages, especially feeling the child move in her belly. Again, there were no sonograms, so they did not know if they would have another girl or a boy.

Karla had been two-and-a-half weeks late delivering Thais and her second pregnancy again passed the expected date of June 5; it was June 29 and still no labor pains. At Kaiser she was told if pains did not start by the 30th, she would be induced. Then, on June 30th in the early morning hours, she began to have labor pains and they went to the hospital. This time the pains were very severe and Karla screamed in agony. She suffered through the pains holding on to Malcolm's hand; he told her later she almost broke his fingers, she was clenching so.

Talbot arrived at 7:45 A.M. on June 30th, weighing in at nine pounds, thirteen ounces, and also quite long. He was beautiful. Karla was very exhausted from the birthing process. She had also had a severe tear and needed to be sutured. She was given Valium after the delivery and conked out She felt she needed a lot of rest, but she was discharged two days later. When she came home, Thais met them at the door; she had a blanket in her hands which she offered to Talbot.

Unfortunately, Karla was not good about speaking up for herself when Mabel said she would leave them alone to bond and would come once the six weeks of her leave were up. Karla was overwhelmed: her exhaustion was so severe she could not eat; she routinely just went to bed. Now Thais was alone in the house, her father at work, her mother in bed, and a new sibling in a crib. She was just about to turn four.

Karla was still in bed when she became aware it was very quiet in the house, Talbot was sleeping, but she heard no movement and knew something was not right. She got up and went looking for Thais. She wasn't in the house! Desperate and scared, Karla pulled on a robe and went outside, calling Thais. Thais appeared, running around the corner, thankfully all intact. From then on, Karla did not stay in bed once Thais awakened.

Her breast milk was not nutritious at first because she ate so poorly and was also dehydrated. Talbot began screaming from hunger and wanted to nurse all the time. He lost some weight. Desperate, Karla started feeding him rice cereal and he quieted. She began eating better and regaining her strength and he prospered.

At the end of her maternity leave, Karla felt things had settled. Mabel was coming back to take care of Talbot. Thais would spend the whole day in preschool. Karla returned to work.

The little family had a happy life. Evenings were spent watching sitcoms and reading. During the trip back to Europe, longing for the rural surroundings of her Austrian home had reawakened in Karla, but she assuaged her nostalgia for the simplicity of country life by watching *The Waltons*. The rusticity of their lives on a farm in Virginia and the strong bonds between the siblings attracted Karla; she could fantasize about the good parts of her life.

About three weeks after she'd returned to work from her leave, Mabel announced her resignation, telling Karla that Talbot cried a lot every day after she left for work. "He only wants you," she said.

The family, especially Thais, very much missed Mabel. In later years, Karla always thanked all the babysitters and remembered them in her prayers. When Mabel's husband was dying of colon cancer at home, she asked Karla to come with the children and say good-bye.

A woman named Angie got the job next. Angie was in her early fifties and appeared very friendly and reliable. But it was no use; Talbot made a dour face every time she approached him. Malcolm and Karla were very concerned that they were going to have to find someone else, even though they actually had nothing to complain about Angie except Talbot's obvious dislike of her.

The next ad brought Allena, a woman in her late fifties, heavy-set, with a very pleasant face and big brown eyes. Her hair was white and cut short around her head. Talbot appeared to like Allena; Karla was relieved. A little younger than Mabel, Allena had a lot of energy and often played with the kids. One day horseplay with Thais resulted in her landing on her shoulder and breaking her clavicle. Karla was shocked, but established there had been no foul play, only too much exuberance.

Karla had meanwhile started a private practice at the urging of a colleague, Marty, who was renting space in a small Victorian across from the Napa library. He was renting the office to the back, which faced a wooded area; Karla could take the front space facing the library.

Her mentor in her residency program had always encouraged Karla to do her own private practice. After discussion with Malcolm, she agreed to the rental and Marty referred a couple of his overflow patients, Medicare-insured, to her. She began a half-time afternoon practice five days a week. Her schedule filled in no time, four patients every afternoon. The pay was minimal, because Medicare paid the lowest fees and required lots of paperwork. Karla herself filed the insurance forms for her patients. She enjoyed the challenges though, and about a year later, she quit her half-time job at the hospital to work from eight to five daily in the private practice.

She treated children, adolescents, adults, elderly, and families. She did play therapy with the children and games with the adolescents. One adolescent in particular, Theresa, provided the greatest challenge. She was fifteen at the time Karla started treating her, and appeared to suffer addiction to drugs; on top of that, she had a fragmented personality with multiple personality characteristics. This young girl had been sexually abused by her father and sadistically punished by her cold mother. Adding to her fragile state was the death of a sibling in a swimming pool while she was present.

Theresa was living in a foster home when she started seeing Karla, whom she came to weekly. Karla never knew who or what she would be working with; at times the girl was very tearful, at times filled with hateful anger. She soon showed a very disturbing symptom of not wanting to leave the office at the end of a session. She would refuse to get up from the couch and only with coaxing finally leave, giving Karla no time to prepare for the next person waiting in the next room. This developed into a regular pattern; if Theresa got upset during the session, she was not going to leave. Karla, alone with her in the office, could not rely on a secretary to help her cajole the teenager out of her office. Karla became anxious every time the sessions were coming to an end, wondering if her patient would leave without a stand-off.

At the same time, the fragmented behavior proved intolerable for Theresa's foster parents. She moved from foster home to foster home. Then one day, Theresa announced that her new foster home was just up the street from where Karla lived. To Karla's shock and dismay, she found Theresa playing with the kids on the street, Thais and Talbot among them. This frightened Karla, for she knew Theresa was having a fantasy of belonging to Karla's family and was insinuating herself right into Karla's home and children. Such actions would interfere very much with her the treatment. Karla became very uneasy. She did not forbid Theresa playing with her children, but she discussed it with her at the office and asked her to step back. Luckily for Karla, Theresa soon exhausted this set of foster parents and moved out of the neighborhood to a different home.

But now the peace Karla had felt in her home had been broken. Worse yet, Theresa proceeded to spend days when she didn't have a session sitting on the bench at the library entrance, in full view of Karla. Karla felt invaded, even as she realized how desperate Theresa was for closeness and acceptance. The teen's abandonment issues reminded Karla acutely of her own unresolved abandonment fears, while the background of a sexually abusive male caretaker and a cold mother were a close match to Karla's own experience growing up. Although she could offer much empathy and support to Theresa, her own feelings were stirred up. Karla suggested that Theresa another therapist, but the girl was adamant she could only share her pain with Karla. Her intrusion into Karla's life had unfortunately broken that objectivity so important in a therapeutic relationship. The situation was unbearable for her, and for Malcolm as well. He witnessed his wife's distress and eventually decided they would have to move.

Chapter 27

They had lived on Arcadia Court for eight years when they started looking for a new home. One day they drove by a newly-built house nestled up against a hill studded with California oak trees. It was a two-story edifice built of redwood. They called the real estate agent, the same woman from whom Karla was renting her office, and found that the price was within reason for them with the sale of their home.

The first floor of the house was a large living area with a bathroom, a small office, and a hidden storage compartment under the stairs. The top floor had a large living room with windows facing north and south, floor-to-ceiling picture windows that gave a view of the entire neighborhood, the bluffs to the east and a large grove of oak trees climbing up the hill. There was a sliding glass door in the living room, the adjoining dining room, and the family room. Light and nature surrounded them. A sliding glass door in the master bedroom faced the trees in the back and a window to the west allowed the sun to illuminate the room in late afternoon; one could see all the way to the mountains at St. Helena. The wrap-around deck had a stair leading to the first floor; a large oak tree rose through the center, breathtakingly solid.

Then there were two wonderful elevated fireplaces with tiles all around, one in the living room and one in the family room. There was a dining room off the main living room with a built-in bar and an eating area in the family room. The large kitchen had tiled counters and plenty of cabinet and counter space. The children's bedrooms on the top floor were good sized and they had their own shared bathroom.

The house was not completely finished when they bought it. The contractor told them the details they needed to attend to would take two months, so they could move in as early as September; it was July now. Malcolm had sold the Arcadia Court house within three days, paid in cash.

At that time there was a real estate boom in Napa, and Malcolm had been reasonable in pricing the house. Now the new owner wanted immediate possession as part of the cash deal. Later they realized an investor had bought their home and immediately resold it at a much higher price, almost double what Malcolm had asked for.

Luckily, their real estate agent helped them out. She had a house she had bought and was going to renovate, but for now it was empty: she and her husband offered it to Karla and Malcolm. So they put items in storage and moved to the old Victorian in downtown Napa. Karla would go to the nearby grocery store with the kids after work to shop. Talbot had a red wagon he loved to pull around and they took it with them and parked it outside. One day when they came out, it was gone. A lesson learned.

They eagerly awaited September and anticipated the new home being ready. Karla hired Mr. Gerne, an interior decorator, to consult; he also brought two smoking chairs and other odds and ends into the mix, all earth tones. He put up curtains that were light in color and kept the brightness of the house. The home felts safe and warm.

They moved in before the beginning of school. The elementary school was down one block on East First Street, walking distance for Thais, now in third grade; Talbot attended a preschool two blocks down the street. They all felt right at home and loved the easy access to everything: First Street led into the middle of town where all the shops were.

Malcolm had located a better job with the Attorney General's office in San Francisco, located in the Civic Center. He worked with the senior librarian supporting the attorneys, and when the senior librarian retired a year later, he took over running the library. He loved his job but hated his commute. He had to get up at 5 A.M. to catch a commuter bus and arrive in San Francisco by 8 A.M. The return trip started at 5 P.M. and delivered him home two hours later. This frustrated him, for he wanted to spend more time with the family. He would come home disgruntled and unhappy. In time he learned to make good use of the four hours on the bus, and started reading all the great literature available in English and some in German.

Reading became his great hobby, and he developed an interest in the entire lifecycle of the book, from bindery and manufacture to buying and selling. He began to invest in first editions. He also began to be a scholar about all aspects of wine—the growing, making, and storing of wines. While touring in France and Germany, he and Karla had visited all the famous wine-growing regions, and Franz had told Malcolm about the great wine areas of Austria.

Karla and Malcolm started a group that had monthly dinners with wine, each couple taking turns creating a meal and serving the wine, usually brought to the table in paper bags. Malcolm would proceed to identify the grape, the year, and the country of origin. It was amazing how he had perfected his knowledge, and everyone had great fun. When Karla cooked, the meals were quite gourmet as well: French cooking interested her in particular, as did Austrian and, of course, American cuisine.

Malcolm found another way to make the commute less painful and spend more time with his family. He signed up to take the bus leaving at 5:30 in the morning so that he could leave earlier and arrive home at 6 P.M. That gained him an hour with the kids even though he now had to get up at 4:30 A.M. every morning. He did his toilet and breakfast quietly as not to awake Karla. She usually got up at around six to get herself and the children ready for the day.

In addition to school, Karla and Malcolm enrolled the children in music lessons starting when they were five. Part of their rationale was their own love of music; growing up, Karla had always wanted to play the violin. When she passed both the general and child boards in 1978 and 1979 respectively, Malcolm suggested she give herself a gift, something she really wanted to do. She immediately thought of a violin, buying a learner violin at the music store. Then she called Lora, a violin teacher in the community, and asked her whether she would take on a thirty-eight-year-old neophyte. Lora agreed and Karla began lessons. She was so eager she had a hard time controlling her exuberance and being patient enough to learn.

Soon Karla brought Thais to Lora, and later Talbot. There was a lot of practicing around the house. Thais and Talbot made very fast progress and had no stage fright during the recitals. Karla did not do recitals after freezing on the stage for her first one. Karla also started piano lessons, since the children's teacher was very happy to take her on. She began music theory classes at the community college and learned the principles of writing songs.

Three violin lessons a week, all after school, and three piano lessons a week before school kept Karla and the children pretty busy. Malcolm was sorry he was not home early enough to help out with any of it, but Karla did not mind. Besides, not only were Lora and Goldi, the piano teacher, excellent at their arts, they became friends with Karla and Malcolm. It was a happy time.

Many Friday and Saturday evenings, the family would walk six blocks down the road and pick up the latest movie release, saved for them by the man who owned the video store. They would sit in the family room and watch movies on Friday nights. When Karla saw the same movies offered on television movie channels thirty years later, she traveled back in time and relished again those evenings; truly a trip down memory lane.

On other Saturday nights, Malcolm would put on an opera on the hi-fi. He and Karla would toast each other with a glass of champagne and listen for a while before falling blissfully asleep in their smoking chairs next to each other while their brains continued to process the music. The children busied themselves with their own interests. They were regenerating evenings, full of good sentiments and peace.

Chapter 28

Just after moving into the East First Street house, Karla found out she was pregnant. She was now thirty-eight years old, and Malcolm thirty-nine. She felt accepting and hopeful about the pregnancy until Malcolm told her he wanted her to have an abortion. He was concerned because they were older and there could be problems, not only with the pregnancy, but genetically. Older sperm and older eggs had more possibility of errors. Also, there was a strong family history of heart disease on his side, which might affect the child. And Malcolm told Karla he was not sure he would be around to raise the child because of his family history of early heart attacks and death. They were not financially secure and would have to go through all the problems getting babysitters again. Karla was shocked; after all, they were married, they both worked, and she had never considered that anything might go wrong. However, she recognized the truths in his analysis. She scheduled an abortion, finding it hard to accept she was going to terminate the pregnancy. When she came home from the clinic, she felt a great sadness.

Malcolm followed this up with a vasectomy and the sadness hit her hard. Karla sobbed; Malcolm was shocked. She did not really know why she cried so much, but found herself thinking of her childhood in Austria where anybody considered unfit was castrated. Did this mean she and Malcolm were unfit in her unconscious mind? But she had been a small child during those times—how could she remember that? She was not aware of consciously understanding Hitler's policy of murdering mentally challenged people, but apparently her subconscious mind had picked up nuances which left a strong impression.

After the abortion, Karla became aware that a small bird was repeatedly dashing itself against the office window when she was present, over a period of a couple months. Was it the spirit of the child who had been aborted? Karla was projecting, she knew, but the guilt was there to be faced.

As she entered her forties, Karla grew restless. She would often wake up around 2:30 in the morning and sit by herself in the living room, not knowing where this disquiet came from. She would go back to bed about an hour later and not tell Malcolm for fear of waking him, as he needed sleep to face the exhausting commute and workday.

When she was forty-two in 1983, this restlessness caused her to feel she needed to move her office. Theresa sitting across the street almost daily was anxiety provoking and her communication with her colleague Marty had become scarce, she no longer felt so connected. She began looking for a different office space.

She found a renovated Victorian, the Migliavacca Mansion, which had stood forlornly in its original setting on the Napa River just down from Karla's office. Now it was beautifully renovated and had been moved three blocks up the street from her office. The first floor was rented by a group of architects but the upper floor was available for rent. It was a large space with a playroom in the turret area, just like a fairytale castle. It was very private and had a back entrance as well as the front, and her clients enjoyed having more than one sitting area avaialble. There was a deck just outside one of the corner nooks; pigeons had a nest there with young in it.

Karla moved her meager furniture and now was on her own.

Chapter 29

*A*llena left the family when Talbot was five years old, complaining of hip pain that gave her difficulty in maneuvering stairs and cleaning and vacuuming. Karla was almost heartbroken; Allena had become indispensable, always prompt getting to work, never taking a sick day, and not involving herself with the family in anything but a pleasant, professional manner. And Talbot did like Allena, who would take him out to the bowling alley and on errands with her.

Now, since Talbot was in kindergarten, he needed after-school care. Both children could walk to their new sitter, Bonnie. Her house was down the street from the school and Karla would pick them up on her way home from work shortly after five. Bonnie took care of Thais and Talbot along with her own children and another infant. She was nice, but a little bit obtuse, it seemed. For example, Karla was paying Bonnie to give the kids a snack, but not too much so as not to spoil dinner. Bonnie took this instruction very literally and gave her own children cookies and brownies, but only fruit or nuts—no sweets—to Karla's kids. Of course, they complained about it at home!

Talbot started first grade at Alta Heights where Thais was in fifth grade. Karla noticed that the public schools in California offered very poor teaching. Thais would carry papers around in her rucksack for weeks and when Karla asked her if she was forgetting to turn in assignments, she said, "The teacher never asks for our homework."

Karla started paying close attention to what the homework was. The textbooks were of poor quality and the question sheets the teacher had handed out did not relate to the textbook. Thais was not learning any grammar. When Karla ran into her teacher at the bank, she said, "Thais is not learning any grammar."

"That is because we are not teaching grammar," the teacher replied with a smile.

Nor were Thais and Talbot learning math; Karla had to supplement their lessons with workbooks. She had the kids fill the books in, then corrected their work and reviewed their mistakes with them. Talbot had not grasped division and Thais had a hard time with fractions and percentages. Malcolm explained to the kids how the government worked, how bills were crafted, and other important facts about the process of a democracy.

One day Karla found that Malcolm had taken both kids, sat them on the front stairs, and explained the Ten Commandments to them. The family attended church sporadically; there was no Unitarian Universalist Church in Napa, so they explored different denominations, but each time were disappointed. The children had not been baptized. This didn't bother Karla, but she agreed it was good for them to have a basic religious foundation.

Thais had now entered the seventh grade at the nearby junior high school, to which she rode the bus. Karla noticed that her daughter, never a good eater, had begun to eat even less. Then one day Thais showed her a paper she had written for her health class on anorexia nervosa.

Karla knew the whole family were very small eaters, the children eating four bites of meat after enquiring what poor animal it was they were eating, maybe two tablespoons of rice and vegetables and salad. She was able to buy groceries for a week for $50. They seldom had leftovers. On Sundays she and Malcolm made wheat bread from scratch which served as the basis for everybody's sandwiches. She herself took a non-fat yogurt and a bunch of grapes for lunch. They did not eat in between meals. Breakfast was homemade granola with skim milk, black coffee, and a small glass of orange juice. No junk food ever graced their home. Sometimes Malcolm took Karla out for dates to restaurants, just the two of them or with friends, but seldom dined out as a family, for at that time there were very few places in Napa for young families to eat at.

This eating pattern had started with Karla, who always had to watch her weight. In Omaha she would eat half a piece of bread for breakfast with her coffee, then take a bag lunch of half a sandwich and an apple. Dinner was not a pleasant time at home as her mother had gone to work by then, leaving Karla to finish the cooking and serve the food. Her stepfather always needled her about something at the dinner table, and this killed her appetite. Then, when she finally left home and had little money to spare for food, she ate even less. It was hot cereal with skim milk for breakfast, a piece of meat and vegetables at the cafeteria for lunch and dinner the same. She avoided carbohydrates and she lost a lot of weight. Even though she felt hungry most of the time, she did not eat except three times a day. Sweets were out of the question.

Now she was watching Thais who began to be very concerned about her figure. Most of her weight was concentrated in her lower body. She had developed breasts around age thirteen, around the time of her first period. She was beautiful, but apparently not skinny enough for the standards of her peers in the seventh grade. Karla's radar was up for a close watch. However, Thais did not lose weight and may have been concerned about anorexia from her experience with a peer at school. Karla never found out.

One day, Karla's friend Jeanne called and asked if Karla could pick up her daughter Sarah, who was in the same grade as Thais. Sarah had sprained her ankle badly and needed a ride home. Karla was free at the time and drove to the school. As she walked to the nurses' office to pick Sarah up, she was appalled by the noise level in the open hallways as the kids went to their afternoon classes. It was pandemonium. She heard foul language and saw rude behavior. Then and there she knew there had to be an alternative for Thais, she could not continue at this school.

That evening she happened across her high school yearbook from South High School in Omaha. The greetings were very civil and kind; most students had written, "God bless you." She suddenly realized how religious she had always been and how that had been lost for years now. She wanted religion back in her life and in the lives of her children; she also wanted the children to be exposed to decent behavior at school.

She discussed her observations and disappointments with the public school system with Malcolm. He agreed fully. Both had heard good things about St. John's Lutheran School, so they paid a visit to the small school. The learning appeared very sound, and the kids looked happy. Thais and Talbot were enrolled at St John's after Christmas in 1983, Thais in the seventh grade and Talbot in the third.

Thais reacted vehemently to this change, not wanting to go to a different school. She protested loudly and when that was of no avail, she woke up one Sunday morning shortly after starting St. John's and she could not see. Feeling her fears of the new school had not been heard, she had a case of hysterical blindness. Thankfully, it passed with encouragement and acknowledgment of how hard it was for her to leave her school.

Soon, she began to love St John's. Her learning improved dramatically and she made some good friends. She starred in musicals they had and found she had a real talent for singing and dancing. The dancing classes she had taken as a small child made it easy for her to learn dance steps, and she loved performing—had no stage fright. Thais began to blossom as a performer.

Talbot, too, was much more challenged and much happier. He had a great time in school and his friendships expanded. He was known as the class clown, for he made everyone laugh.

The summer following this transition to St. John's, Karla wished the children to be baptized and Malcolm agreed. In June, following the ending of the school year, when Thais was thirteen and Talbot was nine, they were baptized. Thais accepted their baptism with great joy and embraced Christ with open arms. Talbot was more reticent but seemed to accept Christ with an open heart if not with an open mind, for he was a skeptic even at that age. It surprised Karla and Malcolm how happy the kids were to be baptized and know Christ.

Chapter 30

*K*arla shortened her office schedule to end at 2:30 every day, picking up the children after school as part of a carpool. For a while she practiced on Saturday mornings, hoping to serve any patients who needed a late or weekend slot, but Malcolm began to object that the family was missing out on together time with her work schedule, and she dropped Saturdays.

Recently, Malcolm had become depressed. He could not pinpoint the exact cause but mentioned that his relationship with his mother had always been colder than he would have liked. Mildred, his mother, scared him when he was younger, making him take the public bus by himself at six years of age across Los Angeles, and even at the age of four had sent him to military school because she thought he was too jealous of his new baby brother, Glenn. Military school was a nightmare for Malcolm and he returned home after a few months because he cried so much. While he was at Offut, he often had courier duty to the west coast. He would call his mother to ask if they could have dinner together, but she always refused, not expressing any desire to see him. Malcolm, a sensitive and caring person, was very hurt by the behavior of the one parent left to him.

His father Philip, a pioneer pilot, was home only after his flying tour for the month was over, resulting in exhaustion after flying airlifts to Japan and back. He would sleep almost the entire time he was home. Malcolm suffered a severe shock when his father, then fifty-four collapsed and died while planting a tree just before his first year of high school began in September. The shock was compounded by guilt because his father had yelled for him to help dig the hole for the tree and Malcolm had procrastinated. He found his father dead when he did go to help.

Malcolm had missed his kind father all his life. Philip was an easygoing, socially adept man matched with his hysterical and anxious mother. Once her husband died, Mildred shipped Glenn off to the private school they were both enrolled in, Pacific Palisades, to board there, and Malcolm had to work after school every day at the school's farm, coming home to face a man's responsibility for his widowed mother.

Soon Mildred began drinking excessively. Malcolm watched as Glenn came under the influence of shallow, pleasure-seeking peers with no real grounding. Meanwhile he had to put up with his mother's constant complaining at home and had to be the responsible one.

Every September, Malcolm became silent and withdrew into himself. Karla saw this happening yearly at the same time and pointed this out. He then told her about his father's death the first day of September and how guilty he still felt and how much he still missed him. She encouraged him to get into psychotherapy. He found a Jungian social worker in Oakland and began seeing her weekly as well as joining this therapist's all-day group session one Saturday a month. He learned much about himself and got a perspective on his relationship with his mother, but soon felt he needed a more professionally-trained Jungian to advance. He transferred to a Jungian analyst in Petaluma; then, feeling he had reached a much better understanding of his psychological makeup, asked Karla to also see this doctor as well. He wanted her to get a better understanding of her childhood experiences, and she agreed.

Karla began making weekly trips to Petaluma on Wednesday just after lunch so she could return on time to pick up the children. In her sessions with the analyst, she focused on the traumas of her childhood, but no earth-shattering insights arrived, other than the analyst clarified for her that her mother was bothered by Karla's presence because Karla served as a reminder of a terrible time in Johanna's life. That insight was not particularly helpful and maybe not even accurate, but it gave Karla another look at how her mother might have related to her after she had started anew with Dimitri.

Happily, life at home had become very pleasant and less stressful because Malcolm got a job working as a medical librarian at the Napa State Hospital Library, a job he had long coveted, in 1984. The new job meant no more commuting on the bus to San Francisco. He was able to take the kids to music lessons and dinner could be earlier, and it meant lots more free time for Malcolm. As he and Karla sat together one day, he said, "You know we are in a really good place now, everything is as it should be."

Thais was now a freshman at Justin Siena, the Catholic high school in the city and she loved it. Talbot was still at St. John's, sailing along smoothly in the fifth grade. Karla was no longer overburdened by her practice as in the past when she had so many responsibilities; she took Wednesday afternoons off and could come home after her session with the analyst to relish some alone time before Malcolm came back with the children after their violin lesson. She found that without really trying, she was losing weight, fifty-four pounds in all; she loved her new shape. She did not have any stretch marks from the weight loss, and she felt energetic and happy. Malcolm took her to buy a new wardrobe. Everything did seem just wonderful.

Then one Friday as they all returned home together, they found that their home had been ransacked. Everything was topsy-turvy, the drawers in the bedroom haphazardly balanced, all the contents in disarray on the floor. All Karla's jewelry was gone, as was the silverware inherited from Malcolm's grandmother, and even the private documents that Malcolm stashed in the cupboard under the stairs were scattered all around. Obviously whoever did this had been looking for cash. Fortunately, they did not keep cash in the house, but the thieves were frustrated and expressed their displeasure.

The police came and took note, but could not identify any clues. Later, pieces of the silverware set were found in the backyard among the oak trees. Talbot remembered going out on the deck in the morning on that fateful day to enjoy the sunshine before going to school and did not remember closing the sliding door, so that is how they got in. The feeling of being invaded disrupted the easy harmony of the family; it created a very unpleasant, vulnerable kind of choking up, which turned to anger and rage. The unseen, unknown enemy was never found or identified, so the feeling of being violated again never left the little family.

Chapter 31

*K*arla was continuing to wake up restless in the early morning hours, becoming aware gradually of a need to move somewhere that was not satisfied wholly by the moving of her office to the Migliavacca Mansion. Now she began to think about leaving California, looking for opportunities elsewhere. Malcolm, too, had become disenchanted with California politics and with how spread out things were. He had gone to Sacramento State for his evening classes in history, but the travel after work and back home was exhausting. Where could he continue his studies?

After talking, they planned a trip to Washington State; Karla had gotten a license there, wishing she could find a job in Seattle. Malcolm might find more opportunities there to follow his dream since it was a large city. They traveled by car on a June day, taking a week for the journey there and back. Karla had found some possible job opportunities outside Seattle at one of the mental hospitals. They liked Seattle: the lodging and food were good, and it appeared to be an upscale town. However, the job at the mental hospital was not what Karla had envisioned and the pay was poor. She would just keep an eye out for other possibilities; there was always private practice as well.

They had been in Seattle three days when Karla began to feel anxious and oppressed. Her chest felt as though some unknown energy had clamped onto it, and a lot of fear entered her mind. She pressed Malcolm to leave and she refused to stop overnight in Oregon as had been planned, telling Malcolm, "I just want to get home. We can take turns driving, but I don't want to stop anywhere."

Malcolm was puzzled, but she was so adamant and so driven, he gave in. They arrived back in Napa in the early morning hours. Karla opened the sliding glass door in the bedroom and saw the oak trees swaying gently in the wind, and found herself saying, "I will never leave you."

She didn't understand where the tension and anxiety in her chest came from and Malcolm wrote it off to the mysterious way Karla often made decisions. Karla felt settled by the energy from the many trees in their backyard, and soon calmed down.

But the intuitive feeling that they must leave California continued for Karla, and Malcolm agreed. She got all kinds of mailers advertising employment opportunities for psychiatrists. Malcolm told her, "I will go anywhere except the South." He feared the the conservatism, the fundamentalism, and the intolerance. However, one day he came home from work and amended his statement, saying, "I will go anywhere you want to go."

This happened to be a summer day in 1985. Just that day Karla had received a letter from a headhunter describing a position in Lynchburg, Virginia, for a child psychiatrist to open a new child and adolescent wing of Virginia Baptist Hospital. When Malcolm made his statement, she pointed to the letter from Lynchburg and said, "Here."

Karla felt an internal shock as she heard herself say this. Had she not promised the oak tree spirits that she would never leave? Where was it coming from, this push into the unknown when everything in their lives was so certain now and so pleasant?

Malcolm and Karla got a ticket to Lynchburg paid for by the head hunting firm and in mid-September they made their first trip. The trees had not donned their autumnal colors, so it was very green and a shocker to Karla for California is brown during summer and autumn. Lynchburg was a town of about 70,000 souls at that time in 1985, located on seven hills and at the foot of the Piedmonts of the Appalachians. The downtown had a few buildings of more than six floors, and it appeared to have known better times. There were few shops and they looked forlorn.

Virginia Baptist Hospital was a handsome building in the Georgian style. It was located off a main street in the wealthy part of town and was nicely landscaped. Karla had a good feeling on visiting the hospital.

Karla met the psychiatrists and the assistant director of the hospital. The assistant director explained the financials: until her practice brought in more money, the hospital would loan her working capital for the first six months. She would share an office with the two other psychiatrists employed by the hospital, Dr. Glass and Dr. Yoon. Dr. Yoon, a native of South Korea, had just recently started working on the adult unit part-time. Dr. Glass was a well-established psychiatrist in the community who had given up his position at the mental health clinic to work for the hospital and open a private practice with Dr. Yoon. There were three other psychiatrists: Dr. Carter and Dr. Grant, who also practiced solo in the community and Dr. Walden, currently the director of the adult unit.

The hospital had gotten permission, a certificate of need from the authorities, to open a child and adolescent unit to service Lynchburg and adjacent counties. Karla was shown the sixth floor of the hospital where the unit would be located. There was a lot of office space and hers would be particularly spacious. It was ready to receive patients, so now the hospital was gathering the staff to run it. They needed a clinical director who would treat patients on the unit and then follow them up in the outpatient practice. The expected salary with the unit in full operation was more than Karla and Malcolm's combined income in Napa.

Malcolm made a side trip, driving sixty-four miles north on Route 29 to look over the University of Virginia and get information about admission to their history department's graduate program. He was favorably impressed and told Karla it would not be a hardship to drive there for classes as he would have his own time and not be working.

Karla admitted to herself that the surrounding countryside was somewhat depressing; the community was also old and established, and newcomers would have a hard time being accepted into the community. She felt oppressed by the closeness of the forests and mountains; it was hard to see anything more than 100 feet away because there were so many trees and hills. The California landscape around Napa was wide open and the trees were not as tall. She loved the smooth, grass-covered hills with a tree here and there, not obscuring the sky.

Returning home, Karla put herself in the running, telling them if they did hire her she would come in June of 1986, nine months later. The kids had started school and she needed time to close out her practice. Deep down also Karla needed time to reconsider if she was doing the right thing. The interviewers were disappointed with the delayed start date she offered; they hoped to open the unit by Christmas, but said they would consider her as a possible candidate.

Karla and Malcolm discussed what this move would entail. They had found that the public schools in Lynchburg had a good rating, but after their California experience they distrusted public schools and had looked at available private schools. Malcolm would be unemployed and would attend graduate school so there would be no income aside from Karla's. Both knew that a librarian job in Lynchburg would be hard to get, and Malcolm was thrilled at the thought of finishing his graduate degree.

Karla acknowledged that she would have to work a lot more and a lot harder than her current easy office schedule. She would have to be in from 7 A.M. until 7 P.M. or later: hospital work in the mornings, private practice in the afternoon, and returning for admissions after the close of business daily. Also she would have to be available to take calls 24/7, considering they had no other child psychiatrist and none of the adult psychiatrists felt qualified to treat child and adolescent patients. It was a serious commitment. The children were another matter: they did not want to leave California, particularly Thais.

Soon the hospital sent her a tentative contract pending the approval of the newly hired administrative director for the unit, Dr. Strong, a doctor of education. She was apparently very hesitant to accept the verdict of the interviewers Karla had seen before her arrival, and made her own agenda: first Karla was to go to Los Angeles and be interviewed by a child psychiatrist there who had professed a mild interest in Lynchburg and whom Dr. Strong knew from past association. Karla flew down to Los Angeles on a very stormy night in early December. The plane was buffeted back and forth like a boat on a stormy sea, and Karla began to question what she was about to do. Was this a warning, an omen of the way it would go?

The psychiatrist in Los Angeles had a very luxurious home perched above the Pacific Ocean. He offered Karla his deceased son's room. Karla saw the picture of the young man who had died from a disorder of the nervous system. Again she felt a strange foreboding in her chest. However, Dr. David was very kind, saying he had been thinking of relocating but was just entertaining the thought. He gave Dr. Strong a good report on Karla.

Next Dr. Strong sent two therapists she had just hired—actually good friends of hers from her previous position in Washington state—to come to the house and interview Karla in her home setting. In the end, only one of the therapists came. He was friendly and talked about the teamwork that would be required of Karla in Lynchburg. Dr. Strong received a good report from him as well, and now she wanted Malcolm and Karla and the children to fly to Lynchburg to have a final interview with her and Dr. Yoon, now director of the adult unit, in January.

Chapter 32

*C*hristmas went by uneventfully in 1985, but one morning shortly thereafter, Malcolm awoke saying he did not feel good—his heart was beating unevenly. Karla felt his pulse and drove Malcolm to see the emergency physician who diagnosed atrial fibrillation, an aberrant heart rhythm. An ambulance immediately took him to Vallejo Kaiser Hospital, and Karla and the children followed.

Karla was in shock: Malcolm had always warned them that he might die suddenly because of his family history. His condition resolved with medication and he was able to come home three days later, on no medication and with a normal rhythm. They did not do a catheterization as his heart resumed normal rhythm, but both Karla and Malcolm were shaken and the children were scared.

Malcolm's hospitalization reminded Karla of a dream she had had a few months earlier. She and Malcolm were sitting at a bar drinking a glass of wine when a man walked in, went right up to Malcolm, and stuck a knife in his heart. He died in her arms. She awoke in a cold sweat from this dream and was hesitant to tell Malcolm about it, it seemed so real.

Malcolm had always warned Karla about the history of heart attacks and death in his father's family. Malcolm would dramatize his own ending, flailing his arms and enacting his own death scene from a heart attack, frightening Karla and the children. Karla had taken this history very seriously. Malcolm got a cholesterol test in 1975; his levels were high, but the advice they got from their physician was to eat a low-fat diet, less meat, more fish. Instead of butter, they were told to eat margarine.

Many of the recommendations from the medical teaching at the time actually harmed Malcolm more than they helped, but at the time it was the accepted medical doctrine. Statin medications to lower cholesterol hadn't been developed at that time.

Karla was concerned: should they be moving? The children were not enthusiastic and Malcolm's emergency dampened Karla's confidence about the proposed relocation to Virginia. However, Malcolm did not want to change the course they had set.

A month or so after Malcolm's hospitalization, Karla had a frightening dream: a German shepherd dog was barking at her side as if warning her. Then suddenly in the darkness, four horsemen appeared—harbingers of an apocalypse in her personal life. The scene then changed; there was a plane crash in which only Talbot and Karla survived. This crash happened as a huge tsunami swept away everything in its path. It was all so real, shaking Karla to the core.

Again, she asked herself, was she making the right move? At the same time, she went ahead as if on autopilot, making all the necessary arrangements, closing her practice, putting the house up for sale, and readying the children with lots of discussions so they could express their feelings and begin to adapt. Malcolm felt very encouraged when he got accepted into the graduate European history program at the University of Virginia, looking forward to a full-time agenda at the school.

On a cold January morning, the family caught the flight scheduled by the hospital in Lynchburg, arriving at the Washington National Airport to a grey, icy afternoon. The next morning, they drove to Lynchburg, a distance of about two hundred miles. Since it had been snowing and conditions had been icy, they saw several cars that had run off the road and were stranded. It was a first experience for the children to feel the biting cold and witness the dangers of winter in Virginia. Descending a steep hill and crossing a bridge over the James River, they were suddenly confronted with the high-rises of the town center of Lynchburg. The children were shocked at this sudden appearance of the skyline out of the very hilly landscape. Lynchburg is located on seven hills that the natives euphemistically liken to the seven hills of Rome.

They passed by a NAPA auto parts shop and the kids got all excited at the name! They were already missing Napa.

The family checked into the hotel in mid-town around noontime and were to have lunch immediately on arrival with Dr. Strong. As they were having lunch the news hit the air: the space shuttle *Challenger* had exploded on launch. It was yet another time Karla had an uncomfortable premonition in her chest; on their first visit to Lynchburg there had been a huge earthquake in Mexico. These disasters were coincidental with their trips, but to Karla they had a darker meaning, like an apocalypse in her life, a foreboding of events. She had learned from out of her past that forebodings and signs meant something for her own destiny. Only later did she come to the conclusion that everything is related in some way and perceptive souls can pick up on this.

Dr. Strong met the family at the restaurant. She was an imposing middle aged woman, tall and muscular with a strong, authoritarian voice. She was encouraging Karla, telling her all interviews so far had been positive. She would wait for the final decision after Karla's interview with Dr. Yoon. The kids later made fun of Karla as they had immediately recognized that Dr. Strong was gay but Karla had not taken notice.

In the afternoon, Karla was escorted to "English Ground," the adult unit, located in the basement of the hospital. At a dining room table, cleared after the patients had eaten, she was introduced to Dr. Yoon.

"What took you so long?" he asked with a friendly smile.

Dr. Yoon was in his mid-forties, of medium height with black wavy hair. He wore glasses which accentuated his striking brown eyes, full of kindness, encouragement, and understanding. He immediately helped her to feel at ease, his questions focusing on her experience and her expectations of the Lynchburg position. To Karla it felt like she was meeting an old friend, but later she recognized that he made everyone feel so comfortable.

Dr. Yoon found no objection to Karla's appointment as clinical director of the child and adolescent unit and Karla was offered the contract, with her chosen start date of June 15, five months later.

That day and the next they had to look at houses, feeling discouraged for none seemed to strike them as all that great until late afternoon of the day before leaving. They were shown a house on Old Trents Ferry Road that struck them as the perfect place for them. It was a Dutch Colonial with a slate roof and a two-car garage. It had a sun porch to the rear with glass windows all around, screened to keep out the mosquitoes and other flying insects so common in the area, and with its own heating system for the winter and air-conditioning in the summer. It looked out on a forest of deciduous trees. Large, mature oak trees surrounded the house; an imposing magnolia could be seen from the master bedroom window, its white flowers exuding purity. The rooms were spacious and well-appointed, and there was a partially-finished basement. The kitchen had a center block with adequate cabinet space and was decorated in bright greens and blues with hardwood floors. The four bedrooms on the top floor had tasteful wallpaper and wonderful views; the master bathroom had a jacuzzi and shower, all nicely decorated. Circular stone steps led up to the main entrance, but the side entrance by the garage would be used most. Everyone loved the house.

They made an offer that afternoon. Because there was such a price difference between these homes and what could be gotten in Napa for the same price, Malcolm did not even counter offer, and by Lynchburg standards probably paid too much. The owners were building a home and were pleased to have until June to move.

The family also looked at a private school for Thais and Talbot, called Seven Hills. They looked as well at the public schools, not going in, but noticing the facilities. They were still distrustful, and after a lot of discussion decided to enroll both kids in the Seven Hills private school for the following year.

On the plane home, there was lots of talk about impressions and feelings. Karla felt enthusiastic; the kids did not like Lynchburg but liked the house; and Malcolm was accepting and excited about the graduate program. They all felt somewhat relieved at being able to picture their new home in Lynchburg, but all felt some trepidation at how serious this move really was.

When Karla put the Napa house up for sale, she asked for an amount that she felt was fair considering how houses were disappearing so fast in Napa, but there were no takers. She did not understand why, but not even one counteroffer came in. Was this another sign? Meanwhile her patients were all grieving her departure right in front of her; all came until the last day of her practice. Often Karla felt as if she were viewing her own funeral, and her heart went out to her loyal patients. They were loath to see her go.

One of Karla's patients was an Episcopalian priest, Annie, recently widowed. She expressed concern when Karla informed her that they were moving to Virginia, telling Karla the South was very different in its social attitudes and mores from those of Northern Californians. The adjustment might be a challenge, she offered. Karla's intuition told her that this was all a sign that all might not be well in Virginia: she had premonitions of danger and vulnerability and the whole family was exposed. She realized that this future they were going into with the move to Lynchburg had no certainties as to its outcome. They were moving from comfort in their environment into unknown territory. Karla, however, placed more importance on her intuition than on cognition. Although she also sensed disaster in the upcoming move, her intuition impressed on her that she must move.

In fairy tales, the hero or heroine is often told not to do the forbidden thing that he or she always ends up doing. It was like that for Karla.

In the months leading up to their departure, Karla and Malcolm had frequent conversations with the children who did not clearly understand why they must leave and what were the changes they had to face. Thais felt resentful and acted out with her friends. She was just entering the time of her life when she might have a first relationship with a boy, gushing one day to her mother that she had been kissed by a boy while playing the piano at Justin and "he stuck his tongue in my mouth!"

Everything was falling into place: the kids had been accepted at Seven Hills, Malcolm at University of Virginia, and Karla had passed all of her interviews and had a contract in hand. Most important of all, the hospital was paying their entire moving costs and would come and pack them up. Malcolm proceeded to throw out all unnecessary items collected over the years, and the kids did the same. Karla was too busy with her work schedule to do much besides cooking and music lessons.

Just a month before they left Napa, Thais won the senior violin competition, the youngest person (at age fourteen) ever to do so. She was very happy; it was a great way to end their tenure in California.

The movers came on schedule the 9th of June and packed everything up until the house was totally empty. After the moving truck left, the family got into their VW Quantum station wagon and said a farewell to the house; they would stay that night in a motel off Highway 29. It was a disorienting feeling knowing they were in their home town but staying at a motel.

Thais looked pale and stressed and was developing some acne. She was less than enthusiastic that first day. Talbot was open for the adventure the trip would offer.

The plan Malcolm had devised was that they would experience the South by approaching slowly, so they went up to Lake Tahoe, down through Death Valley, and into San Antonio, Texas. The night of their arrival in San Antonio, the movie *Roanoke* was playing on television. It was the story of the first settlers on Roanoke Island; all died during their first winter in the new world—another omen, Karla felt.

Was it her passivity that Karla ignored the warning signs she recognized? Or was it that destiny was pulling her and giving her warnings that it would be a difficult pat? Either way, her inner drive made her move ahead with the plans.

The next day they stopped in Dallas for a few hours for Thais to visit her friend Sarah, a classmate from St. John's who had moved there over a year ago, and the families dined together. Thais cheered up after that visit. Next they reached New Orleans. Karla was surprised at the low sea level of the city and the intense humidity. The motel was disappointing; the air conditioning could not keep out the moisture, so the room was damp and stultifying.

Finally they traveled up through Tennessee and east into Virginia. The scenery was impressive, a brilliant deep green, hypnotic. Karla had not known that this part of the mid-Atlantic area was still so pristine in many ways. She had thought it was just all cities.

They arrived in Lynchburg on the 15th of June, and the next day Karla went to work while Malcolm took charge of the details regarding their house. They went to the bank to sign the contract; since the house in Napa had not sold, they did an equity loan until the house sold. It was disappointing to find that the family from whom they bought the house left it quite dirty: the stove and oven were covered in grease. They had to clean house before they could move in.

The movers arrived a few days later. This was final now—no going back.

Chapter 33

*A*new phase of their lives was beginning. Malcolm was home with the kids all day, and they were not happy with his supervision; he could be a taskmaster at times. It was left to him and the children to unpack everything, quite a daunting task. Karla, meanwhile, was busy working with Dr. Strong to hire the staff, doing interviews and devising the working plan. The unit was ready for occupancy.

In the afternoons, Karla drove to her office, about ten minutes from the hospital. To her dismay, she had no windows, but she soon adapted. She was surprised by the almost daily afternoon thunderstorms there all summer and disappointed to find that instead of cool, crisp air, they brought even more humidity. Coming from the dry California summers, she disliked the damp.

She became busy at the office right away; people with children and adolescents had been waiting for her arrival. Dr. Yoon and Glass were friendly and encouraging and Karla soon felt at ease.

Not everything went smoothly. One day she came out of her office to find Talbot and Malcolm in the waiting room. Talbot had a big bandage on his left thigh from a cut he had gotten when he accidentally ran his bicycle into a tree.

June 30 was Talbot's tenth birthday and they went to celebrate at Monte Carlo, a pizza place. They were all hungrily devouring a big pizza when Talbot started gagging. Karla realized he was choking and she rushed to perform the Heimlich maneuver; he spat out a piece of pizza that had caught in his larynx. It was a frightening incident for them all, just a week after Talbot's first misadventure.

That evening Karla had to leave the family to go home by themselves to return to a staff meeting and as she walked toward the entrance she ran face-on into a huge spider whose web she failed to see because of the darkness. Karla had terrible arachnophobia, so this was another slap in her face—literally.

Generally, things progressed well as Karla and the team worked together to devise the treatment strategy. Dr. Strong arranged for Karla to meet the Lynchburg therapists and psychiatrists over working lunches; one psychologist, Darla, became Karla's good friend. Karla also developed a good relationship with the head nurse, a very capable young woman, and the teacher, also a humorous, lively, and intelligent woman. They were in their thirties while Karla was forty-six now. Dr. Strong and her gay partner, Diane, who was the psychologist, were fun to work with during those early weeks. Karla was asked to give a speech to the local teachers and was lauded for her delivery. The paper ran her picture along with an article to inform the community of her arrival. Karla was impressed by the hospitality of the hospital directors, and the community mindedness they demonstrated. She had not experienced this before coming to Lynchburg. This was a taste of Southern hospitality.

There were a few issues, of course. Usually the hospital welcomed a new doctor in the community with a soiree, but they didn't throw a party for Karla's arrival. Apparently, she brought too many books, Malcolm being a book collector—Karla later heard that the director of the hospital, Gary, was quite angry about the cost of the move, which the movers said hinged on all the boxes of books they transported.

One day as the team was all sitting together, working out strategies, Dr. Strong got angry at the art therapist, a recent graduate thrilled to have found a job in her community. In front of the team, Dr. Strong fired the young woman, who became quite tearful. Dr. Strong's behavior shocked Karla; the young woman had no opportunity to argue for her job, and everyone knew how hard it was to find a job specializing in art therapy. Dr. Strong seemed gleeful at her power and used it as an example to show the rest of the team that they were there at her pleasure.

As she witnessed the sadness of the young woman, Karla felt herself getting angry with what she felt as righteous indignation that hardened her toward Dr. Strong. From then on, she no longer trusted Dr. Strong. It was obvious she had to fire the therapist to assuage the jealous feelings of her partner, the psychologist, Karla stopped trusting that woman, too.

The jealousy affected more hiring decisions. Dr. Strong chose a middle-aged alcoholic, whose mind was already half gone, to serve as the social worker. The woman was malleable, clearly no threat to the relationship of Dr. Strong and her partner Diane. A very capable young woman, just out of training, was rejected for the position, which disappointed Karla. Linda, the very open and honest teacher, and Mary, the nurse, also voiced their disappointment at the proceedings, at least to Karla; none of them wanted to confront Dr. Strong.

Once all the staff had been hired, the deck was stacked: Dr. Strong's partner held the psychologist position; her friends from Washington were in secure positions to report to her; and a loyal social worker, Arnold, was the one to whom she delegated authority on the unit. Karla began to feel boxed in, a fear shared by the nurse and the teacher.

Despite this stress, Karla kept her judgments regarding Dr. Strong and her entourage to herself and focused on the work to be done. The staff as a whole was very receptive to her teachings and she felt respected. Dr. Strong did not interfere with her clinical work, so this was Karla's neutral area. She worked well with the team and felt a sense of accomplishment. The first patients began to arrive in July, just two at first; the unit had a capacity of fifteen. Karla evaluated the patients, wrote orders and then met every morning first thing with the interdisciplinary staff for their observations and treatment planning.

Chapter 34

Late that summer, Karla would often come home for lunch with the family. She frequently noticed that Thais ate almost nothing. One day, Thais went upstairs to take a nap after lunch, and complained that she got a slight headache walking up the stairs. Her pace was slowed and she lacked energy. Karla looked in on her before returning to work; she was deeply asleep and snoring loudly. Karla had never heard Thais snoring.

In July Karla dreamed that Thais was a little girl again, holding eye contact while moving away from her toward a tunnel in a mountainside, and as she moved toward it, she sang such a hauntingly sad song that Karla's heart ached. Her heart still ached when she awoke. Her tenderness toward Thais became more marked, from then on tinged with sadness.

As Karla grew older, she became more conscious of signs and intuition. They had been present in her childhood, but at the time she could not yet gather the meaning. That came with further development and awareness.

The second week of August had almost come to an end. Karla and her family had their usual Friday pasta dinner and were sitting in the family room relaxing. Thais asked Karla to come to the bathroom with her; she needed to show her something. She pulled down her pants and put Karla's hand on a hard mass in her groin near the pubic bone. Karla's face went ashen.

"How long has this been here?" she asked, alarmed.

"I just noticed it about a week ago," Thais replied. "I thought it would go away, but I think it has gotten bigger."

Karla's throat tightened as alarms went off in her head. Trying not to upset Thais, who was closely watching her face, she said, "Let's let the doctor take a look at this."

But in the middle of the night, thinking everyone was asleep, she quietly crept down to the basement and got out her Nelson's pediatric book to look up lymphoma. The description fit and Karla went stock-still, her heart thumping in her chest, her breath caught on the inhale.

"What's wrong, Mom?" Thais had followed her down the stairs. Karla had not heard her.

"Nothing, honey, just go back to sleep," Karla managed, calming her voice sufficiently so that Thais went back to her room without question.

The next morning Karla called the pediatrician's office and asked if they could fit Thais in, even though it was Saturday. They were closing at noon, but offered to make an appointment for Monday if it was not an emergency. She had to accept.

That weekend seemed like the longest in her life. When Monday arrived, she took Thais to see Dr. Black. He took her history, including Karla's report of the exhaustion she had noticed and the lack of appetite and listlessness.

"Probably mono," he guessed.

The lab work did not show mono, but her white count and hemoglobin were low. He looked at the lymphocytes on the blood smear and came back, a serious expression on his face.

"I am sending you to a hematologist in Charlottesville, he will see her tomorrow morning, and he will probably do a bone marrow exam. Thais has abnormal lymphocytes."

Karla felt as if a death sentence had been handed down on Thais: lymphoma was often fatal, even with all the tools available to modern medicine. Again, she tried to show calmness on her face when she reassured Thais that they would wait until tomorrow to see what was next.

The trip to Charlottesville on Tuesday morning was marked by silence and trepidation on all their parts. Thais was looking for reassurance from Karla and Malcolm, her face pale and beseeching. Her blue eyes revealed the same sense of foreboding Karla felt in her heart.

They arrived at the hematologist's office. He proceeded in a straightforward manner to perform the bone marrow extraction from Thais's hip. Karla held Thais's hand as she cried out in surprise and pain pain when the large needle was pushed in and the bone marrow withdrawn. They were all asked to wait while he read the slide he made from the cells.

The wait seemed to last forever, fear hanging in the air like a thick black curtain over the little family.

The hematologist returned and without any prelude announced, "Thais has lymphoma. Given the severity, there is a 90% chance it will prove fatal."

He said this in front of the whole family—Malcolm, Karla, eleven-year-old Talbot, and of course Thais, who turned ashen. Talbot began to cry.

It was as if the sun had been eclipsed: unrelenting darkness and settled over them, as if they had suddenly fallen into a deep well with no escape foreseen.

The doctor asked the stricken couple to come into the consultation room, where he further explained that many couples with severely ill children eventually divorce from the stress. So now they had not only been told their daughter would not survive her illness, they were told their marriage would not survive either.

Karla knew that the medical teaching of that day was for openness and honesty about diagnosis and prognosis, but this physician had no art in his medicine, no understanding of how his pronouncements hit this family like a bombshell. His forthrightness was not helpful at all; if anything, it may have been detrimental to everyone's state of mind.

The hematologist arranged for Thais to be admitted that day to the University of Virginia hospital just up the road from his office in Charlottesville. En route, the family attempted to rally from the emotional blows they had received. Thais kept looking for reassurance that this was all a bad dream and soon she would wake up. Talbot could not say anything; he was so scared for his sister. Malcolm and Karla went through the admission proceedings in a daze, numb and hardly able to respond to the questions.

The doctor who met them at the hospital was Dr. Karen Brooks, the pediatric oncologist. She was a pleasantly plump woman in her forties, blonde, with smiling blue eyes and a competent and empathic manner who took to Thais immediately. The surgery to remove the lump was scheduled for the next day, and the doctors would biopsy the lump to further identify the cancer. Dr. Brooks also ordered a spinal fluid extraction to see if the cancerous cells had gotten into the fluid.

There was a lot of activity going on around Thais. At the time, the old hospital was still in use as the new one had not yet broken ground. The rooms and halls were crowded with extra chairs and beds, the hallways dark, and there was little to cheer up the patient or the family. But that matched their emotional state anyway: grey and drab, no sunshine.

That first day at the hospital was heart-wrenching for Karla. The prospect of surgery in the morning was bad enough, but she also worried, knowing the intense pain and sickness that chemotherapy might cause later. Thais, oddly, developed a runny nose, something she usually did not have. All that night, Karla was running for another box of tissues. *A replacement for tears?* Karla wondered.

That first evening, Karla insisted that Thais get dressed and join them at The Virginian, for dinner, a small restaurant across the street. Dr. Brooks hesitantly agreed to let her go, so all four could dine together. Thais was very relieved to escape the scary hospital setting even for a little while and regain a sense of normality as they sat together at table and had light conversation while eating.

The surgery was scheduled for 7 A.M. so Karla stayed at the hospital that night. Malcolm and Talbot returned home; they would come back early the next morning.

Thais was told by the resident while waiting outside the operating room, that one of the side effects of anesthesia could be death. Her eyes widened in anxiety and looked to Karla for reassurance. Karla told her it was a routine warning for all patients before surgery and that she would be fine.

Malcolm and Talbot arrived as Thais was wheeled to recovery. Dr. Brooks met them on the elevator up to Thais's room. Putting her hand on Karla's arm, she said quietly, "I am afraid it is bad news. The mass was all cancerous cells, which means the prognosis is very bad."

Shocked, Karla and Malcolm and Talbot went to Thais's room to wait for her return. When she came in, she wanted to know what the biopsy had shown. Karla told her that it was very serious, but everything would be done to make her better.

Toward noon, Dr. Brooks returned to the room to see Thais. "I have egg on my face," she said with a big smile. "An expert in hematology who is visiting the university took a look at this morning's slides and yesterday's bone marrow. He says it was acute lymphocytic leukemia, not acute myelocytic leukemia, which is a *much* worse form." She looked from Thais to Karla and Malcolm, then back, and continued, "The spinal fluid unfortunately did show some cancer cells, but we found it very early, which is good. We will still need radiation on the spinal cord and brain as part of the treatment. However, everyone agrees the disease is in the very early stages."

An audible sigh of relief ran around the room, and everyone relaxed; even though the news was bad, it was not the worst, and they were all grateful for that.

She was able to come home after that first week of induction; the other treatments could be administered by Dr. Aires, the pediatric hematology oncologist at Virginia Baptist. Thais would need to return to Charlottesville for certain outpatient administrations that needed to be done there.

Chapter 35

I t was a September afternoon. The slanting rays suffused the bathroom windows with a glowing afternoon sunlight. Karla was filling the big jacuzzi in the master bathroom so that Thais could take a relaxing bath. She was too weak to scrub herself or wash her hair. She had lost a lot of weight with the chemotherapy, which caused her to vomit whatever she ate, and she lost her appetite as well.

As Karla washed Thais' beautiful curly strawberry blonde hair, clumps of it came out in her hand. Karla had to suppress the anguished tears welling up in her chest, her heart breaking. Thais noted the clumps and asked her mother to cut off her "tail," the fashionable length of hair that teenagers allowed themselves to grow while the rest of the hair was shorter. Karla cut it and Thais kept it in her jewelry box in her room.

On her return from the hospital, she had an IV line in her subclavian artery above her heart. The placement area had to be cleansed daily with iodine solution. With this line in place, IVs could be administered quickly and accurately without using any needles in her arm. Malcolm took over this job as Karla was overcome with all that was going on. Expertly, and with no show of emotion, he cleaned the line every morning. Malcolm also treated Thais as if she were not ill, encouraging her to take part in everything that was going on, never coddling her or cajoling her. Thais followed Malcolm's lead, indeed doing everything she could as if she were not ill. This actually helped her to forget her situation and take one day at a time; she could still laugh and joke and learn and be active, although at times chemotherapy rendered her temporarily immobilized.

Thais went into remission in early October after the required number of radiation treatments to her head and spinal cord. There were no cancerous cells in her nervous system now or in her blood.

Karla was in no mood for Christmas that year; she preferred self-denial, as celebration would be too daring. But not for Thais. She asked her parents to take her Christmas shopping, her spirit infecting the whole family. They ended up decorating a tree and were full of happiness inspired by their daughter. It felt like the usual Christmas, always anticipated with excitement.

So much love came from Thais! She appreciated life to the fullest and drank every moment in as if it were her last.

Malcolm took Thais to Charlottesville for her chemotherapy in the outpatient hematology oncology department while he went to class. Thais and her dad developed a relationship that was never possible in Napa because of his long work hours and his fatigue after work. Karla realized this was a silver lining to the dark cloud of Thais' cancer.

More treatments to ensure remission followed. Thais was hospitalized for a chemotherapy course lasting three to four days. During one of those stays, during which time Malcolm could visit when he was in Charlottesville for his studies, but Karla could not, the guilt overwhelmed her. Karla developed stomach pains and was given medication to calm her tense gastrointestinal tract which was reacting to her stress. One evening, she could not let go of the thought that Thais needed her. Ignoring Malcolm's warning that she was too tired to travel, she drove to Charlottesville. Thais was feeling very low and lonely and was thrilled to see Karla, but began to cry silently when her mother had to leave an hour later. Karla could see the longing in her daughter's big blue eyes.

Distracted by her mood, Karla got lost driving home and ended up on an unfamiliar highway, disoriented and discouraged. She felt worthless as a mother, abandoning her daughter when she most needed her. Unknowingly she drove through a red light; a driver whose car had already entered the intersection sideswiped her. The crash brought Karla to her senses. She apologized profusely to the man, admitting her guilt, and told him about her daughter's illness. He was understanding, but she still got a ticket and had to go to court.

As she crawled into bed about an hour after midnight, she said quietly to Malcolm, "I had an accident with the car, but I'm all right."

He said, "Go to sleep. We'll discuss it in the morning." It was so cold and uncaring; he never held her or comforted her, which she badly needed.

In general, Malcolm couldn't handle any more problems; there was just too much for him to process. It was only later that Karla recognized that his way of handling all this misfortune in the family was to internalize it and "keep a stiff upper lip."

Chapter 36

Thais missed a lot of school. She was enrolled at Seven Hills, private school, but because she was absent so much she missed most of her sophomore year. Karla and Malcolm realized that public school would serve her better, allowing for home schooling and providing more teachers available to give her extra time. She transferred to E.C. Glass High School in the spring of 1987. She spent her junior catching up on her classes, receiving excellent help from her math teacher in particular. The other teachers were also sympathetic and donated extra time to help her come to grade level. Several even came to the house when she was too weak to put up with a long school day.

Thais began to blossom at E.C. Glass. She was thrilled to get her learner's permit, and Malcolm gave her the blue Volkswagen Rabbit that they had brought from Napa. She developed friendships with diverse people from school and from the community, and she handled responsibility well.

She was interested in continuing her music writing, so her parents installed a Yamaha keyboard in her room on which she composed both lyrics and music. She had friends with whom she shared her music interests. Lynchburg College offered her an opportunity to give a performance of her pieces to an audience, mostly friends and family. The songs were lovely, including one called, "To My Mom." Whenever Karla listened to the video recording later, she choked up and could not finish it all; it was heart-wrenching, the songs so haunting.

Thais also won the poetry contest in 1988 at E.C. Glass with a poem entitled, "The Walk," which she composed on a walk with her parents, stopping to pick spring flowers and presenting the bouquet to Karla. Her music and writing conveyed exquisite perception and emotion; Karla knew that Thais' works were reflections of her soul.

Talbot was doing well in private school throughout this time. Seven Hills had a strong sixth grade program, and Talbot had a classic introduction to Southern peers and their antics. He made a good friend, Felix, and they spent much time together. One time, after seeing the movie *The Exorcist,* he demonstrated the famous turning-neck scene to the delight of his peers, all boys, and ended up having to wear a neck collar for a week, having hyper-extended his neck. His classmates were a rowdy bunch, much different from the well-behaved fifth-graders at his Lutheran school in Napa.

However, Talbot began reacting to the lack of attention he received as Thais and concerns about her health were foremost in his parents' minds. He was angry, and Thais and he had it out: he accused her of getting all the attention just because she had cancer, and she slapped him hard. Thankfully, they made up and it was never an issue between them again. Later, when he was older, Talbot let his mother know how hard that time was for him, but his attitude toward Thais was ever humorous and gentle and supportive.

Karla, meanwhile, was working very hard: the unit was soon filled to capacity and the work was joyful. In the mid-eighties to mid-nineties, insurance companies did not terminate hospitalizations before the patient was ready to be discharged, so the children and adolescents had enough time on the unit to work on their problems with their parents and staff. Once discharged, usually after a month, there were very few returns—the "revolving door" syndrome had not yet begun. But Karla was the only child psychiatrist, so had to field calls from the unit as well as from her outpatients with no time off. The first break came at Christmas in 1986, when one of the adult psychiatrists volunteered to give Karla a week off from call.

Something was also going on with Karla's health now. She was taking the birth control pill to regulate her periods, but they were very heavy and prolonged. Her gynecologist told her he felt a mass in her abdomen; it could be just fibroids but there was no way to know if there was also a malignancy due to the fibroid's size. He sent her to two other consultants and they said she may have a sarcoma, a very invasive cancer of the uterus. When her abdomen grew larger and felt heavy, all three physicians agreed she probably had a sarcoma. Surgery was scheduled for early March; she would be off work six weeks and would possibly need chemotherapy. She donated two units of her own blood leading up to the surgery. Her physician told Malcolm and Karla that he may be doing radical abdominal surgery if nodes were involved. He recommended removal of the ovaries as well, to which Karla agreed.

It is hard to imagine the stress this little family experienced with this news. That dark cloud hanging over their heads was getting darker, no silver lining in sight.

The surgery was performed at Virginia Baptist Hospital on a blistery, wintery March day. Malcolm never expressed what he felt, not wanting to add his own fears and concerns to the mix. Instead, he put all his energy into putting the children under his wing and doing all necessary responsibilities for them and the home.

After the surgery, she woke up, pale and weakened. Her blood was transfusing into her arm. Malcolm arrived with the children, each of whom brought Karla a small gift and who both looked very concerned. The doctor arrived just after the family and told her the wonderful news: she did not have cancer! The fibroid had filled up with more blood at each period and there was no exit for the blood; had she waited much longer, it would have burst the uterus. Her ovaries were disease-free but were removed as a caution.

It was about fifteen years later that Karla learned from her Aunt Mitzi, dying of ovarian cancer herself, that Karla's paternal grandmother had also died of ovarian cancer. Karla was relieved knowing she had escaped this hereditary link.

Karla needed the full six weeks to recuperate. Her continuous hard work and the emotional stress had taken her strength away. Malcolm was incredibly supportive, bringing Karla a breakfast tray every morning before going to Charlottesville for classes and taking care of the children's needs as they went to school. He also prepared dinner the first few weeks of recuperation.

Karla found during this time that she was very hungry for art, reading art and museum books in bed. Something inside her had been starving for this kind of cultural involvement since they came to Lynchburg.

The family was surprised at how many people sent flowers during her recuperation; these gestures of support were very welcome.

Chapter 37

*A*fter a year, the other psychiatrists decided they could cover the child and adolescent unit on weekends. Karla joined the on-call roll, meaning she had every weekend off except when she was on call covering both the child and adult units. Finally, the family was able to take weekend trips out of town. She would also be covered for vacations. This was a very welcome change and occurred as the psychiatrists became more familiar with the needs of the child and adolescent unit, which were not much different from the adult unit.

Her relationship with Dr. Strong worsened, however, as the teacher and head nurse joined Karla in objecting to the director's tactics. Dr. Strong took a hostile stance toward Karla, openly giving her a diagnosis at staff meetings of Oppositional Defiant Disorder. This diagnosis is given to children and adolescents when they deliberately go against parental dictums. This "diagnosis" was a clear insult, and reflected more on Dr. Strong's attempt to ridicule Karla than on Karla's actual behavior.

Finally, Dr. Strong told the staff on the child and adolescent unit that she was getting rid of Karla. She even began the interview process. One psychiatrist who came to be interviewed told Karla he did not want to be used as a foil against her, as Dr. Strong had told him he would need to do. He did not take the job. Then Dr. Strong found a child psychiatrist she felt was a sure replacement for her and began the process of hiring him.

Just at that time, Karla admitted a child, a boy of about ten years old, for anger problems. He and his mother told Karla he was sexually abused by the same child psychiatrist Dr. Strong was in the process of hiring. When this was reported to authorities, Dr. Strong had to withdraw her offer to this doctor.

Soon after that, Karla was called to see the assistant director. He informed her she was on probation, but gave no reasons. This was totally unexpected; she knew she had fulfilled all requirements of her position, and even more than was asked of her. She sat listening to the director, uncomprehending, seeing a door slamming closed in her face. However, she contained her tears, releasing them in bitter sobs only when she reached home. Malcolm, not knowing what had happened, asked her what was wrong. He listened quietly to the story, not commenting.

A few months prior to this, Malcolm had encouraged Karla to take a trip to Boston for a Harvard continuing education course. While there, she visited a book shop and was drawn to a box containing *I Ching* cards with an explanatory booklet. She noted it but did not buy it. The next day she felt an irresistible impulse to go back to the store and again this item drew her in its direction. She gave in and bought the cards. While in the hotel in her spare time, she posed questions and sorted the cards. As she did so, her anxiety lessened considerably; she was shocked at how exactly the cards represented her situation, the feeling of being trapped with no way out on several fronts. She had made a friend of the *I Ching* then; while describing her predicament it also began to hint at ways out.

After telling Malcolm about being put on probation, Karla turned to the *I Ching*. It told her she had support in unknown places that would come to her aid. But who and when remained an open question.

Two years later, she found out from Dr. Yoon that Dr. Glass had testified against Karla at Dr. Strong's request. Dr. Glass was instructed to tell the administrator of the mental health department that Karla was disrupting the team, that she was disrespectful and insolent. Of course, this was far from the truth, but since he was a long standing member of the medical community and was known to be honest, his word was taken as fact and that was the reason for the probation. Dr. Glass later confessed to Karla that he regretted his complicity with Dr. Strong and had borne false witness against Karla.

This testimony felt to Karla like another betrayal, bringing back memories all the way back to childhood. The community member who described Karla as "seductive" when she was eight was no different from Dr. Glass. These false testimonies did tremendous harm to Karla.

Now Karla was in a real bind; she feared working with the patients: if anything harmful happened to a patient under her care, Dr. Strong would be sure to lay the blame at her feet. She felt outnumbered and defeated.

How could she survive in this environment and still keep her integrity? Dr. Strong was playing games openly to get rid of her.

One morning, sitting across from Dr. Strong at a staff meeting, Karla made a decision. She would rely on the truth, and she would not resort to playing games as Dr. Strong was doing. Now she felt she had an inner resolve, a way of proceeding through the maze. She also felt an unknown support when she consulted the *I Ching* on the problems she faced. Every evening after dinner she would spend some time sorting the cards. It helped her work through the issues. Malcolm made fun of her obsessive need to consult the cards, but it was in good natured humor and he did not discourage it.

One day in the first week of December 1987, as Karla awoke, she again had that certainty in her chest of what she must do. She turned on the word processor and typed out her resignation, writing, "Without the support of the administration, I cannot safely continue to do my job."

Malcolm was shocked when she showed him the letter, but he said nothing.

She delivered it that morning to the assistant director who had put her on probation three months before. Everyone was shocked, especially the administration now caught with no one to replace her. They had to find a *locum tenens* temporary child psychiatrist as of January 1988 to fill her position.

How could she resign? Her family depended on her as the breadwinner while Malcolm was unemployed and a student. But that intuitive message from her deepest self was stronger than the reality confronting her. She told the hospital that she would continue with her outpatient practice but would not admit inpatients because she had lost confidence in Dr. Strong's support. In dividing the team, Dr. Strong had disrupted the unity so important for good treatment.

Now Dr. Strong vowed that she would drive Karla out of town. She did not keep her hostility to herself but let everyone know. However, within a few weeks of Karla's resignation, Dr. Strong was relieved of her position; she and her partner Diane left town.

Karla's next step was to hire a lawyer to look at her contract with the hospital; she was convinced she had some financial items they were still responsible for. Indeed, they ended up paying for one year of her office rent as compensation. It was a small amount, but since her income had now dropped considerably, it helped a lot.

Karla had dug in her heels, bordering on rigidity. Dr. Yoon came up to her in the kitchen of their office one day, stepped very close to her, and said in a confidential, quiet tone, "Please, at least admit adult patients to my unit. It will also help you."

His plea entered her heart and she started admitting adult patients, thus bolstering her income and mollifying the hospital administrators and staff. Had Karla asked, they no doubt would have given her back her clinical directorship, but she was too proud. She felt it was probably best in the long run if she left the hospital and moved to another location in Virginia. She applied for several positions at the University of Virginia student health but was disappointed at the small salary, which would not be enough for the family expenses now.

She asked Dr. Yoon for a letter of recommendation and was shocked when she read what he wrote. He commended her for her job skills, then added what a wonderful wife and mother she was, hoping she would not leave the community. Karla read the letter aloud to Malcolm, saddened by its contents and again softened. She ended up not moving.

Chapter 38

The surprising benefit of her leaving the clinical directorship was a lot more time with her family. They were finally able to travel, not only to visit supportive relatives Malcolm had in Pennsylvania, but also to Europe and California.

Since the kids missed California so much, Karla took them to San Francisco and Napa. Thais and Talbot loved this reconnection. Thais was able to spend time with a wonderful, supportive friend, and Talbot looked up his old schoolmates from St. John's.

Malcolm said he would never visit California again after his mother got very angry when he left. The letters she wrote him, full of anger and jealousy at his move away, depressed him each time. Her jealousy related to the fact that her sister Eleanor, with whom she had never gotten along, lived in New Jersey. Malcolm visited her and developed a relationship with her; she was an interior decorator and helped Malcolm find wonderful pieces of furniture and carpets at great discounts. Karla began to secretly throw the unopened letters away, as full of poison as they were. Malcolm instead began to focus on his future as a history teacher at a university setting.

Karla and Malcolm started looking at colleges for Thais the summer before her senior year. Malcolm was not in favor of large colleges, looking instead for a small, informal atmosphere for Thais. They visited Antioch in Ohio and also Oberlin. While at Antioch, Karla visited the bookstore on campus. There she saw Wilhelm Reich's *I Ching* translation of the sixty-four hexagrams. Again, she felt as if the book were calling to her. She ignored it the first day, but returned the next to buy it. This was the scholarly translation by a German scholar who had acquainted himself with the Chinese language. It would replace the cards she had been using.

Eventually, Karla memorized the hexagrams. She also learned the wisdom through much trial and error and daily study. Before making any decision, she would consult the hexagrams using three coins. She was surprised to find that doing the *I Ching* not only gave her sage advice, but, mysteriously, the situation she was questioning changed also.

Karla had a feeling her life was changing again, some big change, but she knew not what or how. She was becoming aware that as a family they would not stay in Lynchburg once Malcolm got his doctorate and found a job as a professor. He alerted her to some changes that would occur once he graduated.

"Be ready to be poor again when I get a job, for then it is your turn to do something you want to do; you can quit working and I will support us, but teacher's salaries are lower than what you are earning now," he advised.

Thais got accepted at Oberlin. She was a little hesitant about the distance; what if she needed chemotherapy? She had been in remission since fall of 1986, but she still needed updates of the chemotherapy and blood transfusions if her hemoglobin dropped after a treatment. Dr. Brooks said the treatment was minimal since Thais had been in remission three years. She would only need checkups.

But Karla also felt anxious about how far away Thais would be. She consulted her partner, Dr. Yoon. He agreed with her and suggested they get Thais into college in nearby Roanoke, only an hour away.

Karla did not tell Malcolm she had consulted with Dr. Yoon. She knew Malcolm felt very sure Thais needed a break from overprotective parents, needed to find herself in her own milieu, and Oberlin was also a conservatory where she could follow up on her violin and piano talents besides getting a good liberal arts education. So she buried her concerns in her heart and did not share them with Thais either.

Thais graduated in June 1989 with National Honor Society membership, a real accomplishment considering how much school she had actually missed. This was also partly due to her wonderful teachers who concerned themselves with her progress. What a happy occasion that graduation was! It was a celebration that she was alive and in remission, and that she would soon gain a lot more independence.

This was a time of transitions for everyone. Talbot entered high school as Thais entered college. Malcolm earned his master's degree in history in 1987 after only one year of study, and now he easily passed his oral exams for his Ph.D. Now he was busy collecting data for his dissertation; his focus was the Austrian novelist, Robert Musil. If he was successful with the collection of primary sources, he would complete his dissertation and graduate in the summer or fall of 1990. It was all happening so fast.

Thais transitioned to Oberlin, the whole family accompanying her and setting up her half of the room. She had a roommate, also a music student, but once the girl found out Thais had had cancer, she moved out. Thais was not a person who liked being by herself, so she made nightly phone calls to Karla, looking for reassurance. Then she branched out and developed friendships with some gay men and also made a wonderful friend named Sara; she was beginning to adjust. She thoroughly enjoyed her classes and especially the music. She joined a choir in a church in the vicinity and was a regular attendee there.

When Thais came home for Christmas break, she and Talbot developed a closeness with Malcolm as he was home most days now doing his research. He was finished with his class work, needed only trips back and forth to Charlottesville for more books for his notes. He would pick Talbot up at the bus stop every day. Now Thais added enjoyable talks with her Dad about her studies; she had become a refined young lady, always friendly and pleasant, respectful of her parents.

Just before Thais left to return to college, Karla arranged a family picture. It was a Sunday; they dressed semi-casually and went downstairs to the formal living room to pose. The photographer took pictures both inside and outside the house.

Chapter 39

Malcolm was also blossoming, very happy with his studies and his fast progress. One day he told Karla, "I realize now I am a scholar." He scheduled a trip to Austria to look at unpublished papers related to his inquiry, in February of 1990. His return ticket was to be scheduled later once he knew he was finished with his research.

The day Malcolm was to leave was a beautiful winter day. Karla was returning home from her morning session at the training center in Madison Heights, an additional job she had taken, across the James River Bridge from Lynchburg. As she drove toward home, she was interrupted by a funeral procession. A strange foreboding welled up in her, making her very uncomfortable. For a moment, looking at the hearse, she felt herself suspended in time.

When she got home, Malcolm was folding the laundry, his last act of kindness before leaving. Karla went upstairs to the bathroom, looked in the mirror, and started crying. The tears were overpowering her, and she had to tell herself to stop. She went downstairs and approached Malcolm and hugged him, which felt so good, but also so sad. He said not a word, immersed in his own sadness.

They picked Talbot up from school and headed for the airport. Malcolm's plane to New York was scheduled for 4 p.m.; from there he would catch his evening flight to Vienna.

Karla did not know why, but she did not accompany Malcolm to the gate, telling him they were going to watch the plane from a hill near the airport. As he walked down toward the waiting area, he did not look back. Karla drove up the hill and she and Talbot stood at the fence overlooking the runway. As the plane took off, she heard words involuntarily come out of her mouth: "I don't think we'll ever see him again."

It was an inappropriate thing to say to Talbot, a symptom of her passive resignation that bad things happened in her life. Her son, not having had such experiences, was puzzled. They went home, and soon had settled back into their daily routines. Before Malcolm had left for Europe, he had arranged for a woman to clean house on a weekly basis to ease Karla's life.

Then one day, Dr. Selig, the psychiatrist who was then working on the child and adolescent unit, told Karla that the administration wanted her to resume the directorship of the unit. They hoped she could forget what had happened two years before. Karla, happily shocked by this invitation, agreed and wrote Malcolm about the good news. He was very happy to hear it. Soon she was back again, working late hours and finding herself very pleased to be back up on the unit, the staff welcoming her back with open arms.

Thais was also doing well; she found some good friends at Oberlin, was much more comfortable this second semester, and called far less frequently.

Then one day early in March, the coffee maker stopped working, and around the same time, so did the TV. It puzzled Karla. Malcolm had always made the coffee their whole married life; the TV was also always under his control. This seemed so odd. She could not help associating these mechanical failures with Malcolm.

On the morning of March 13, Karla suddenly woke up from a deep sleep with a feeling of impending doom in her chest. She had never felt such a weighty darkness in her chest before. The clock at her bedside read 2:30. The pressure in her chest was so overpowering—a new experience, a kind of an inner implosion—that she went and sat on the toilet seat in the bathroom, waiting for the feeling to pass. Finally, she returned to sleep.

All day she was spooked; it seemed that all her patients were sobbing about adverse life events. Even though the patients related their own adverse events, their sadness pulled at her heartstrings as if it were her own.

Karla and Talbot were at breakfast the next morning, Wednesday, when the phone rang. It was Fritzi on the line. "Please find a chair and sit down," she said.

Karla perched on the bar stool by the telephone and heard Fritzi say, "Malcolm died. He collapsed at the train station waiting for the train to take him back to Vienna. We just had dinner with him on Sunday before he took the train to Klagenfurt. He seemed fine."

In an instant Karla's world stopped, becoming quiet and dark. She remembered what Malcolm had told her on their first date, about returning to the light at death. She also felt a certainty about their togetherness that would not be broken by death.

Then she became concerned about Talbot. He was quiet and numb, lying down on the couch in the family room, falling into a dead sleep. Later he told her he was hoping it was all a bad dream and on awakening, everything would be as it was before that morning.

Karla called the hospital to let staff know what happened and that she would be away for a few days. Everything moved in slow motion, the heaviness of the sadness and grief weighing her down every step. She wished someone could assist her to handle everything, but there was no one, just herself.

The minister and a staff member from the hospital came and stayed for an hour. Karla then had to call Thais and arrange for her to fly home that evening. She was in a state of shock on hearing about her dad, but said she would fly at the earliest time available. She had been exchanging letters frequently with her dad, and he had seemed fine.

Karla began the process of getting to Europe. Why did the American Embassy not notify her of Malcolm's death? She put this question in the back of her mind.

Then Karla went to buy three tickets to Klagenfurt with the local travel agent. Only Pan Am tickets were available, stopping over in Zurich with a connecting flight to Klagenfurt on Lufthansa.

Karla had an aisle seat in the mid-compartment and Thais and Talbot sat across the aisle in the window section. Both were crying intermittently, talking in low voices to one another. Karla, enveloped in her own disbelief and grief, was rudely jolted by the children behind her who kept grabbing on to her hair and kicking the seat. When she asked their mother to keep her kids from kicking the seat, she was rudely reprimanded. It was a most uncomfortable flight. The movie told the story of a boy who lost his father; in those days there was one screen in the front of the plane for each section, so one could not help but view the screen. Sleep was impossible for the three tearful travelers.

Arriving in Zurich, they barely had time to go to the bathroom before catching the plane to Klagenfurt. There, Karla and the children were met by a policeman and by Karla's half-sister Kristl. Where was Fritzi? Karla was expecting to see her at the airport. Instead Kristl told her they would stay with Aunt Mitzi after going to the morgue to make arrangements for the body.

When the morgue director brought out Malcolm's personal belongings, it was weird to see them without the person known to have carried them for years. Karla was given his wedding ring, his watch, his wallet, his little address book, and his passport. When Thais saw his wallet, she became ashen and could not contain herself; she was shaking. The morgue director said, "I think your daughter is very fragile. We should postpone the viewing until tomorrow morning."

Karla finished making the arrangements quickly, paying for the services, arranging for cremation and for the ashes to be transferred to the United States with help of the American Embassy. Kristl then drove them to Aunt Mitzi's house, about an hour north of Klagenfurt. Mitzi met them, along with her other daughter Elfi, and Elfi's twelve-year-old daughter Tanya, on Thursday evening around ten.

On Friday evening, Fritzi and her husband came to the door of Aunt Mitzi's house bearing an armful of red roses and embracing Karla with the words, "Let me bear your pain." After a brief talk, they left, saying they would see them next day.

As Karla and the children collected themselves, Elfi and Kristl played cards and talked quietly. Aunt Mitzi gave Karla some milk with rum and honey and tended to the children. They went upstairs to bed, sharing a large bed. When the lights went out, Talbot broke into sobs; intermittently there was crying through the night, and they barely slept. Nobody could quite believe what had happened.

The next morning, Aunt Mitzi had to attend a meeting at the Chamber of Commerce in her community, honoring her for her many years of business in the community. She was seventy-five years old and soon would hand the business over to a relative to continue.

Kristl packed Karla and the kids into her Volkswagen and drove back down to Klagenfurt to the morgue again. After they announced themselves, they were escorted to a makeshift room and the attendants carried out the wooden casket with Malcolm wedged into it. He was too large and long to fit into the casket entirely, looking uncomfortable even in death. It was awkward and insulting at the same time.

Karla approached him as the children stood off to one side. Their sadness at seeing their dad like this was humbling. He had always been their confident father, but now he was frozen and immovable.

"I am here, Malcolm; we are all here," she said as she touched his frozen hand. His eyes had been taped shut, so she could never look into those honest blue orbs again. His face was not discolored, luckily; it merely looked as if he had fallen asleep. Karla kissed him. The children approached and each touched his hands and kissed his forehead. Then it was over.

Karla went to the police department to sign papers. The policeman in charge that day was gruff and dismissive. "He was standing looking at the train schedule when he suddenly collapsed: there were several physicians in the crowd waiting for trains that morning, and they immediately administered CPR but to no avail," he said in a businesslike manner, shocking Karla.

Later Fritzi related that the police had called her on the day of Malcolm's death and asked her to call Karla. Fritzi did not want to do it—it was too awful—so she called Franz and asked if he would call Karla. He likewise refused. By this time a day had passed and so it happened that Karla got the call next day. Even their behavior puzzled Karla; why all this hesitancy?

Karla, overcome by grief, was looking only at her side of this, not really aware of the position her brother and sister had been put into by the police. Being the bearer of such disastrous news was too much of a responsibility to place on them. Much later, she realized this, but at the time, she needed their support too much and could not acknowledge the distress this caused them.

Karla looked at Malcolm's passport. Clearly written in it on the inside of the first page was their home number as well as the number of the American Embassy in Vienna. Neither had been called; instead they had looked through his little address book and found Fritzi's number. This continued to bother Karla, but she could not get anyone to clarify for her why she was not called directly and why the embassy was not notified.

The next day, Fritzi picked up Karla and the children to spend the afternoon with her and Horst, her husband. She had people over, and Karla and the children sat amidst them at the table. They were laughing and joking; no one mentioned Malcolm. The children were puzzled. Was this an Austrian custom, a kind of wake? None of them wanted to question this openly at the table for fear of showing displeasure. Karla began to feel very tired, and she could see the children were exhausted. Fritzi suggested that she and the children go upstairs to their bedroom and lie down. They did so, their energies totally spent, and they fell into a half sleep.

Karla was upset with Fritzi. She was hoping that she could spend some personal time with her, but Fritzi avoided her. When Karla asked her to clarify her involvement in getting the news out and to give her more details, she grew silent. At one point, Fritzi said that Malcolm was in a phone booth when he collapsed. When Karla reacted with surprise to the statement because it differed from the police report, Fritzi became tight-lipped, giving no further details.

Malcolm had visited Aunt Mitzi and Fritzi on the weekend before his death. Aunt Mitzi reported that he appeared very happy visiting them on Saturday, and was sincerely saying goodbye to everyone on leaving; he even went to the inn a block from Aunt Mitzi's house and bade his farewell. On Sunday he had dinner with Fritzi and Horst. Karla heard from her brother Franz later in the day: he wanted her and the children to take the train to Wurflach once all details were taken care of in Klagenfurt; he would then accompany her to Vienna to the embassy to report the death and to Malcolm's apartment to close it up and gather his belongings.

Karla was more and more puzzled. Did Malcolm die of a heart attack? Also mentioned in a letter mailed the day of his death (which she received after returning from Austria) was the appointment he had at the University in Klagenfurt where he was requesting to look at Musil's private papers, unpublished. He wrote that he was very rudely received and that they did not give him access to the papers. He was very upset, and this happened the Monday before the he died. He wrote how confounded he was at the rudeness of the professors. They refused to honor the letter of request which Malcolm's professor in Virginia had provided.

Karla did not know those details at the time she was in Austria for the funeral arrangements. She had been mystified because of the attitudes of everyone involved in this: the police, her sister, Aunt Mitzi. They all acted as if nothing had happened; she saw no tears being shed by anyone except herself and the children. It was so appalling, for Malcolm had treated them with the utmost respect and kindness always. Karla could not ascertain what they were feeling, but she felt relieved by the way it had all been structured to ease the strain on her.

Karla became worried that there had been foul play and contacted the morgue again, requesting an autopsy to be done before the body was shipped to Villach for the cremation.

She was on the way to Wurflach to meet her brother when she got the report from the medical examiner who performed the autopsy. The examiner said, "He had extreme arteriosclerosis of the coronary arteries, equivalent to a ninety-year-old man. There were no other findings, except mild involvement of the arteries in the brain." In a way it was reassuring. She and Malcolm both knew that he had heart disease; this was almost the natural result of that predisposition.

Before he left on his trip to Austria, Karla had arranged for him to see a physician to have his heart checked. When he came home from that visit, he told her he refused a recommended stress test, which had been recommended, and he was not going to have bypass surgery if it was suggested. She listened quietly as he talked, but, not wanting anything to be the matter, she did not press further. Now she wondered, was he not telling her everything about how serious the doctor thought his condition?

Chapter 40

Karla's intuition told her she was heading into a downward spiral emotionally, feeling paralyzed, feeling pulled, pushed, and sucked into a trajectory of disaster. She did not rally herself to change the trajectory but allowed herself to fall. When Malcolm told her what the doctor said, she should have insisted he delay his departure and do more thorough investigating. Again, Karla's feelings of responsibility were blinding her to the fact that Malcolm made his own choices and was more than capable of doing what he thought best.

Malcolm asked her before he left, "Is there anything you are going to do differently after I leave?"

"No wine with dinner. It's no fun to drink alone," she blurted out.

He laughed, "And what will that do?"

"Help me lose weight," she said.

After he arrived in Vienna, he wrote copious letters. Karla responded sparsely; she had always been a poor correspondent. He told her he had rented a nice kitchen-bath-bedroom ensemble including a television and he had brought a short wave radio with him, but had not installed a telephone—too costly, he said. In those days it was necessary to go to the post office and rent time in a box to make the phone call. So he would call her usually when it was noon in Vienna, which was 6:30 in the morning in Virginia, knowing she had not left for work yet. He called about once a week to update her on his progress.

She sent him money via a check, but he never got it and it was never returned. Soon he was short of money, neither one thinking of sending money via the express way. Actually Malcolm had told her that once his

135

mother wired money to him when he was traveling as a student. Why neither one availed themselves of this simple solution is baffling.

He began to send desperate letters that he had not received the check. In one letter he sent a cartoon of himself hanging himself out of desperation. Malcolm was a good cartoonist and had drawn many for Karla and the kids, often expressing black humor. But Karla got from this cartoon that he was feeling desperately alone. This desperation was not expressed in his phone calls, the last one being very upbeat as he had reserved his return ticket home on Karla's birthday in April. He did still have money enough to pay rent and food.

It was at this time she reassumed her position of clinical director on the child and adolescent unit, so she was much busier than before and never home before 8:30 at night. She was caught up in her own whirlwind.

All of this came painfully back to her after he had died. He had suffered abandonment emotionally during his childhood with his cold mother and was poorly equipped to deal with loneliness in a foreign city, but Karla, not realizing this, pictured him as an experienced traveler for whom loneliness was not a problem. She was wrong. She had thought him more resilient.

Karla and the children arrived by train in Wurflach; Franz met them at the station. They had taken an evening train so it would not disrupt his work schedule. Exhausted, they slept again in one bed in his home.

The next day, Franz drove with the three of them to the outskirts of Vienna, then hired a cab to bring them to the apartment block where Malcolm had lived. The second-floor walk-up was near the Westbahnhof train station, as Malcolm needed to travel often. The super let them in. The apartment was very neat, as well as very roomy and comfortable; Karla felt relieved. In the kitchen was a bottle of red wine and a pound of spaghetti and olive oil. He had been eating sparsely, fearing running out of money, but also keeping to the low-fat diet. To Karla's surprise, on the mantel was a picture postcard of Jesus Christ suspended on the cross in the sky. Malcolm had not been religious, had avowed himself an agnostic. She wondered, had he gotten his faith back in his loneliness? On the mantel also was payment for that month's rent which Karla gave the super. It was the exact amount owed. Apparently he had made sure to have enough to pay the rent at month's end.

Curiously, when Karla collected his suitcase and belongings, there was not a single note regarding his searches at the library. This shocked Karla, for he had told her things were going well as far as the data collection. He was a voluminous note taker; she did wonder if his notes had been removed. They would only be of value to someone who was interested in the same period in Austrian history, but there was no way they could get access before his death.

What she did find in the apartment were artworks that he had collected in his forays. One was a lithograph of an Austrian country woman, holding a child in her arms. Another was of St. Elizabeth, a very pretty painting on glass.

After taking the small bag packed with his belongings, Franz took them to the American Embassy in Vienna. They waited in line for admission to the building. Finally Karla got to speak to a clerk there, but she was very impersonal, telling Karla no one had notified them of Malcolm's death. Karla, having dealt much in her past with bureaucracy during those waiting days at the International Refugee Organization, was not shocked at how little Malcolm's death or its report mattered to officials. Karla signed papers allowing them to transport the urn from Villach to Washington, D.C., where she was to pick it up.

They returned to Franz's home in Wurflach late that afternoon. He insisted on taking Talbot to the barbershop for a haircut. Karla and the children were to leave for Lynchburg the next morning.

Karla looked with sadness and longing at the potted geranium Malcolm had given to Poldi before heading off for Klagenfurt. Neither Poldi nor Franz shed a tear in front of her, nor did they even mention Malcolm. Karla herself, being a warm, demonstrative person, would become tearful on others' behalf, would offer sympathy. But all her life, Karla had looked for more warmth than she had received; her ability to give it was based on how wonderful it feels when a person comforts another in distress.

On the family's return home from the funeral arrangements, Karla received Malcolm's last letter, dated the day he died, in the morning. He reported indigestion after the heavy meal at Fritzi's house on Sunday. Then he reported on the unpleasant reception regarding the primary sources in Klagenfurt. That was the last she heard from him directly. In the letter he stated he was very disappointed at the behavior of the professors at the University of Klagenfurt and he was frustrated with their rude treatment.

In this letter he had also said he believed there would be wars in the Middle East, escalating throughout the area. At the time he wrote this, there was as yet no warfare except the ongoing struggle between the

Palestinians and the Israelis. Karla wondered how he was able to predict war. That he even brought this up in his last letter puzzled her—it had nothing to do with his research. Still, his 1990 prediction came true over the next decades.

After returning home, she received a call from Linda, her teacher friend from the hospital. She reported that they had gone to Vienna as part of their European trip, especially to connect with Malcolm as they knew he was there. They arrived at Malcolm's apartment on Saturday, the day he had left for Klagenfurt. They found him not answering his door and left a note stuck into the door informing him of their visit, waiting to hear from him when they could meet. Karla found no such note in the door when the super opened it for them.

The strange discrepancies mounted. Not one note referring to Malcolm's research was found in the small bag he took on his travels. Nor were there any notes whatsoever in his apartment. Malcolm usually took notes both in English and German, leaving a shoebox full at home before he went on his trip. He would have been very accurate in identifying his sources, but not one piece of paper was found on his person, his apartment or his belongings. About a year later, a book was published in Austria dealing with the same material on which he was writing his dissertation pertaining to Robert Musil's literary relevance to Austrian history.

But more than just intellectual theft, things didn't make sense. The way the police had notified her about his death along with their failure in notifying the United States Embassy about a citizen's death abroad meant they had not followed protocol. Also, the way Fritzi suddenly became mute when she was telling Karla about him being in a phone booth when he died—she was covering up something. Karla could never find out what.

Karla had gone to the railway station in Klagenfurt and asked the attendant if she could speak with someone about the death that had occurred there that week. He referred her to the bathroom attendant, an elderly woman. She went with Karla to the place in front of the arrivals board and described how she had been sweeping up in that area when she noticed a tall gentleman suddenly collapse. She rushed to help him, collapsing herself with his heaviness. He died as she held him, both of them on the floor. Some doctors waiting for the train immediately administered CPR to no avail.

A couple of years later, Karla realized the same woman was still resident in the bathroom and that was her *only* ongoing duty, to collect money and clean the toilets after they were used. She would not have been sweeping the floor near the arrivals and departure board. When Karla used the restroom about five years later, the woman was still there, turning on Karla in a hostile way, having become senile. So Karla had doubts about her story, too.

She had planned to pick up the ashes when they arrived a week after her return, but finding she was still too numb to deal with the bureaucracy, she arranged for the local funeral home to bring the ashes to her. They did so with more show of respect and regard for her feelings than anyone heretofore.

It was the final step, receiving the urn. She put it first on a small table in the formal living room where Malcolm had enjoyed reading by the window in his chair. She felt a need for a religious acknowledgement or ceremony, or at least a priest to bless the ashes. She called their minister at the Unitarian Church, but was not offered the visit she asked for. She then turned to the Episcopal Church in Lynchburg because of the association with her priest friend, Annie, who had visited them recently. The priest came and sat with the three of them and said some prayers. Karla felt better.

The memorial service was not held until May, two months later; Annie came to perform the service. Annie stayed at the house with them and offered solace as she busied herself with printing a pamphlet and arranging the service in the small chapel of the Episcopal church in Lynchburg. The gathering consisted of Malcolm's graduate school classmates and professors, and Karla's colleagues and friends. His professors dedicated their monthly journal issue to Malcolm that year.

During the reception afterwards at the house, Karla missed her colleague, Dr. Yoon, who arrived late because he forgot the reception and had to be reminded by his staff. Annie met Dr. Yoon at the house and spoke with him before he found Karla. Later Annie remarked to Karla in a letter, as if in a warning, "Dr Yoon is a very handsome man, but he is married." Karla was puzzled. What did Annie see that she did not?

Many spiritual conversations took place during Annie's visit. At one point Annie, in referring to Karla's having no church at the time, remarked, "I wanted to take you to task for not attending church, but God told me you are His."

Another memorable evening that Karla never forgot was when Thais asked Annie, "What happens after we die, and what is it like to die?"

"It is just like birth," replied the reverend. "You are born to a spiritual life."

Thais remembered that. She got a rosary (Karla did not inquire from where) and she prayed with the rosary at night. Her faith became very strong. She did not further confide her fears about death to her mother and Talbot, but Karla was sure it was a matter of discussion with friends.

Chapter 41

Thais had taken the loss of her father very hard. In May, just a few weeks before the memorial reception for Malcolm, Karla got the dreaded phone call from Thais. She had been feeling weak; when she was tested at the clinic in Oberlin, it was found she had cancer again.

Karla immediately had her come home by plane that very day. Thais looked pale and wan. She had been grieving for her dad a lot, she told her mom.

She resumed treatment in Charlottesville with Dr. Brooks. She informed them that the more deadly form, myelogenous leukemia, had now surfaced. Thais would definitely need a bone marrow transplant to give her a chance of survival.

Karla was beset with fears. A bone marrow transplant was fraught with side effects and after effects, some of which might not show up for years. Unfortunately for Thais, neither Karla nor Talbot was a match. Malcolm might have been as they had the same blood type, but it was too late to know. A non-related donor transplant was harrowing and experimental. Karla prayed a lot and tried not to show her fear, for Thais needed all the courage she could muster for this exhausting therapy.

One day, Thais said that Dr. Brooks told her that sudden death was often the immediate outcome of a transplant as tissue rejection set in and all the organs were challenged to the utmost.

"But God would not do this to us," she had reassured Karla. "He took my Dad, so he is not going to take me now." The hope in her innocent blue eyes radiated love.

When they heard there was a donor match, they were overcome with gratitude. Now they had to wait for the cancer center to schedule a transplant, probably shortly after the new year. Meanwhile, Thais continued to get chemotherapy which allowed her to live as normal a life as possible. She needed blood transfusions more often now, though. She was also hospitalized at Virginia Baptist for treatments that could be done locally.

It was sad and disheartening that none of Thais's peers ever visited her when she was in the hospital. Her stays there were very lonely, watching TV all day while Karla worked, seeing Karla for a brief time in the evening before she went home with Talbot. But Thais bore it all cheerfully. In between treatments she helped out at home, visited with very nice friends she had reconnected with since coming home from Oberlin, and even got a part-time job at the store of a friend's father. The job made her very happy even though the pay was very little, because she felt productive and could talk with people. Out of her first paycheck, she bought Karla a decorative wooden Chinese box which became one of Karla's most cherished items.

Thais did not lose weight with her chemotherapy now, and with a reddish wig she looked the picture of health in between the treatments. Karla prayed for a miracle, that Thais have a spontaneous cure.

Chapter 42

$\mathcal{D}$espite the dark cloud looming over Karla's little family, she became concerned about her colleague, Al Yoon, after the memorial service in May.

Karla actually had not been aware of what happened to Al until she saw him sitting dejectedly at his desk one day. Stopping to inquire what was wrong, she heard his story. He had come home one evening from work about two months before, and a policeman was at the door to accompany him as he picked up some belongings; he had to move to a motel as he could no longer live at home. His wife had taken out a restraining order on him, and he was to have a court hearing regarding the charges.

Al and his wife had three children; one recently married daughter, a son in graduate school, and a daughter in college. They had been married twenty-eight years at this point.

Although Al was Karla's colleague, they did not socialize outside work. They shared the costs of the practice with Dr Glass, including secretary services and office space. She knew relatively little of his life outside the office. She was shocked at this series of events, especially given that he had just had bypass surgery in January of that year. Karla had visited him in the hospital at that time. Now he was kicked out of his own home.

It seemed incredible to her that he could have done anything wrong; he was a very respected practitioner and colleague. All she knew so far of his family life was that he was very devoted to his wife and children, but that his wife accused him of infidelity and had done so for years, even hiring a private detective on two different occasions to shadow him and report to her. When the detectives found nothing to report, she claimed he had bribed them. The restraining order charged him with physical abuse.

Karla was quick to reach out to him, feeling that even if she did not know what went on in his private life, he was her colleague and she supported him emotionally. She invited him over one evening to share a meal with her and the children, which he accepted. He was living on fast food and sleeping in a motel, having just one suit of clothes he had managed to grab before being escorted out of his house.

Karla had a practice of making bone soup with broccoli and cauliflower for Thais: it seemed to help her, for she did not appear sick at all. Al seemed to enjoy it, although he seemed very sad, not knowing his next steps. He didn't want to divorce, but was separated by force. He was debating if he should he return to Korea. But his children still needed his support and he wanted to be there for them. Karla heard from another colleague that he had also been considering suicide.

Karla felt compassion in her heart and reached out with friendship, which he reciprocated. The kids also liked Al, who developed a habit of visiting Thais during her chemotherapy hospitalizations, which cheered her up.

So in the midst of her own crises and losses, Karla found a friend in Al—although there was very little actual contact between then outside of the practice.

Chapter 43

$\mathcal{A}$s the end of summer of 1990 approached, Karla, Talbot, and Thais spent precious time together. Thais had become a beautiful, charming young lady, a smile ever-present for everyone, with sparkling blue eyes that shone with innocence and good will. She was quick to uplift and support, did not spend any time moping or bemoaning her fate. Her faith had grown strong; she trusted that all would turn out well.

"God would not let anything bad happen to us after Dad," she reminded her mother each time she saw her worrying.

She made some very nice friends in Lynchburg, sincere young men and women who gave her much comfort and happiness with their presence. She also looked after Talbot, chiding him good-naturedly for not being attentive to his homework. Over the summer Thais finished her freshman curriculum at Oberlin and would now be a sophomore should she be able to return to school.

She was also busy trying to patch up a lost friendship from her life in Napa. As a freshman in high school, she had started a band, with herself as the singer. They were able, along with other teenage bands, to give a performance at Justin Siena High School. Her good friend Nancy, whom she loved dearly, was the string player. As the piece they composed between them came to an end and they were about to take their bows, Thais joked with Nancy, "You were out of tune," or something to that effect. Nancy took this very seriously, as did her mother in the audience—the mother actually told Thais, "You should die for this!" From then on, Nancy refused all contact with Thais and did not accept an apology. Thais mourned the loss of a friendship that had meant so much to her. Repeatedly she wrote letters to Nancy, asking for forgiveness, despite Karla's advice to just forget it.

Finally, in 1990, Nancy agreed to meet her at Reverend Annie's house in Benicia during a planned visit to California. There Nancy and Thais made up; Thais was tearful and so grateful that this wound could be healed. That was how Thais was.

It was Thais who pointed out to Karla one day after Al had visited her in the hospital, "Dr. Yoon likes you, Mom."

"Of course; we're friends," Karla said.

"No, Mom, he likes you more than as a friend," replied Thais.

Karla became thoughtful but could not relate to that statement and let it drop.

Al had offered to pick the three of them up at the airport on their return from California that summer, and Karla was chagrined because they missed the connection in Atlanta and he had to come back again several hours later. It didn't matter to him, though; Al was cheerful and felt no inconvenience.

One afternoon that summer, as Karla was enjoying a cup of tea at home after work, she suddenly felt a strong urge to put pencil to paper. She closed her eyes and let the pencil move on its own accord. It felt as if she was scribbling, but when it stopped, she opened her eyes and to her amazement saw, "I shall return to Lynchburg on August 29. Malcolm."

This was indeed shocking and was the one and only time this happened to Karla. She had no previous experience with automatic writing, although she knew of it from her readings. She kept the date in her heart and waited to see what would happen on that day.

On August 29th, at the end of her office day as she cleaned up her desk for the next day, Al came into her office. He asked if he could have dinner with her. Overcome with emotion, she could just muster, "Please ask me again tomorrow." It was obvious that this was what the note had talked about: Malcolm through Al; Malcolm uniting her with Al.

Why the postponement on Karla's part? She was excited because of the association with Malcolm, but apprehensive about Al being the one.

Our intuitive self is connected to everything that is and sends its messages in diverse ways. In this case, Karla would not have been able to get such a clear message unless it was on a piece of paper clearly written.

The next day was Friday. Al saw her as she was leaving the hospital after rounds and again he stopped her and asked her to have dinner with him. Smiling, this time she replied, "Yes, call me later, after work."

Karla knew intuitively this was not just a dinner date, but beyond that she had no idea what might happen next.

He called around 4:30, saying he would like very much to take her out to dinner, but he did not think it was a good idea at this time. Instead, could they meet at the office around six for a talk?

Karla told the children she was going to a meeting with Al and left after an early dinner. She waited in her office. He came a short while later, carrying a can of Diet Coke.

He sat across from her, she in the chair and he on the double loveseat. They began talking about their personal lives, she about her sadness, he about his failed marriage and his loneliness. He told Karla the court hearing some months ago merely stipulated that they were to live in separate spaces—hence his apartment.

"Do you think you will get back together with your wife?" Karla asked hesitantly.

He shook his head. "I don't think so; it has gone too far."

He proceeded to relate details of the troubled relationship from its very start. Many attempts to improve the relationship failed. He was very concerned about the effects their marital problems had on their children and had wanted to leave the relationship many times but always stayed to make sure the children reached adulthood before acting on his need to have a less troubled life.

He was having health problems: high blood pressure, heart symptoms of angina and his blood sugar was out of control. He had a heart attack in January of 1989 and a double bypass operation was performed.

He had been told by his physicians another bypass might be necessary within five years. He felt tired all the time and was anxiety ridden about what his future held.

Karla had not been aware that Al had such serious marriage and money problems. She had heard some staff on the adult unit refer to his problem with his wife, but she never asked questions, feeling it was none of her business. Now she wondered how she had missed all of this while practicing with him every day. The reason was that he never complained.

She also recognized that in Korean families at the time, husband and wife frequently lived separated but did not divorce. That has since changed since then, but in the nineties, divorce was still rare, especially in immigrant couples.

She felt as if she had stepped into a wasp's nest in getting closer to Al. She feared that his wife would never divorce him or that he would simply acquiesce to her ways and even resume married life. As she got up to leave, he let her go, but not without saying, "Please let me see you again."

Chapter 44

She drove home, her head spinning. What had just happened?

In meeting with Al, she had opened her heart to him. She truly wanted to help. Moreover, feelings of attraction were developing in Karla. They had long been friends, but now she saw Al in a different light, as a suffering man whose health was deteriorating from stress in his marriage. She cared.

He met with her later the next day and they sat in his car. His face was sad and serious, talking about leaving the city and going far away, maybe Guam.

The next day, Sunday, he called and said he was going to the funeral of a colleague in the medical community who had shot himself in a depressive phase of his bipolar illness. The funeral would be on September 2, a Monday, also Labor Day. She agreed to meet him at the church.

She was about ten minutes late entering the church and had to take an available seat at the back, whereas she saw him sitting up in front. She sat looking pensively at the coffin, realizing how suddenly one's fate can change. Their colleague was a brilliant man respected in the community, but that did not save him from losing his own battle with bipolar illness. A foreboding took over in Karla; she felt sad, not only about the colleague who took his own life, a genius in his field, but also about her own future, reading this funeral as a sign she did not really want to accept.

It may be hard for the reader to understand the forebodings Karla had about future events. It is simply a fact of her existence that she had these limited views into the future, often accompanied by the emotions that would accompany the future event. In some ways, it could be considered a gift, although a terrible one at times.

Al and Karla did not see each other that day as Karla stole away, overcome by the fear she felt.

Another day he asked to meet her again in the evening, at the office, when no staff was there. This time he inquired about her sexual history, looking very serious, a sadness in his eyes that she could not read. As she related the important events in that history, he made no comment, but listened attentively. Karla was surprised. *Does he have some awareness of my past without my having told him?*

When she finished, he rose, walked to her, kissed her, and held her in his arms.

They met at the office again on Saturday morning, after rounds. This time he brought a translation of Korean poetry for her to take home and read, relating his own desire in his youth to become a poet. Instead, his father urged him to study medicine, and Al considered that request a command. Still, he had devoured books from early childhood, reading in a bookstore where the owner, a friend of his mother, indulged him. He read incredibly quickly and had a good memory of what he read, considering it meaningful information related to his life.

After that, Al and Karla would meet once or twice a week in the evening to talk and embrace and love each other. He would also take her for drives out on country roads. Karla, always happy to be in natural surroundings, loved the slender oaks that reached their arms into the sky and their foliage, a cool green mixed with a palette of reds and yellows.

She was amazed how much she loved him; after all, Malcolm had only been dead for six months. But she often wondered how the relationship began, with the channeling she received from Malcolm, and thought it possible his spirit was there as well, encouraging her to open her heart.

Al's health was not the best; he told Karla he expected he would need another bypass in five years. He was on medications for high blood pressure, high cholesterol, and depression. He was told to change his diet drastically to help the blood sugar normalize. He ignored the directive to use the treadmill for daily exercise. He also suffered from anxiety about his future; how long did he have to live? What would happen to his children as a result of the divorce? All these thoughts whirled through his head, he told her. He also contemplated returning to Korea, starting anew there, but he knew he could never leave his children and they were established here, fully integrated in the American way of life. They were young adults now, all of them still in higher education, and developing important relationships for their future. He did not want to take that away from them.

Karla began pointing out to Al how he could eat healthier, but he really was not prepared to listen; he had more important issues to occupy his time. He was too overwhelmed to take his own health needs into consideration. He continued his maladaptive patterns.

Karla also noticed that Al had never mastered the English language well, speaking in what Karla called "Korean English." He confused personal pronouns, which made his communication hard to follow; he also often left off the subject. His communication improved much with frequent reminders and nudges like, "Who are we talking about?" Karla often wondered how he communicated with his patients, but realized it was his warmth and supportive manner that patients related to more than his language. He was also a good listener. He was very popular with patients. Karla learned in her later studies of acupuncture that patients come to a practitioner "to sit by his fire" and heal themselves. Thus his speech reached the listener's heart; it was often quite poetic, and people remembered what he said. Karla herself had often been struck by how his words went to her heart, long before they became more than friends.

And it continued as they became lovers. "Your eyes are like the ocean; they express a broad mind and tolerance." He looked deeply into her eyes, his own filled with such warmth. They saw each other's souls.

Chapter 45

*F*all was coming, the leaves turning a flamboyant gold and red, setting everything ablaze on those sunny days of October. Karla became very concerned that Al was living in his house again, knowing there were daily angry arguments with his wife. Karla knew that for a person with a heart problem, anger was very bad; this held true as well as for diabetes, because the fight-or-flight response pours sugar into the bloodstream.

However, Karla now became consumed with waiting for a transplant date for Thais, planning for the eventual temporary move to Seattle and informing the hospital mental health director of the need to find a replacement for at least a six-month period. Dr. Brooks had originally suggested the University of Nebraska as the transplant center because, she said, "They do wonderfully with adolescents." In Karla's mind there would be an advantage in that she knew Omaha and the university medical center was her alma mater. The disadvantage was that her parents still lived in Omaha, meaning dealing with the dysfunctional family. It would be too great a burden for all of them. So she chose the Hutchinson Cancer Research Hospital, a center limited to bone-marrow transplants and thus having the most experience with that procedure.

Dr. Brooks' responded to Karla's choice with silence, since clearly the University of Nebraska was her first choice for Thais. However, Karla stuck to her decision.

Karla would long remember the Christmas of 1990, her heart bursting with love and anguish whenever her memory took her back. She did not feel emotionally ready to celebrate Christmas without Malcolm. She told the children she would not bring in a Christmas tree; it would be too sad, remembering how wondrous the Christmases had been for the family when Malcolm was alive.

Thais was to be discharged from the University Hospital in Charlottesville two days before Christmas. Karla was so happy to bring her home, and as they drove along Highway 29 south to Lynchburg from Charlottesville, everywhere there were festive lights. It was gloaming, and the atmosphere was filled with a soul-expanding serenity.

The day before Christmas, as she arrived home from work, she found a beautiful tall Christmas tree decorated in the living room, standing in the same place as years before. Thais and Talbot had pooled their cash and spent $75 for a tree, shining and splendid with the ornaments and lights. On that afternoon as Karla worked, Thais and Talbot had invited their friends to help them decorate the tree. They were so happy and Karla caught the spirit. That brought back the wonder of Christmas once again, all that love.

Karla then shared with the children that when Malcolm's mother had lost her father at the age of ten—he had bladder cancer, apparently as a result of having been exposed to carcinogenic chemicals at his job as a chemist—her mother, Malcolm's grandmother, decorated the Christmas tree that year as she had always done before, letting her girls know that life goes on. That grandfather was Malcolm's namesake. Now Malcolm's daughter was doing the same thing.

Karla learned much from Thais about forgiveness, about love that does not end, about kindness and consideration, and about the joy in life. Though Thais was threatened with death and sickness, she embraced life to the fullest, taking joy in everything she could. She listened to and wrote music, sang, read, danced, and learned, all with determination and joy.

On Christmas Day, Karla felt sad, overcome by memories of Christmases past. Thais suggested they visit a winery about twenty miles up north. They got into the car and as they drove, Karla's spirits rose. The children were so happy about that; they were very concerned about Karla's grieving, although she generally hid it from them, crying quietly in her bed or going to the bathroom and sobbing. Maybe it would have been better just to let them see her grief, but she thought all the happiness they could muster would make her happy as well. After all, there was a sword still hanging over them. Every day now was so precious.

Chapter 46

*I*n March of 1991, Karla made the detailed arrangements for the trip to Seattle. The neighbors across the street offered to let Talbot stay with them for the duration of their stay in Seattle. Talbot, however, chose to go along to Seattle.

A secretary at the office whose own daughter had had a successful bone-marrow transplant at the Hutchinson Cancer Center referred Karla to her volunteer worker in Seattle. The volunteer arranged for one week's free room at the Sheraton in the city. This would allow Karla ample time in which to find an apartment for the family.

Karla had worries about the house being left unattended for up to six months. Arranging and paying for continuing yard care eased her concern about the outside, but what about any problems that might occur inside? Anything could happen, even someone breaking in knowing they were gone.

At work, she had to make sure there were follow-up programs in place. Dr Selig, her benefactor in getting her directorship back, was taking over the unit in addition to the long term unit he was already managing. She felt very lucky for his help. Oddly, the hospital did not excuse her from paying her monthly office rent even though they let other professionals use her office during her absence, and this was a sore spot for her.

Al had kindly agreed to take care of her patients for the duration of her absence and even to take over an extra job she had at the local training center, saving the job for her return. She was immensely grateful to him for this, for she depended on her office and hospital practice; there were no substantial savings she could rely on when she returned, and in the meantime she would have all the extra expenses of the apartment and car they would have to rent in Seattle.

Al also arranged for a farewell party consisting of colleagues and the office staff, who came to the house the day before the family left, helping to spread good cheer and vowing all their support. Thais was appreciative and hopeful, talking to her friends, absorbing their good wishes and love, while Karla nearby hid her tears and her anxiety. The picture taken of Thais that day shows a beautiful young woman, her hair glowing with a reddish tint (a wig, of course) and looking radiant and healthy; looking at the picture, it was hard to believe she was at death's door.

Thais had bought extra-large t-shirts to wear at the beginning of her treatment before having to switch to hospital gowns. She was practical in her packing, taking only necessary items. Her room was left as tidy as always.

The morning of the departure to the airport, Al picked them up; the office staff and another colleague followed along, planning to stay with the family until the plane left. At the time there were no security checks, so they could sit with them at the gate until the plane boarded. As they sat and chatted, Karla noted that Thais had a look on her face that said, "Please God, let me see this airport and these people again."

Upon arriving in Seattle, they connected with Sherry, the volunteer from the Hutchinson Cancer Center, and checked into the Sheraton for the week. It was one of the simple rooms with extra beds put in and looked out on to a hotel across the street that had flags flying from many different nations. Karla focused on the Korean flag and thought of Al. What would happen to their relationship during her absence? *He might forget me,* she thought with trepidation.

It was the last day of March, and it rained gently all week in Seattle. Karla left the children at the hotel and went looking for apartments, guided by the need to be close to the hospital while finding enough space, and of course a kitchen and laundry facility. She looked at four or five small, cramped apartments with lofts, but she knew Thais might be too weak to climb up. She felt discouraged when they only had three days left at the hotel before they would be charged for their stay.

Finally she found a suitable apartment. It was walking distance from the hospital and clinic, and it also had shuttle service to and fro. It had two bedrooms and a fold-out couch in the large living-dining area, with a small kitchen and even a small washer-dryer. The apartment was bright and airy and clean. All the families living in the building were going through the same experience, with a loved one receiving treatment at Hutchinson.

They immediately took possession of the apartment, everyone very relieved. She had also rented a car on a monthly basis at an inexpensive car place and was given a Toyota with a shift and some dents in it, perfect for their requirements and much cheaper than some others she had found.

Karla went to tell the volunteer that she'd found an apartment. Sherry worked at the Sheraton as a bookkeeper. She was a woman in her late thirties who had lost a sister and mother to leukemia. She had a preteen son and lived with her boyfriend in the suburbs. She was also an alcoholic, which Karla associated with Sherry's experiences losing a sister and mother to cancer. Sherry was wonderfully supportive, though, and started by giving Thais a lovely ceramic music box. She was in touch with them almost daily, letting them know where to eat while at the hotel; she was a godsend.

They also met a second volunteer, Terri, a woman in her forties who was rather self-involved, talking with Thais more about herself and her troubles. However, she also took them out to parks and to see places outside the city while Thais waited for admission on the 8th of April.

That first week was very busy with welcome attention from the volunteers and completing the move to the apartment. However, Karla was also very concerned about Talbot's continuing school; he was two weeks behind already in his second year of schoolwork. The education clinic that was offered to siblings of patients as part of the program at the Hutch was hit and miss, and Karla wanted more for her son. She explored the area and found a Catholic boys' school within walking distance from the apartment and the Hutch. She inquired about possibly admitting Talbot for the rest of the year, and after deliberation, the administrator enrolled him for the rest of the term as a sophomore. There was tuition to pay, but Karla thought it well worth it. And it was: Bishop O'Dea, turned out to be a boon for Talbot, for he spent the full day there, engrossed in learning and interaction with peers his own age. He loved it.

Al called every day to inquire about their progress, reassuring Karla that the relationship was continuing. She always felt supported by his positive attitude that all would work out well. Everything seemed to be getting settled the way Karla had hoped.

Chapter 47

April 8 arrived and Thais had already finished all of the legal, financial, and other documentation required for her admission to the hospital. She was pleased to tell Karla that she would be getting SSI support during her treatment and convalescence.

Karla and Talbot accompanied Thais to her hospital intake. A doctor sat down with them, informing her that her donor was a male and she would have male red cells. What impact that would have was unknown. He also discussed the imminent threat of death due to the severity of the treatment, challenging her body to the utmost. It was sobering and a bit terrifying for them all, but they were grateful for the information.

Then the nurse assigned to be Thais' primary took her to be bathed to sterilize her before she could be put to bed. The nurse later told Karla she had never taken care of such a magnificent body, since admissions were usually pretty sick, but Thais had an appearance of vibrant health. *Must be the broccoli bone soup*, mused Karla.

Once Thais was in her bed, Karla and Talbot had to gown themselves and wear masks to be allowed into the room. It was uncomfortable, but this would be an everyday requirement from now on.

So far, so good, Karla thought to herself, *but what will be next?* She soon found out that the process would involve total body irradiation and combination chemotherapy to kill all of Thais's red and white blood cells. Karla was staggered by the attack on her daughter's body this treatment entailed. They were told the side effects possible, which included sterilization. The doctors asked if she wanted to have eggs harvested and frozen for future use.

Thais looked at her mother for an answer.

"Is the harvesting painful?" Karla asked.

"Yes, unfortunately there is a lot of discomfort to bring the eggs to harvesting."

"Then, no, I don't want my daughter to have any more discomfort added to what she is experiencing already," Karla said firmly, locking eyes with Thais. She could see in those eyes the sad statement, "Mom, you are giving up on any grandchildren." But Karla had a single goal: getting her daughter through this alive, with the fewest assaults on her body.

When she had time to think, Karla felt downcast. Total body irradiation, exposing every cell in Thais's body to potential cancer-causing fire—and Karla was helpless to mitigate it. Thais, too, was shocked at the intensity of her treatment and the dangers lurking in this life-saving procedure.

On the day of the radiation, Karla sat in the waiting room. When Thais was brought back out, she was as red as a cooked lobster and looked exhausted, barely mustering a few words. Now she would have no viable blood cells anywhere in her body.

The bone-marrow transplant was scheduled to take place overnight, beginning April 30 and ending May 1. It entailed a slow intravenous drip of the donor cells. Thais would be sedated to lessen some of the shock she would feel.

The little family was full of hope that evening as the drip was started toward midnight, Talbot and Karla watching and praying, both for Thais and for the donor. It was a very sacred moment of time, entailing gratitude of an immense sort for the unknown donor, being witness to an exciting step in the progress of medicine, and most of all, a feeling of saving Thais from the brink of death.

Karla had been working with the *I Ching* throughout this time, containing her anxiety as she threw the coins, hoping that the manipulation of the hexagrams would intervene in a positive way as had been her experience in the past. Interestingly, the hexagram she drew for the transplant was thirty changing to one, the same as the date of the transplant.

When it was over, they prepared for some serious effects of the transplant: the host versus graft rejection and the possibility of infection while the blood cells established themselves. She was given intravenous amphotericin, an antifungal, because of the danger of Candida infection during this vulnerable period. This antifungal could damage her kidneys, they were told. Thais was exhausted, very pale, and scared.

On Mother's day in mid-May, Karla and Talbot were with Thais. They were dressed in the sterile gowns and masks. Suddenly, Thais went pale and stopped breathing. The nurses immediately called a code and medical staff rushed in, closed the curtain, told Karla and Talbot to leave the room, and began resuscitation.

Karla and Talbot were in shock—it all happened so quickly. Half an hour later, Thais was breathing, but she was in a coma. Karla stayed the night, sleeping on a loveseat in the waiting room, just around the corner from Thais. She didn't really sleep, going every hour to check, being told, the condition had not changed.

Now the vigil began, every day sitting at Thais's bedside, holding her hand, talking to her as if she were awake, telling her how much she was loved and asking her to please come back. Karla was told that the reason for the coma was an invasion of Thais's brain by the Candida as her immunity was very low until the transplant could start producing immune cells.

Two weeks later, Karla had gone home to pick up Talbot and bring him to the hospital; as they walked to Thais' room, they saw her sitting in a wheelchair with supports to her back, just inside the door, waiting for them with a huge smile on her face. Overjoyed, Karla donned her gown and mask and hugged her daughter, a grateful prayer in her heart. Thais had two drawings she had done just before they came: one was of Talbot, wide-eyed with his mask, and the other of Karla, sitting with one hand behind her back, with an inscription, "To my lovely Mom." Karla's heart burst with joy and relief. Talbot was tender and attentive to his sister.

Thais gained strength from the many cards and letters she received from the Lynchburg community, which covered a whole wall in her room. She enjoyed looking at those good wishes from so many people who cared about her. Karla herself was amazed at the number of teenagers and adults who reached out to her daughter and her heart was grateful.

Because she was very weak, Thais' muscles had to be trained so she could walk again. There were daily physical therapy exercises to get her strength and mobility back. But soon another complication made itself known: her entire skin came off in fine, sunburn-like peels. Underneath the old skin was the new skin, soft and fine like a baby's. The process took about three weeks. She was having a severe rejection response despite the medications to counter this.

Talbot would come from school in the afternoon and lift everyone's spirits with his comments—he was their resident stand-up comic. It was so wonderful, this laughter on top of all the serious events going on with Thais. She also needed dialysis now, as her kidneys had suffered not only from the amphotericin but also the host-versus-graft response. But she was so happy to be alive, to be able to move, to converse, to love. And she had reserve enough to be concerned about Karla, about her long hours at the hospital every day. "Mom, do you think you could let one of our family who are visiting come and stay with me while you get some rest?" she asked. Karla couldn't believe how considerate her wonderful daughter was, even when she felt so ill.

By the beginning of the last week in June, Thais no longer needed dialysis, but the doctors continued close monitoring of her kidney function. The pulmonary specialist announced that, despite a cardiac rub he heard, he felt Thais could go home to the apartment and be followed as an outpatient. On June 30th, Talbot's sixteenth birthday, Thais was discharged. Talbot saw the homecoming as his greatest birthday present ever. In the evenings the two would sit together and pray, thanking God for her life and recovery.

One day the nurse from the Hutch was there for the home visit; she asked Thais about her near-death experience back in May. Thais told her she would tell her in private, not in front of her mother and brother. Karla was taken aback but did not say anything. She never found out what Thais did experience and why she could not relate it in front of her family, but there were several clues Thais released without identifying them as such.

They were now preparing to return to Lynchburg sometime toward the end of July. Karla bought a large suitcase and showed it to the kids, telling them she was going to start packing and also order airline tickets.

"Don't be too sure, Mom," Thais offered but said nothing more until a few days later. Karla was talking about Al and Thais said, "Mom, you are going to marry Al and I will be at the wedding."

Again, Karla wondered where this came from. Karla herself had grave doubts whether Al would ever actually divorce, and marriage seemed an improbable step for the two of them.

Thais and Karla went on a little outing in the car one day, to the downtown Seattle section, finding a bench with trees all around, a pretty place. Karla sat down on the bench, but Thais stood behind her: Karla felt watched. It felt like Thais was trying to communicate something to Karla, but decided it was better not to, leaving the air gravid with intent and unspoken warning. She felt it but did not say anything to her daughter, but it did not augur well. Karla felt immeasurably sad, and stealing a look at her daughter's face, saw it mirrored there.

Karla and Thais visited the nearby library from which Karla had gotten books. Karla again had that familiar feeling of being drawn to a book, a Taoist story which deeply impressed her. The story told of a teacher whose female student accused him of impregnating her. The parents, infuriated, brought the child to him to raise. Without any objections or protestation, he raised the child. When the child was grown, the parents came again, demanding the offspring back, because they now knew he was not the father. Again, without protest he allowed this son to be taken from him.

Karla knew the message: accept fate, for its mystery is beyond human understanding.

Chapter 48

One morning, the 19th of July, Thais awakened, saying she did not feel well. She appeared swollen and exhausted. They went to the clinic and as Thais was waiting for the doctor, reclining in her chair, she told her mom, "I'm having trouble breathing, Mom."

Karla rushed to get the doctor. On examining Thais, the young doctor said, "She has cardiac tamponade. The sack surrounding the heart is filled with fluid; it needs immediate surgery to relieve the pressure on her heart and lungs."

As they waited for the surgery to be completed, Karla and Talbot felt their own hearts full of anxiety and fear. It had all happened so suddenly. Karla was grateful that Thais was already at the clinic when her symptoms occurred, for if she had been at the apartment, it might have been too late to save her life.

The surgeon came into the waiting area. "She is still in grave danger," he said. "She had a lot of fluid around her heart."

Thais came out of recovery, conscious but clearly uncomfortable with her breathing. She was hospitalized at the Swedish Hospital where the clinics were located and where the surgery had taken place. Talbot and Karla stayed at her bedside.

"I'm having trouble breathing again," she said in the early evening. The physician who came said they would have to intubate her.

Because of the pain from the tube in her throat, she was given heavy doses of narcotics and she passed into a near coma. Another physician came in an hour later and assessed her fluctuating blood pressure and erratic heart rate. He told Karla, "She may not make it through the night; her vital signs are very unstable."

Karla held on to Thais's hand, watching the monitors. Thais was fighting for her life with all the strength she had left. Karla was numb, praying, beseeching God for Thais's life.

Talbot's anxiety and disappointment were also very worrisome. He had been so thrilled when his sister was at home and they had made plans to return to Lynchburg. Karla had to send him back to the apartment alone at about 11 P.M. She needed to get someone he could vent to, so she called the social work department, but everyone had gone home. It was an insane bind for Karla, both her children needing her desperately—there wasn't enough of her, not enough hours in the day.

Talbot called a few hours later, saying he had thought of jumping out the window at the apartment, he was so distraught and scared. She ordered him to come to the cafeteria, where they sat and talked until he calmed down. He went home with a promise of not harming himself. They would see this through, she told him.

Back at the bedside with Thais, she held on to that dear little hand, the hand she had always feared was too soft and yielding. The heart rate went up to 180 and 190, then back down to 90 and 100, the blood pressure accompanying it. It was dizzying to watch the instability of her heart.

Morning came. Karla had closed her eyes for a few moments when it looked like the heart was stabilizing, but it always only lasted for a few minutes. The staff from the Hutch came to transport Thais back to the center where they could give her expert care. As they wheeled her through the connecting hallway with an oxygen tank attached to her bed, the tub in her throat was jostled and she contracted in pain.

"We will give her periods without the oxygen to see if she will breathe on her own," they explained to Karla.

Thais awakened as they did this and motioned for a pen and paper on which she tried to write, but had not enough strength and Karla could not make out the words at first. Finally she got the message: "Please take out the tube."

Karla explained to Thais what the staff would try to do periodically to see if she could breathe on her own, but if she could not, so she had to remain intubated to save her life.

Because of fear of infection, they did not perform a tracheostomy, and to tolerate the pain of the tube in her larynx, Thais needed to be heavily sedated. Still, periodically she would open her eyes and smile lovingly at Karla and Talbot. Her nursing care had now intensified, with a team of nurses rotated sitting, one at a time, in Thais's room, monitoring constantly.

Karla and Talbot and of course Thais in her dreamlike state got to know these nurses individually for they conversed as they kept watch. All of them were very kind and most attentive to Thais's every need.

The doctors were more impersonal and spent little time with Thais directly, being more concerned with lab values and progress or the lack thereof. As Thais failed to improve, one doctor even rudely told Karla it was time for Thais to die.

Karla insisted on getting an outside consultation for Thais's heart. Reluctantly, the chief nurse agreed and a cardiologist came and assessed Thais. Off to the side, he remarked, "You could sue them; they discharged her from the hospital too soon. She had a cardiac rub which indicated she needed attention to the heart before she left the hospital."

Under the consultant's care, Thais's heart stabilized and resumed normal rhythm and blood pressure. But the lungs did not respond, and an MRI revealed no lung function. She had developed respiratory distress syndrome stemming from the challenged heart.

On July 22, Thais's twentieth birthday, she was on a respirator and getting dialysis, and her liver enzymes were elevated. Her body was failing her. But she fought on, together with Karla in denial of the death specter at the foot of her bed.

Talbot was in therapy with a psychologist who was preparing him for Thais's death. She also recommended Karla begin therapy to deal with the reality of the situation. Karla's answer was prayer and the *I Ching*. She prayed night and day, and when her anxiety got so great because Thais did not improve, she resorted to the *I Ching*. The advice was, "Go with the flow." Very disheartening.

She got some encouragement when she was told by one of the lung specialists that Thais could regain her lung function, it was not a static condition. Her heart had stabilized; there was no longer a rub and rhythm was strong and good.

Karla held Thais' hand every day, now on this side of the bed, then on the other side. She talked to her daughter, knowing that at some level the communication was reaching her. When she opened her eyes, there was such love in them that Karla felt immense gratitude for those brief encounters.

The staff was now pressuring Karla to discontinue life support, for they saw no hope. Thais had signed a Do Not Resuscitate order, a right-to-die directive before she started her treatment. Karla would not give the staff this document when they asked for it, claiming she did not know where it was. She realized they knew she was lying, that she did not want her daughter's life to be terminated. The staff, seeing Karla's reluctance to let them terminate life support, arranged a meeting in which the treatment team met with Karla in conference and discussed with her the limited quality of life Thais would have on a respirator. Karla still felt strongly that one day Thais would get weaned off the respirator and come home to Lynchburg with her.

A minister spoke with her, describing the beautiful afterlife. He claimed to have proof of heaven from patients who were dead and came back to life, imparting what they had experienced. The nurses were all cajoling her, telling her Thais's quality of life would be so low that she could not enjoy any of it. August 15, 1991, exactly five years to the date when Thais had her first symptoms, they wanted to turn off life support. One could say she had a reprieve of five years as she was told she would die when she was first diagnosed. Karla and Talbot gathered around Thais that evening, accompanied by the minister to say their last farewell to Thais before they would turn off the respirator.

As Karla talked, Thais opened her eyes and smiled a warm, loving smile. That smile told Karla there was still hope. She had also been told by the lung experts that conditions like adult respiratory distress syndrome could turn around. Hope, rekindled again by that smile, made Karla change her mind; Thais needed some more time, maybe she could still breathe on her own. Karla prayed continuously, with a sinking feeling in her chest that she was losing the battle with the unseen enemy. The hospital staff was firmly planting that thought in her mind. She had avoided entertaining it, only allowing hope in her heart and faith. When the anxiety made her feel like a wild animal in a cage, she resorted to coin throwing to ask the *I Ching*, her faithful friend, if Thais could survive. The hexagram that showed up in answer to her query repeatedly was Hexagram 17: Following, which meant it is best to follow the course. The course, though, was that Thais was not judged to be a survivor of her transplant by most of the medical personnel. It was disheartening and Karla felt more fenced in by pessimism all around her.

Karla knew that her hope was keeping Thais alive against great odds, but was it strong enough to triumph over destiny? Although Thais was in a deep slumber, Karla and she were one in thought that she would return home with them.

The week following, the staff told Karla, who had been staying over in the room, that she smelled and needed a shower. When she returned an hour later, the staff was in tears. They told a startled Karla that because she did not come up with the paper to terminate Thais's life, they had awakened Thais and had asked her if she wanted them to continue her care. She had told them she wanted to live. Karla could only guess what had made everyone cry: Thais had been looking for her Mom who wasn't there. She must have thought she was all alone. The horror in her heart at what her daughter had just experienced made Karla nauseated.

Karla knew that the insurance company was constantly pressuring for the treatment to be terminated, just like there was pressure to send her home from the hospital prematurely, eventually leading to her re-hospitalization. Now that pressure intensified; every day someone at the hospital would bring up the question again about the quality of life and how happy Thais would be in the afterlife. Karla did not relent and kept an ever-closer watch. One day she found that the nurses had not cleaned Thais's face in the morning; it was as if they were giving up, seeing it as a futile endeavor. She complained and began to clean her daughter's face.

One evening Thais had a large amount of blood in her urine collection bag. Karla asked for a physician to come and take a look. He had an Australian accent and Thais, on hearing this, smiled broadly and lifted her head to see him, only to recoil in pain as he manipulated her catheter. Karla wanted to scream.

Now Karla saw it was getting very bad for the urine in her blood meant kidney functioning and bladder were affected, and she was already on dialysis. Al had gotten permission from Karla to call the nurses on the unit to inquire about Thais. He called almost every day. When he was told that the prognosis was very poor, he offered Karla to let him give the decision to terminate Thais's life, to spare Karla that life-ending decision which is so against any mother's nature. Karla thanked him but declined; it was something she needed to do for Thais if there was no hope.

Chapter 49

September 2, Labor Day, was exactly one year from the time when Karla had gone to the funeral service for her colleague in Lynchburg and had that foreboding feeling that scared her so. She and Talbot came in the morning to find that Thais was moving her head in a torturous, decerebrate manner. She did not respond when Karla spoke and did not open her eyes. Karla asked the nurses, who told her it was the Candida fungus invading her brain again.

Now Karla knew that Thais could not recover; she was too weakened, her body systems were decompensated, broken. She told the staff she would agree to terminate life support that evening, but she needed time to call her friend, Reverend Annie.

Annie immediately got in her car and drove non-stop from Benicia to Seattle, arriving around seven that evening. Finally, Karla, Annie, Talbot, and Sherry, gathered around the bed.

Thais had already been given an IV of Haldol in the morning after Karla had told the staff she would agree to terminate her life; after that she had stopped moving her head and became comatose. Around 8:30, Karla began to think of all the times in Thais's childhood that she had sung her to sleep with a lullaby around this very same time. She told her daughter that she was going to go to sleep and wake up with God, and she sang her the lullaby. Annie administered the blessing. Karla and Talbot kissed Thais and held her hands, one the right hand, the other the left.

The nurse unplugged the respirator and took the tube out of Thais's throat. The heart monitor kept showing that her heart was still beating, and Karla verbalized her distress: that faithful heart did not want to stop.

The nurse then disconnected the monitor. Karla could not cry; she just felt as if she had driven a knife into her daughter's heart, like an executioner.

Karla and Talbot asked everyone to leave the room. Karla held Thais's right hand. It continued to feel warm while the rest of her was getting cool. She held that hand for a long time, in shock, looking at her daughter's face as if to engrave it on her memory forever.

Talbot asked to be alone with his sister and Karla left the room. She never asked him what he said to his sister, but she was sure he was crying. When she went back in, the hand was warm still where they had held it.

As they all reluctantly left the Hutchinson near midnight, Karla suddenly felt free. She knew Thais was free, the release death offered brought freedom.

But she was not free of her memories.

Chapter 50

*L*eaving her daughter's body to the nurses who reported washing it with tears and love, feeling completely empty, Karla walked out to the car. It did not sink in right away that the necessity for the pager was gone, that there would be no more sitting by the bedside holding Thais' hand and loving her.

In the early morning hours of the next day, Karla was asleep. She saw Thais walking toward her, bending over and kissing her on the mouth. It was so real that only when she awakened did she realize she had been asleep.

Both she and Talbot arose early. Talbot was nauseated; he was still in denial and disbelief, not wanting to assimilate and digest the reality of his sister's death.

Annie was staying with them in the apartment. She did not say anything and busied herself watching a video. Karla started to pack. Annie told Karla that the heavens opened up to receive Thais at the moment of her death.

Karla spent the morning and afternoon of Tuesday calling family and friends. She spoke to Yumiko, a family member through marriage, who had come twice to the Hutch for moral support. Yumiko told Karla that on the night of Thais's death, of which she was not aware at the time, Thais had called her as she was sleeping, and had appeared to her.

The staff from the Hutch called and asked to do an autopsy. Karla refused. She did permit them to aspirate some tissue from her lungs, but otherwise she did not want anyone to disturb her daughter's body anymore.

She made arrangements with the funeral home, going there together with Talbot. She wanted Thais cremated, no showing, the simplest coffin, the least preparation—for she considered those things funeral homes did to bodies as a desecration.

On Wednesday morning, the day that Thais was to be cremated, Karla felt a strong calling to visit Thais. She did not ask Talbot to come; he was still feeling unwell. Later he told her he regretted her not asking him as he would have wanted to see his sister's body one more time.

The funeral home had put the cardboard casket in a cramped side room, not a viewing room. Thais was ice cold. Karla's tears streamed from her face as she beheld her daughter's body. Gradually, but amazingly, Thais's face began to emanate light, until she glowed with an ethereal energy. Karla again touched her face, for the light streaming from it made it look alive and warm, but the face was cold to the touch. Karla melted into that light, transfigured by the beauty of it. Her tears knew no end. She kissed her daughter's face and her hands and felt her soul melting into that of Thais. Finally she made herself leave.

After the cremation, Karla could not bring herself to pick up the urn, just as she had been unable to get herself to pick up Malcolm's urn. Instead she told the funeral home to hold on to it, and she would pick it up on her way back to Lynchburg. She needed to adjust herself to what was left of Thais's beautiful body, some ashes in an urn.

Annie left and Karla and Talbot were completely alone. They were utterly exhausted and needed rest before returning to school and work. Karla went to a travel agency, and she and Talbot decided to spend a week in Hawaii. Talbot liked beaches, and they thought that they could let their tears flow freely and talk about the changes that would come to their lives now.

The flight was uneventful. They had a room in a beachside motel, just a short walk from the sands and the warm water. When they arrived and checked in at the desk, there was a phone call: Al. He wanted to know if they had arrived safely. Al had the uncanny ability to always know exactly when Karla had arrived somewhere, as if he was watching her with his third eye.

Karla and Talbot both felt tense, the sudden letdown making them feel at a loss what to do. Thais' death left a huge empty black hole at the center of their lives, into which all their spirit and energy were sucked. They went and got massages. As she was massaged, she felt incredible pain in her entire body, as if all the grief and stress of the past two years had stored itself there. She wanted to scream but restrained herself.

For the rest of the Hawaiian stay, both she and Talbot were in a fog. They actually did not talk much; he spent much time on the beach and she sat on the deck of the room, just staring into the sky.

They returned to Seattle to pick up their stored suitcases and the urn at the funeral home for the trip back to Lynchburg. It was now mid-September. Sherry picked them up at the Seattle airport, her final volunteer service, and as she drove them to her hotel for their overnight stay, she was under the influence and drove wrong way on a one-way street. Karla gasped as cars approached them and they swerved on to the shoulder. She saw then that for Sherry this was a really difficult encounter, for she knew the pain Karla was feeling, having experienced it herself, the emptiness and despair. They kept in touch via yearly Christmas cards. It was so wonderful to hear years later that Sherry had been able to overcome her alcohol addiction and was happily married to a wonderful man.

Al met Karla and Talbot at the Lynchburg Airport; he was accompanied by the office staff and Dr. Glass. He briefly came upstairs to carry up the luggage, grabbed Karla and planted a kiss on her mouth and hugged her with relief, thankful that she was safely home. Then he left, leaving her with the car he had driven for her while she was away; Dr. Glass gave him a ride home.

It was unfortunate that they had arrived home at nearly midnight; the house was dark and felt so empty. But they were tired, and quickly went to bed. It was as if the house, too, was sympathetic for Karla felt enveloped and comforted by its walls.

The next morning Karla hesitantly walked into Thais' room. Karla looked around and on a small table in the corner was a card: the Queen of Spades, harbinger of death. Thais had put it there before they left for Seattle. Had she known her fate? Thais often played cards with one of her friends and had no doubt experienced the Queen of Spades as a negative portent.

Karla was unable to cook; she had too many memories of the happy meals the four of them and then the three of them had shared together. Meals now consisted of the huge muffins from the bakery section of Harris Teeter for breakfast and eating at a fast food restaurant for lunch and dinner. She still fixed a sandwich for Talbot to take to school, but that did not entail cooking.

Now, Karla was assailed by her grief over Malcolm and Thais. There had not been time before. Now she had lots of solitude to cry, pray, and meditate over the losses of two people so dear to her heart and soul. She cried daily, tears streaming down her face at any memory, pleasant or unpleasant, having to do with her life before the deaths. Thais' suffering was a cross she bore. That dear, innocent young woman offered up in a research hospital in the hope of saving a remnant of her life burst in on Karla's memory every day in myriad ways.

Chapter 51

$\mathcal{K}$arla was scared about her finances on her return from Seattle. Although she had received income deposited to her account from the money owed her by insurance companies during her absence, her costs—both from what was not paid by insurance in Seattle plus the ongoing costs she was facing now—worried her. She sat down with an accountant and looked at income versus output; at least she was breaking even, and after paying the rest of the hospital bill in Seattle, she would start to generate income again. They had survived financially.

She returned to work on the first of October, resuming her clinical directorship of the adolescent unit and her outpatient practice. Amazingly, Al had really saved her practice. Because he treated her patients during her absence and reminded them about her imminent return, all her patients began coming back to her. For that she was very grateful.

Getting back to work turned out to be the best medicine, for it kept Karla's mind in the present and helping adolescents and kids get better helped her self-confidence. The work hours were grueling, usually starting at 7 A.M. with rounds at the hospital, meeting with the staff, then starting at the outpatient clinic around 10 A.M., and working until noon. She took a one-hour lunch break during which she went home and ate leftovers from the restaurants the night before, reclining in front of the TV, then returned to work for at least another eight hours. It was during those brief moments of rest that Karla realized she was exhausted, more mentally than physically. Still she kept on: back to the clinic, then back to the hospital for admissions that had come in during the day on both child and adolescent unit and the adult unit, she finally left the hospital around 8:30 P.M.

The unit staffs of both the adult and adolescent units were kind, supporting Karla in any way they knew how. Her own unit staff arranged to have a different staff member bring a meal every Wednesday, a meal they had lovingly prepared, and that is actually what kept Talbot and Karla going, for they stretched those meals to last half a week. The nurses on the adult unit took Karla to their home for an afternoon on the lake they lived by or offered to invite her to the lunches the unit gave the patients once a week.

Karla knew Talbot was having a rough time at school. He had enjoyed Bishop O'Dea in Seattle as it made him feel he was living some semblance of reality. Often, after school was out, he would drive around Seattle in the rental car by himself with a learner's permit. Seattle was a large place and he could explore different parts of the city. Sometimes he would go to the University of Washington's library and browse, also doing research for his homework. In the early evening, he would come to be with his sister.

Returning from Seattle and settling back into the mundane concerns of high school in Lynchburg was like driving a race car and then walking. He felt his peers were not interested in what he had gone through; it was awkward when they did ask, as if they hoped he would not answer. They were in the heyday of their lives and Talbot was in the pit of his. A very stern English professor, Dr. Locke, showed little empathy and piled on the work, conveying the message, "You've had hands-on experience of what is talked about in the literature, so consider yourself a step ahead." Anyway, that is how Talbot reported reading his insistence that Talbot turn in first-rate work.

However, in some ways it was true. Talbot had turned sixteen in Seattle. He had seen suffering, not only that of his sister, but all the other patients on the unit at the Hutchinson with whose fates he was familiar. He had to live in a make-shift apartment for six months and attend a Catholic school for the first time. While he was making attempts to date girls, he was grappling with his sexuality, but Karla was too preoccupied to notice.

Talbot was on his own from the time he got home from school around 2:30 until Karla finished her work. They were long days. Karla was concerned about Talbot being alone so much in the house, but he had his driver's license and drove the Saab for hours out on the many roads around the area. He got a speeding ticket in Appomattox and Karla and Talbot had to go to that historic courthouse, where his license was suspended for three months. Then he was confined to the house unless one of his driving friends could pick him up. Karla was concerned until she realized he had many friends; they picked him up to take him to school in the morning as Karla was already at work, and he took the bus home.

Talbot shared with Karla that being alone in the house so many hours stirred up too many memories and he could not handle it; he had to get out and distract himself. He was suffering at school as well, because some of the rumors were that Thais had AIDS instead of cancer, and people who thought that treated him badly.

Talbot saved his homework until he and Karla were home together as he avoided being alone in the house. He was often up until midnight, rushing through it. School was hard for him now. He had already missed a whole month of his junior year as they returned from their Hawaii trip and took a couple of days to take care of things at home, but was expected to make up all of it. He often recounted how strange it was to be back at E.C. Glass. He found that no one mentioned his sister; it was as if she never existed. It distressed him that his beloved sister's death was a taboo subject; he felt disconnected and lost, for he could not be as carefree as his peers who had not had a tragedy in their families. It was similar to what Karla and her children had experienced with her relatives in Austria.

He got a girlfriend, and they spent much time together. Karla saw them once holding hands when she picked Talbot up after a school activity. Judy was a lovely person with whom Talbot could talk about everything. Her family also welcomed him and Karla.

In his room Talbot had put up posters of girls in bathing suits. He had friends who were girls and he was interested in dating more, as he considered his relationship with Judy more platonic than romantic.

Karla was alone when not at work. Although Al was still separated from his wife, he was still living in their house. He felt hopeless about getting a divorce, convinced his wife would never go that far.

Karla saw Al only at work now. She would look forward to Saturdays, hoping he might spend a few hours with her, but he avoided her, claiming tiredness. He was never available on Sundays. She was lonely and desperate, not knowing if the relationship was at an end. He was always very kind and courteous to her when they did encounter each other, but he was obviously distracted by his own problems.

Her loneliness after Thais died was excruciating. She would sit in the master bedroom in front of a window that faced west, with her back to the light. She was tired, she realized, and it felt good to just sit and do nothing, to close her eyes and retreat into the quiet spaces of her soul. She continued to indulge an avid interest in spiritual books. She was searching for ways to reach her departed loved ones.

At times she would sob, lying down, her face on the pillow. At night she could not fall asleep easily no matter how tired she was, often dropping into an exhausted slumber only to awaken a few hours later. In the early morning hours she would get dressed and take a walk, about a mile's distance, again walking and praying, as was her habit now. She prayed a lot, hoping it would reach her loved ones.

One night as she was gradually waking up, she felt a vibrating energy in her right hand. It felt wonderful and loving, and she knew it was Thais or Malcolm holding her hand. She had several more experiences similar to that. She knew she was not alone then.

In the fall of 1992, Karla saw an article in a medical journal about acupuncture, along with information about getting instruction to learn that skill. She read it as a directive for her: the study of acupuncture could take her mind off her grief and the stagnation of the relationship with Al. She enrolled in Dr. Helms' course for medical acupuncture for physicians, in Santa Monica, CA. The first week was introduction to acupuncture, its history and all the points. Karla was one of about ten women in a class of about seventy people, all physicians. Most were family practitioners, with some neurologists, anesthesiologists, surgeons and psychiatrists.

The training was intensive, with lectures for nine hours every day for six days. It was followed by an assignment to take home fifty VCR tapes and answer questions for each tape. When done, the tapes and answers had to be sent back for scoring. In the spring of 1993, Karla returned to Santa Monica for the practice sessions with the needles and various other techniques.

Karla took to acupuncture like a fish takes to water. She was thrilled by the philosophy, which takes for its hypothesis that we have energy channels running throughout our bodies that can be affected by placing needles in the major points of these channels. The points can create positive changes in the physiological, emotional, and spiritual well-being.

It took many hours to learn the points and their significance and the application to healing. But for Karla it was another gift she treasured, this new knowledge. She began using acupuncture in her practice in Lynchburg to a limited extent, selecting patients who would be open to trying this adjunctive treatment. Her patients found that the treatments relaxed them, helping to alleviate psychological as well as physical pain, and appeared to strengthen them as time went on.

She had developed a new art. She practiced extensively on herself so that she could evaluate how this tool effected change. From then on, at the first sign of any disturbance in her homeostasis or well-being, she used the needles on herself. This gave her confidence in treating others.

Chapter 52

*I*n February of 1993, Al told Karla he was moving out; the fighting and arguments with his wife were affecting his health. He could not sleep; the anger was taking its toll on his body. He rented an apartment a few blocks from the hospital and moved out with one suitcase.

Now Al began actively dating Karla. On the weekends they would spend a few hours together, eating, talking, and embracing. Her lonely life of the past three years was coming to an end. Often they drove out into the beautiful countryside around Lynchburg, finding it relaxed and calmed them.

One of Karla's partners in her outpatient practice, a doctor who had replaced Dr. Glass, who had retired, had resigned to return to his native state, expressing disappointment in his experience in Lynchburg. One of his patients was transferred to Karla as she returned to her practice in October 1991. Lucy was a clergywoman and was in her early forties at the time. Lucy was her name.

In the therapy, Lucy revisited her family pathology and the suffering she had endured as a victim of ritual sexual abuse at the hands of a cult, a clandestine group of which her father was a member. Karla soon realized that this woman dealt with her considerable psychic pain by using pain-killers, which she was taking in ever-greater numbers. She was also chronically suicidal, so that Karla was often in contact with her by phone outside office hours. She saw Lucy weekly, often twice weekly during her most stressful times.

As the therapy progressed, Lucy opened her considerable psychic abilities to Karla. She was a channel for messages from the spiritual world.

One day she brought a message which was scripted and framed. She told Karla she was walking through a store and the frame fell off the wall into her arms as she stood there. Intuiting that it was from Thais, she gave it to Karla. It read as follows:

Imagine
stepping onto a shore and finding it heaven
Imagine
taking hold of a hand and finding it God's hand
Imagine
breathing new air and finding it celestial air
Imagine
feeling invigorated and finding it immortality
Imagine
passing from storm & tempest to an unknown calm
Imagine
waking and finding it home

The signature very lightly sketched at the bottom was unclear even with a magnifying glass but appeared to be, "Ancubi."

Tears welled up in Karla's eyes and she choked up. It was exactly what she had imagined Thais might have experienced on dying, this freedom from pain, from breathlessness and inability to speak.

Karla was in session with the psychiatrist and remarked to him, "The saddest thing about the house is that Thais's room just stays the same. Nothing changes."

That afternoon when she returned home, she heard a commotion. Someone was in the house! Checking every room, she came to Thais's last. It was in total disarray. Karla was scared; she heard some movement under the bed, so she went over and slowly lifted up the bedcover . . . only to find herself face-to-face with a squirrel! It had gotten in through the chimney and explored the house; for some reason, it had left all rooms intact except for this one.

Karla quickly closed the door and waited for Talbot to get home. They nudged the squirrel into a laundry basket and carried it outside to release it.

Karla was thrilled: Thais had heard her and responded.

Lucy told Karla her tears were a bridge to Thais that bound them together. She also told Karla that she would like to be the minister marrying Al and Karla. Shocked, Karla looked at her. She still thought it highly unlikely.

Then the staff on the adult unit began whispering in Karla's ear, "He is one in a million." When the staff had a party, they asked Al to bring Karla. At first he was very reluctant to do so because of the community reaction, but the staff were adamant in their conviction that the two belonged together. A psychologist friend whom Karla valued and to whom she had sent her children when Thais fell ill the first time, asked Karla one day, "When are you and Al going to get married?"

It was strange that friends and staff had them married while Karla and Al had grave doubts they could ever get to matrimony. How did everyone feel so certain when Karla herself felt so shaky? It seemed an impossible dream, which Karla feared would remain merely that.

She had support from staff for another issue: her grief. The head nurse on the children's unit asked Karla to join an informal group held at one of the therapists' office on Friday afternoons, during which all matter of things pertaining to the members were discussed. Karla joined, and focused on her grief. The women in the group upheld Karla during this difficult and lonely time.

Another group asked her to join them, a group made up of the psychologist who was her friend and two other professionals, both women. This group got together once a month, changing the meeting place on a rotating basis to the members' homes; the member whose home was offered that month also cooking the meal they shared. They all shared an interest in culinary arts so the meals were unusually creative and fun. The members of this group were into psychic phenomena.

One of the women asked a question of the other two women on how things were for Karla seeing her sadness and expressing concern about her. "All is as it should be," said the psychologist.

This cryptic answer left Karla wondering, how would she know whether it was as it should be? Also, things were not looking good at that moment for Karla's personal life. She decided to focus on her professional life instead, devoting herself to her patients.

Lucy soon ran up quite a bill seeing Karla; insurance paid very little for Karla's service and Lucy's funds were not sufficient. Karla went to the secretary and told her to erase the balance, at that time about two thousand dollars, deciding that Lucy's life was worth a lot more than what she owed on her bill and knowing that owing this money only added to Lucy's problems in dealing with her life.

Karla realized the border was a little blurry in this particular patient-client relationship. The patient's psychic ability, counterbalanced by Karla's supportive and clarifying stance, made a strange combination. But Karla had always been a maverick, able to handle complexity.

So had Karla stepped over the line? She tried to make sure she did not, focusing only on Lucy's ongoing dialogue, not allowing any of these psychic breakthroughs to muddy the waters, but listening carefully to what was being communicated, for it felt trustworthy.

It appears that the client-psychiatrist relationship is unique; looking deeply into the psyche of another person is always accompanied by that person getting glimpses of the psychiatrist's make-up. It goes both ways, and that is the fine line that Karla and Lucy both treaded.

Karla's co-workers had also overstepped the line, telling Karla and Al that they were meant to be a pair. Again, Karla could listen, but not respond. She had to leave matters in the hands of destiny, that unknowable force.

Phone calls at the house were for Talbot or for Thais. Karla had to tell Thais's far-away friends, some of whom she did not know, that her daughter had died, listening as the voice on the other end of the line became still.

Karla often felt lost; what was next for her in her life? What would happen to the relationship with Al as time went on? Could she finally leave Lynchburg, which she intuited was not going to be her home in the future, if she didn't know where and with whom her future path lay?

Chapter 53

One October day in 1992, Karla gave Al a ride for an early morning departure at the airport. He was going to visit his parents and brothers in Seoul for two to three weeks. He felt like he was going home again, seeing familiar sights, visiting old friends, sleeping in the same house with his parents and middle brother and his family.

It was her week of being on-call for the adult and child unit, admitting unassigned patients from the emergency room or self-referred. Every Wednesday she kept an appointment with her psychiatrist in Charlottesville, about sixty-four miles north of Lynchburg on Route 29. She had begun seeing Dr. Rosenberg after Malcolm died and resumed sessions after returning to Lynchburg from Seattle, because she felt awash in an unplanned fate and needed help with her grieving.

She had her cell phone next to her on the car seat. At that time in 1992 cell phones were bulky, elongated, heavy machines. She was driving the brand-new red Saab convertible Talbot had nudged her to buy on their return from Seattle, saying she needed to follow her dreams. Since she was a teenager and could drive, she had always wanted a convertible. So buy one she did.

The top was down on that balmy October afternoon, around three in the afternoon. She was rounding a curve, going about fifty-five miles an hour, and grabbed the cell phone, thinking to dial the hospital to check up on things. Suddenly she spun out of control, she saw the car heading front end toward some small oaks, rushing headlong into them. All she could think was, "It's not fair! Talbot needs me."

Then came the tremendous impact, flying with the car through the air and down an incline, landing on the bottom, with no awareness of landing, right side up again. She did not know how long she was unconscious, finding herself sitting in the car when she came to. The windshield had been bent and had cut a bleeding gash into her forehead. In a daze she ascertained that, yes, she was alive, and no, she had no broken bones, and she could move. She undid her seat belt and got out of the car.

A nurse from the hospital who had been traveling on the road as well stopped her car and walked down the incline. A man who was driving on the separated road on the opposite side had also seen her car flip, and he came to offer help. An ambulance came, and she was taken to the University Hospital in Charlottesville where she was checked out. X-rays were negative for bone breaks, and her gash didn't require stitches. A policeman took a report, charging her with improper driving, and she was released. A court date would be scheduled.

At around six in the evening she called Talbot. His voice shook as he asked if she was ok. Could he pick her up with the other Saab? Could he bring a friend? He arrived accompanied by his friend Jimmy. Karla looked a sight, her dress blood-stained, the butterfly bandange on her head a stark white reminder of the accident.

After buying hamburgers for Talbot and Jimmy, she returned home. She showered, changed, and went to the adult unit. Incredibly, she had ten admissions total that day and she stayed until midnight doing the workups.

She was badly shaken but also extremely grateful. She had been heard; she was alive, and she could be there for Talbot. This gave her such a boost of energy that she felt no pain or discomfort that night as she worked. It was the next day, twenty-four hours later, that she had excruciating back pain, but still she kept working.

The nurse who witnessed the accidents told the staff that it was a very serious crash, so they were amazed that she was at work as if nothing had happened.

Back home a few evenings later, she felt she needed to tell Al what had happened; he would want to know, she was sure. She called his number in Seoul and his mother answered. Karla just gave her name. He called later and, after hearing what happened, said he was very happy she was safe. He told her to be careful. Would she still be able to drive to the Dulles Airport and pick him up that weekend? She would and did.

Karla asked herself, *Am I suicidal?* She could answer no, but she had been careless, and would not be making calls while driving in the future.

Chapter 54

March 1993, marked another anniversary reaction of Malcolm's death approaching. On the morning of the 13th, Karla awoke to a heavy snow that had fallen during the night and was still coming down in busy flakes whirling and dancing. The phone rang as Karla contemplated how she would make rounds; the snow was about two feet deep. It was Fritzi on the phone from Austria.

"Our father died this morning around 8:30. He collapsed while shaving and died shortly after," Fritzi said.

Karla wanted to fly to Austria for the funeral, but the weather made that impossible. She would have to visit his grave later, maybe even a month or two later.

Once Karla had collected her thoughts, it occurred to her that Malcolm and her father had died on the same date and the same time of day, her father exactly three years exactly after Malcolm! Karla shed no tears on the news of her father's demise. It seemed she had none left.

Karla did go to Austria two months later and visited her father's grave in the mountains, nestled against a big elm tree and overlooking the valley down below. She prayed her last farewell to a man who led an unfulfilled life. His only pride was his children.

Shortly after she returned from Austria, she went to a conference out of town. She was in her hotel room that evening making out the on-call schedule for the psychiatrists, her job for a year, when Al called.

"I am divorced," he said.

Karla's pen dropped to the floor. She thought she was hearing things. How did all this happen when she least expected it?

He related that his ex-wife had filed for the divorce and he had signed the papers. She had demanded that he give her all of their properties and saved money, leaving him with eighty dollars in his pocket. She had completely emptied their savings account before she filed. He was left with a large alimony in addition to mortgages and many bills to pay, as his children had school expenses. He had no cash to his name except what he earned from now on.

He felt he could no longer afford the apartment he had been renting, so he was looking for just a room, some distance away from the town so as to pay less. He showed Karla a house located in a hidden place in the nearby mountains, up a winding dirt road. It looked hazardous, especially at night and in the winter. Karla had taken Talbot for a ride to show him the house after Al told her where he was going to be living next. It looked dismal.

Talbot spoke up. "He could live with us, Mom. This is too dangerous for him up here. I'm going away to college, so there will be room, and he can park his car in the garage."

Karla was shocked; she had not considered asking Al to move in with them, and here Talbot had offered it.

"I will ask him," she retorted, realizing how much Talbot cared about Al.

In September Karla broached the subject with Al, sincerely inviting him to live with them, no rent payment expected. Al, too, was shocked to hear the offer from Karla. She told him it was Talbot's idea when Al expressed concern about Talbot's feelings in the matter. He accepted, saying he would move in at the end of October after returning from another trip home to Korea.

He arrived with his meager belongings: some shirts, slacks, underwear, and socks, and a jacket and raincoat. He also brought the few pots and pans and dishes he had been using at the apartment.

She was thrilled that he would be living with her. Talbot had started his first year of college at the University of Maryland, living in the dorm there. It would be good to have a man in the house again, a man she trusted and loved.

They relished their time together, after work and on weekends. Karla was surprised to find Al was adept with his hands. He repaired the hole in the attic which was allowing squirrels to nest there. He constructed a cover for the basement entrance so water and snow did not collect there anymore. He even helped with setting the table and doing dishes.

Their time together was filled with holding each other, making love, telling each other their dreams. Karla told him she wanted to leave Lynchburg, but she had no idea where to go. He also wanted to leave, since the children were all on their own, and he, too, had sad memories of his life in Lynchburg.

For the most part, they got along easily, seeing life as humorous despite its tragedies. Al felt a loss after the divorce, a loss of family cohesiveness. One day his ex-wife called, demanding he pick up the family dog, because she was leaving for a one-month spa vacation. He told Karla he was bringing the dog home, but she objected, she did not want a dog in the house.

"It is the dog and me or nothing!" was his ultimatum.

She knew this demand was very unfair, but recognized his attachment to his dog and relented. However, she made it clear it was only for the time the dog's owner was away. When his ex-wife returned, she told him she no longer wanted the dog, so now he was to keep it. Karla again raised her objections. They were away from the house for long periods of time every day and the dog was a nervous type, needing lots of attention; she would become destructive in her frustration at being alone.

Al found a solution in a woman who adopted stray dogs and cared for them well. She agreed to take the dog and Al and Karla would visit at times, paying for the dog's food.

Al continued to reiterate to Karla that he wanted them to get married. He asked her to set a date, and since it was June of 1994 now, she chose August 6 of that year. Years later it dawned on Karla that it was the very same date she had originally set with Malcolm in 1966, before he had to move up the date to June.

Karla reminisced about Al's words to her from the start of their courtship. He was so impressed when he saw how hard she worked all day but never lost sight of the needs of her family, cooking for them and taking excellent care of them. He admired her family very much. And now she was going to be his wife as had been forecast by people from diverse backgrounds and circumstances a few years before she ever dared to hope.

Karla was totally overcome by Al's amorous advances. He told her he had been impotent for some years now but since they began courting, he had a constant erection in her close proximity. Their kisses were passionate and he touched her all hours of the night. He slept poorly, falling asleep suddenly, then an hour later waking, fully recharged. The lovemaking was of an ardor she had not experienced before. The sexual tension between them was there from the first, so that just hearing his mellifluous voice set her to vibrating internally. She surrendered to him totally.

Against that background of their intense love, his anger when it surged baffled her at first. There were clashes that were destructive and damaging. Al had a hot temper and would throw objects when angered—not directly at Karla, but in her direction. He somehow assumed she would be sensitive to his cultural issues without knowing about them. Karla had only been in one fight with Malcolm in which he had thrown something and made a motion to strangle her with a pillow, stopping after a few seconds but scaring her out of her wits. After that incident, there was no recurrence of a physical altercation in their marriage of twenty-four years; instead, Malcolm would distance himself after a verbal altercation, lying down in bed and thinking things through. Karla was timid and non-violent, and these episodes with Al were frightening. Also, it took Al days to recover himself from a fight, whereas Karla regrouped in half an hour, an hour at the most. She was ready to make up, to discuss their differences, and to come to a conclusion, but he was unreachable, and if she pressed him, he returned to throwing things to scare her off.

In time, she, too vented anger, rebutting him, setting him straight as to how she saw the situation. The degree of rage in her overwhelmed Karla: she found herself slamming doors, getting into her car, driving out and not returning until the anger was spent. At one point, she started taking dishes out of the cabinets, dashing them on the floor, feeling she would not stop until every dish was broken. She needed to see something break the way she felt her soul, spirit, and body had been broken. His anger had released her long-buried frustration.

One fire kindled the other, the sparks flying, exploding, all the pent up anger at their fates, coming together. It was one post-traumatic distress order meeting its equal with no referee. Could they weather these storms, adjust to each other's cultural norms without hurting each other emotionally? Karla was so in love she could not conceive of living without Al. He threatened to leave constantly, would storm out the door and be gone for several hours; she never knew if he was going to come back. Whereas he was always reachable on other occasions, he would not return her calls when he was angry with her. This rekindled all her abandonment fears; these times challenged to her trust in him.

When Karla announced to her psychiatrist that she was going to marry Al, his response was a shock to her. "I don't want to see you anymore. Your marrying Al is a mistake; come back when it is over," he said, dismissing her then and there, interrupting the session. He refused to discuss the matter further. Karla, deeply embarrassed and feeling betrayed by his inability to handle her decision, got up and left.

Karla was to have another shocking surprise a few days before the wedding. Talbot had just returned from international studies abroad in Austria after completing his first year of college. Driving home from dinner one evening, he announced, "I'm gay, Mom."

Karla was speechless; it was a jolt. She had really not suspected him to be gay. She did not say anything, but let him know she heard him. It was going to take a while for her to process this change, for she had not suspected it. But then she had been too preoccupied with other problems in her life to notice his struggle.

At college, from then on, Talbot began to advocate for gay students, cementing his own identity as a gay man. Once Talbot was certain of his sexual identity, he met with Judy, his girlfriend. She was hoping they could get into a serious relationship. He told her about his sexual orientation, asked her not to remain in contact with him, and encouraged her to find another romantic involvement and forget about him. It was very hard for her. He told his mother it had been sad for him as well, but unless he let her go, she would not open herself to other relationships with a heterosexual man.

Chapter 55

Karla and Al did not agree on who should perform the wedding or in which church it should be held. He wanted the hospital chaplain to wed them in the Virginia Baptist Hospital chapel. She wanted Lucy to marry them in a chapel located in the woods about thirty minute drive from Lynchburg proper, the Laurel Grove Presbyterian chapel. Annie also wanted to marry them if Karla could fly her out from California.

Karla made the final decision about the clergy and the place, and Al conceded but at a price: only Talbot, Al's son Michael, and their retired partner Dr. Glass and his wife were to be present. Karla's staff had given her a shower; she felt bad about not being able to invite them, and they were sad (as well as a little resentful) about it, too.

The week leading up to the wedding on Saturday, August 6, at 11:30 A.M., was a week of daily rain. As Karla awoke up on Saturday morning, the sun was bright and the day beautiful. She donned an off-white calf-length dress, and Al put on a suit and red tie. Talbot dressed in an orange sport coat and looked dashingly handsome. He wanted to sing a song for them during the ceremony.

The church, a small red brick building set among large oak trees, was simple but so suited to Karla's temperament, unadorned like herself. From the orchard across from the church, the smell of fresh peaches and summer fruit wafted over to them. Karla had left the ceremony up to Lucy, who had gotten them both to name their favorite music and had made a tape of the collection. Karla and Al walked down the aisle together. Talbot and Michael were seated on each side. The only guests, Dr. and Mrs. Glass, sat in the empty pews.

Both Karla and Al became indescribably sad as the music played, tears streaming down their faces, each immersed in some memory of the past. Talbot sang most beautifully, and Karla cried even more. They said their vows and shared a cup of wine and held candles. Lucy performed a beautiful, stirring service, filled with hope and promise and acknowledging a painful past for both bride and groom. She had brought a wooden angel to be present at the wedding, to represent Thais. At last they exchanged rings and kissed, their love fulfilled.

They shared a lunch with the minister and their sons and the two guests at a place called Peaks of Otter Lodge, located in the national park at the foot of the Blue Ridge Mountains, just twenty minutes from the church. They all quietly enjoyed that ride into the mountains for the luncheon.

Then they returned home; Al was actually on call, and after he drove his son to the airport, relieved his colleague who had covered for him that day. Talbot returned home with them. Al was gone most of the afternoon catching up on work at the hospital. Their partner Dr Glass had remarked, "That was the smallest, longest wedding I have ever been to."

Pictures! They had forgotten pictures, Talbot reminded them that evening. They decided that the next morning, on Sunday, they would drive to the church and take pictures, only outside; Lucy had videotaped the service. Karla took the flowers from the day before and pinned some to Al's lapel, and off they went again to the little church where Talbot took some lovely shots for them. The photo of Karla and Al standing in front of the signboard for the Laurel Presbyterian Church now sits on the dresser in their bedroom and reminds them yearly to take a trip to Bedford and again find the church across the street from the fruit orchard.

She was now Mrs. Yoon. It sank in slowly, and she relished the thought that they were together to share their lives, come what may.

Chapter 56

Karla knew very little about Korea. She had heard her mother talking with the journalist from the German paper in Omaha, discussing the Korean War so long ago; Johanna feared Dimitri might be drafted. Then there was a young physician from Korea, a Dr. Lee, who was doing a surgical residency at Creighton University in Omaha. He was engaged to marry a friend of Karla's, and she was invited to the engagement party. When Dr. Lee called off the engagement, he asked Karla to stand by his now ex-fiancée during this time. Impressed by his concern for Darleen, Karla invited Dr. Lee to dinner with her and Malcolm. He explained there were too many cultural differences and Darleen did not want to return with him to Korea.

Her next experience with a Korean was with Dr. Kim, one of the psychotherapy professors at her residency training program at Napa State Hospital. Karla was impressed by his calm, pleasant manner. She baked a cake for the class to enjoy during one of the sessions. Later, in Napa, a piano teacher had a large number of Korean students. They lived in Angwin and were Seventh Day Adventists.

Marrying Al now immersed her in Korean society, culture, history and most of all, his family relationships. Her first trip to South Korea was in August, just after their marriage. She knew no Korean and was told the family spoke limited English; Al assured her she would be welcomed.

It was a steaming hot summer day when they arrived in Korea. After a stint in a fancy hotel for a medical conference, they checked out and were picked up by Al's sister-in-law to go to the family home.

Al's father met them at the door. Al translated his father's greeting, "Welcome to our Korean home." Both Al and she then did the formal bow on the floor in front of the parents, Karla closely following Al's example.

Al's mother was a woman in her late seventies, and his father was in his eighties. Karla's mother-in-law impressed Karla with her agility, sitting on the floor in the traditional manner and easily arising. Al and Karla slept on the floor, the wonderful cushioned futons softening the hardness and rolled pillows which cradled the neck. The house was just below Korea University, next to an ancient Buddhist temple. They could hear the bell that called the monks to prayer and meditation early in the morning.

The next day, Oma Nim, Al's mother, grabbed Karla by the hand and led her into the small kitchen to make the vegetable appetizer dishes Korea is famous for called *panchan*. She involved Karla in every part of the preparation for the meal they were all to share.

Living in the house at the time were the parents, Al's middle brother and his wife and two children, college age. A third daughter had recently married and moved out. Al's younger brother lived across town with his family, but he slept in the house while Al visited so the family could be together. Everyone spoke Korean; Karla understood not a word. Oma Nim explained that a smile was sufficient communication. She could be like a baby, picking up a word here and there. And truly, Karla did not feel isolated, for the family members engaged her, the two college-age students speaking English with her at times to ease her understanding, and Al translating with much consideration.

Al's father had been a Minister of Education in Korea after the Japanese occupation ended; he had also been a congressman. He was known for his strictness, his insistence about stressing a science curriculum in the schools, and desire to bring back traditional Chinese medicine into the society. He never took a bribe, refused to change his name to a Japanese name during the occupation, and was even imprisoned for his refusal to follow Japanese mandates—he was an ardent patriot. When he refused to partake in the Park dictatorship, he was placed under house arrest and was never active politically again. He spent the rest of his life collecting Korean history, involving himself in the publication of it.

Al's mother had been a teacher and principal all her life, retiring at age seventy-five. She was also a painter, having aspired to attend art school, being denied that opportunity by Al's father, who believed it was beneath a woman's dignity to paint. She often lamented this to Al in her letters. However, she learned on her own through books and showed considerable talent in panel-painting and other art. She was an accomplished seamstress and needleworker, again using that art to express herself.

Oma Nim brought Karla fully into the family, telling Al she could die in peace now knowing he had such a wonderful, caring wife. She made skirts for her of lovely materials, gave her gemstone rings, and taught her cooking as ways of showing her love. This warmth in her life was new to Karla. Her own mother was not demonstrative and Malcolm's mother had not been either.

This welcome, which was repeated every time Karla and Al went home to Korea, encouraged Karla to strive to learn Korean, a task that took her many years. Al kept telling her it was too difficult an undertaking with all the things she was doing and he never expected it of her, but Karla was adamant. Her hearing problem stood in the way of learning the spoken language, because she could not pick up the different sounds easily. She realized it was a very poetic language full of onomatopoeia, with wonderfully repetitive and musical sounds.

Koreans love to sing and have a great talent in all aspects of music. Karla had loved to sing in the past and wanted to join the karaoke that was part of every social gathering, but unfortunately she had lost her singing voice after Thais died. Finally, about fifteen years later, her musical voice started coming back, but never again with the clarity and high soprano she used to vocalize.

Karla found the Korean culture had much to offer her, especially the marvelous, healthy cuisine. Also, the politeness demonstrated by the society and by Al made her realize she had been a barbarian before. Korean generosity and the beauty of their presentations awed her. Gifts were always beautifully wrapped and presented humbly. Gatherings such as weddings were dress-up affairs in which everyone sported their best. Karla, a simple Austrian by birth, at first felt outdone by all the finery, but she soon learned a few tricks of her own. Al often took her shopping and picked out clothes for her, encouraging her to wear appropriately sized clothing, not skimping on the size to convince herself she had lost some weight. Always Al told her she had big bones and needed the weight, that it would detract from her beauty if she lost too much. Oma Nim loved to have Karla do acupuncture for her and eventually every family member tried it to relieve various ailments and conditions. This eagerness gave Karla much confidence in her skills. Karla felt Al had given her a great gift when he introduced her to his family and his heritage as a Korean. Overall, she was always encouraged to be herself with Al and his family and was appreciated for who she was.

Chapter 57

Finances were a problem in their marriage. Karla asked Al if she could read his divorce agreement, to see about all his bills and alimony obligation. The agreement was horrendous: the alimony was more than he could afford, as the psychiatric practice was now taking in less money due to new insurance limits called managed care.

Karla began shaking as she read the agreement, telling him, "There is no way you can survive this. We have to go to your lawyer and see if we can at least decrease the alimony, since she already got everything you ever had without any financial responsibilities on her part."

He nodded and called his lawyer. Then began the process of assessing everything, his income, his assets which were all hers, and trying to come to an agreement with which he could survive. It was time to get realistic. His former wife was in perfect health, spoke English well enough, and could actually help by supporting herself at least partially. However, she had never worked outside the home in her life and had no marketable skills, nor any desire to work.

Before Karla married Al, he insisted they see a lawyer to draw up a prenuptial agreement as he did not want to touch any assets Karla had prior to their marriage. Other than that, she helped Al in every way she could, sharing his bills, helping with his taxes and saving him any house payment as she was taking care of that. She had no debt other than the mortgage.

After one year of negotiation between the two lawyers they reached a lower alimony payment, limited until the time his former wife could start collecting Social Security on his account at age 65. However, she continued to have her lawyer, whom Al also had to pay, agitate for more money. Finally, in desperation, Al appealed to his children to put pressure on their mother to be reasonable and accept the altered agreement. This was successful and his son sent a letter to the attorney urging him to desist suing, saying that his mother was very confused about the reality of the situation.

Karla was actually surprised that, other than phone calls demanding something, Al's ex-wife actually never made any contact on a social level.

She moved near her daughter and sister in Boston; then, having worn out her welcome, moved in with her son and daughter-in-law in Philadelphia. Whenever Al and Karla visited his son there, though, she was nowhere to be seen. Al also found out she confiscated all the family pictures, and that she cut out his picture in all of them.

At last, in 1995, after the final agreement, Al could pay attention to his new life for there were problems there as well. After their marriage, the hospital became very cool regarding its professional relationship with both Karla and Al. Soon their secretaries were more partial to the needs of the other colleagues. Finally, Karla and Al felt they needed to have their own office with their own staff, and ended up moving across town. Now their office expenses increased considerably for they no longer shared the expense of the secretaries as members of a large group.

At the hospital it was no better; the administrative directors of the units presented opposition to ideas they had and started limiting conferences in which Karla and Al could take part. Two new colleagues appeared to take over the units for which Karla and Al served as the clinical directors. It became clear they were no longer wanted. The nursing staffs of both units were an exception to this cold treatment, as they warmly embraced the new couple.

A friend of Karla's had told her once, "If you marry Al, leave Lynchburg. They don't have any tolerance for interracial marriage." How true that was! Both Karla and Al also felt it would be better to relocate. Where to go was now becoming a frequent conversation.

In the spring of 1995, they started making weekend trips to the Washington, D.C., area, and began interviewing for jobs.

While still in Lynchburg, Karla got a letter from Kaiser in Fairfax, inviting her for an interview for a child psychiatry position there. It would have to be full-time. Karla had hoped to take a part-time job so she could follow some of those interests Malcolm had alluded to before he died, something she could do that was a hobby or activity to enjoy. Al fully supported this, so he suggested she also apply in other areas for part-time positions.

By July, their solo practice in Lynchburg was well established. Should they weather it out there? Managed care, which was now in full swing, consisted of constant monitoring and advising about patient care by amateurs who worked for the insurers. It was an insult to any self-respecting professional to have the person on the other line, not a physician or even medically trained, tell them they needed to switch to a cheaper drug alternative, usually a generic. Then there were the so-called treatment reports in which all the patient's private information was divulged to the insurance company, and again an employee, not a professional, decided how many visits an individual could have. It seemed that the insurance companies were not aware that most patients did not go to the trouble to see the doctor if they did not need it!

The hospital, to counteract this intrusion by the major companies, decided to form its own insurance corporation which would do the same thing, but would decide locally how many visits were appropriate. This plan was sold to the employers and the doctors. Karla saw it was no different from what was already happening with the major insurers.

Karla thought the distraction of a vacation might make the decision-making process easier. She and Al signed up for a trip to Turkey that October of 1995. Al knew nothing but work; he had sacrificed and had not taken trips except home to see family, satisfying himself with reading the travel section of the Sunday paper, whereas she was a firm believer that vacations nourished the soul and helped an overworked person to realize there was a world besides their work environment. Al was happy with the plan; they were looking forward to this time away.

One weekend in July, Al, Karla, and Talbot, who was home for a weekend, took a car trip to northern Virginia. Al was reading the *Washington Post*, looking at apartments, and suggested they follow up on one that was reasonably priced. They contacted the owner who was living in the apartment at the time. He was looking for someone to take over the apartment while he went off for his MBA at Harvard, a two-year stint. It was a condominium in Fair Oaks, close to the freeway and shops, had a golf course visible from the kitchen and living room window. The young man was cordial as they looked around and took his number to contact him in the near future should it still be available. It was very small compared to the Lynchburg house, but it would be a start and would give them a chance to look around for a house during a year or two years' time.

They also contacted a real estate agent, who gave Karla an armful of listings of houses and townhouses for her to look through as she returned to Lynchburg. At the time there was a real estate glut in Fairfax and surrounding area.

Karla again wondered, *What are we doing?* It was unsettling but there was also some inner urgency connected with it, of moving on, the next step.

She was relieved to come back home to Lynchburg and sleep again in that house that had held her while she went through her sorrows, comforting her with its large rooms, the bedroom window looking out on a blooming magnolia and the large trees that sheltered the house with their leafy arms. They could just stay and put up with the unspoken abandonment of the hospital administration, the bane of the insurance company that had been formed and would transform the practice, the revolving-door hospital practice that would require much more work and accomplish much less, and working daily from dawn until dark, until noon on Saturdays and Sundays. But both Al and Karla were tired of this new business plan of the insurance companies; even though it had just begun, they saw no future in it for their practice. They also needed time for their new relationship as a married couple.

They decided that it would be best to move to a larger metropolitan area because of their interracial marriage. Karla felt compelled to contact Kaiser; they set up an appointment for her in September. Now that Karla and Al had made a decision to move, they quickly realized Northern Virginia was the most logical place. It had a much bigger population and both could hope to get work there. Also, Talbot was at the University of Maryland and lived in Silver Spring, and Al's youngest daughter lived in Arlington and worked in the District as a teacher.

She made an appointment with Kaiser in Merrifield for 10 A.M. on a September Monday. On Sunday, after arriving in Fairfax, she contacted the condominium owner to set up the contract with him for his condominium.

That Sunday, she drove the 1992 Saab convertible, the replacement of the one she had crashed. As she headed for the turnoff for Washington off Route 250 in Charlottesville, the accelerator stuck, and she could not slow down the car to make a very sharp turn for the on-ramp to 29 North. Horrified, panic rising up in her chest, she kept pumping the brake and shifting the gears. Just as she neared the turnoff, the car slowed down and worked as if nothing had happened. She was very shaken, thanking God she had not run herself or someone else off the road. She would have to take the car in to the dealer in Laurel and she called them to be there first thing on Monday morning. Was this a sign? Was this a message that she was heading into more disaster? Anxiety-ridden, she ignored it, going full steam ahead.

The next morning she rose early. By eight she had dropped off the car in Maryland. It might be the master cylinder, they told her, a very expensive repair, but it would have to be done considering the acceleration problem. She picked up the loaner and got into heavy traffic going south. She despaired of making her appointment on time and she had no phone. However, at five minutes to ten she had arrived and was standing at the elevator to go up to the third floor at the Kaiser Merrifield Office.

How had she managed this trip back and forth across the beltway, all the way from Fairfax to Laurel and back to Merrifield? Surprised herself at this feat, since she was always easily disoriented, she thought that being guided was the only way she could have done this.

Her interview went well and she told them she could not come to work until December. In the afternoon she talked with the condominium owner and signed a contract beginning September 25.

She returned to Lynchburg, job in hand and an apartment for them to live in.

Al went the following week and interviewed with a private practice group whose members were congenial and the practice appeared to be thriving. He would have to work for what the insurance paid, no health insurance, no benefits. This might be a challenge for the same reason it was no longer profitable to practice in Lynchburg: the insurance managed-care scissors.

Now they were going to move. Al and Karla invited the hospital mental health administrator to lunch and handed him their resignations. He seemed very pleased, as if he had just won the lottery. They would work until the day before the move. They also informed their patients and staff so they could do the paperwork to assure the patients received continuing care with other practitioners. It all went smoothly.

Chapter 58

Karla was overwhelmed by packing. The basement was full of unopened boxes, some of them full of important letters from the past, mementos and such. She still felt as if she had been dumped into a pool of molasses, the thought of moving all the stuff burdened her so. So Al took over, cheerfully going through the things in the basement, getting her permission to throw out unimportant papers.

Talbot had also gone through things when he heard they were serious about moving. In the basement he discovered a whole box of pornographic videos, surprisingly all having overweight women as the sexual objects. Karla was shocked until she thought about it: she was so tired from work all the time that her sex life with Malcolm had gradually dwindled to almost nothing. He satisfied himself with these videos. Too late she recognized the damage. Talbot, embarrassed but helpful, packed all the videotapes and took them to the dump.

Karla had always gotten the impression from Malcolm that he did not like her gaining weight, for she had gained weight eating fast food and sugary muffins for breakfast, not having time to plan meals well. He must have been turned on by her chubbiness, she realized.

Malcolm had emphasized weight loss with Karla during their married life until they moved to Lynchburg, when it became unimportant compared to the life events they were facing. He had been shocked at how fast she gained weight with excess calories and how hard it was for her to lose it. Karla was often hypoglycemic, but the light-headedness and weakness was alleviated by carbohydrates pretty quickly. While in medical school she had studied the Krebs cycle in physiology, learning how excess carbohydrates lead to fat storage. So she began limiting her intake, avoiding breads and other starches, focusing on protein and vegetables with sparse helpings of fruit. She experienced dramatic weight loss but she loved breads and couldn't maintain the diet. A few years later, in the seventies, Dr. Atkins came out with his low-carbohydrate plan: Karla tried it, but it was too full of fats and she could not stay on it; she had always avoided excessively fatty food. She gained weight with both pregnancies, using the low-carb diet to lose, especially since it appeared to help her hypoglycemic episodes the most. She never returned to her pre-pregnancy weight, however. The glass of wine with every evening meal did not help, as it is metabolized as sugar. While in Lynchburg, the two glasses of champagne every Friday and Saturday night, a habit she had begun in Napa, plus some cheese and crackers, followed by crashing in bed, countered any restrictions she placed on carbohydrate consumption otherwise, and she had trouble losing any weight.

After the hysterectomy and oophorectomy, she was placed on estrogen, which is a fat-building hormone, and it made dieting too arduous for her. Karla worried Malcolm would be less interested in her when she was what he referred to as "pleasantly plump." During the last six months of their life together, after having passed his orals, Malcolm was finished with all class work, just doing research for his thesis, going to the library to stack up on books, and then reading and jotting notes—a whole shoebox full of index cards. He had taken over the cooking, going to completely fat-free dinners. He also fixed Karla's lunch every day, a turkey pita sandwich on a plate filled with celery and carrots—really low-fat food. He fixed Talbot's lunch as well and for Thais when she was home. He roasted almonds for his snack and stayed away from all junk food; he began to look youthful and was in excellent physical shape. Karla, however, had gained weight. Too late, Karla realized Malcolm had appreciated her figure and felt attracted. She need not have worried so much.

The basement content revealed some other secrets. Notable by their absence were the documents his mother had given Malcolm a long time ago, containing information about land she owned in Arizona and her other assets. Malcolm had never told Karla, but apparently his mother had asked him to send everything back to her after she disowned him. Karla also found a life insurance policy taken out on Malcolm when he was a baby; it expired in February of 1990, one month before his death—ironic.

Al and Karla made a plan: they would take only what they needed for the small condominium, leaving the large pieces of furniture in the house.

After they had a house in Fairfax they would move the rest. Al dove into the work at hand, packing sometimes into the midnight hours, carefully doing so as not to damage anything. Karla was surprised at how much responsibility he took for stuff he had not collected himself, for it was all hers from years of accumulation. He had nothing but some clothes and a few dishes.

Next came the packing all the charts, for which they had to rent extra space up in Fairfax. Again, Al proved himself a very organized and able packer and decision maker. Karla had considered Al depleted, both physically and emotionally, the first marriage and subsequent divorce having siphoned off his considerable strength. It amazed her how capable he was of hard work and dedication to a task despite these physical and mental challenges.

She knew she was weak, feeling constant sadness over her losses, moving slowly, each step harder than the last. Still, she remained determined to keep moving, fearful if she stopped she could not get herself going again. Moving to Fairfax represented building a new life together for these two people both in their fifties, both carrying not only physical but emotional baggage.

Al spent a whole week at his new job filling out forms to sign up with the major insurers, as that was the only source of pay he would see. Karla had unpacked and put the apartment in order. The kitchen was miniscule, room for one person only, but she found enjoyment looking out on the fountain at the golf course from the kitchen window. She found a grocery store five minutes away by car and planned inexpensive meals, setting a budget of fifteen dollars per day for their food.

The trip to Turkey was amazing. In the middle of all this turmoil they had gone through in their first year of marriage, seeing a new part of the world was rejuvenating and lent them perspective. Even if their lot right now was very hard, and it was, they were better off than a lot of people.

On their return, in November, they focused on the problems at hand again; Al had to pay some back alimony that he had been unable to fork up in the past few months. They were paying for two cars, a house payment in Lynchburg, rent on the apartment, and Talbot's educational expenses as well as a student loan for his oldest daughter. Al found there was no income in the first two months as insurance payments always lagged; not only that, but they also paid less than 50% of his charges. They survived on the ongoing income from their practices in Lynchburg, and on Karla's savings. Al began to look for additional work, scouting the area to get hours at nursing homes in addition to his daytime job. Karla began working the first week of December 1995.

In April, at tax time, there were no funds to pay the taxes they owed for the previous year. They had skimped on paying estimates for the last quarter, so there was a penalty, and all of Karla's last savings went to pay those taxes that year. Now they only had the income from the practice, which was decreasing monthly, and Karla's salary. Al's daily work remained mostly unpaid. He began receiving more income from his after-hours work at the local nursing homes, because at least Medicare paid on time. At one time on weekend rounds, he had to visit four local hospitals to see all the hospitalized patients from the practice. It took most of the day on Saturday and Sunday, and he still didn't receive his reimbursements in a timely manner.

It was grueling, that first year. They had spats because she felt neglected while he pursued all the different places he worked. They had very little enjoyment and spent spare time resting to get ready for another demanding week. Her work at Kaiser was very exacting, her schedule overbooked; the children and families she treated were overwhelmed, the kids seriously ill psychologically. She had to make accurate, speedy decisions, for if the child did not improve, the school would get concerned and the parents grew more stressed.

Karla would take the household bills to work with her on Fridays. She had two hours free then, during which she was supposed to pursue continuing education, but she needed to write checks to pay their debts.

Karla also spent a large part of that year house-hunting. At that time, Fairfax had a housing glut. The real estate agent gave Karla a pile of papers and she had to go through them and decide which to see. They saw about 100 houses that year on Saturdays and Sundays. Often Karla went out with the real estate agent while Al did his on-call rounds. She would always intuitively know if a house was right for them and in this she and Al always agreed, because he would experience the same intuitive reaction. Twice they signed and paid a deposit on a house because it satisfied their physical needs, but after overnight reflection, both admitted to each other something didn't feel right. Al was also deeply intuitive and responded to energy vibrations rather than sales talk or features.

On a Saturday in July, 1996, Karla found the right house. Al was on call again. The real estate woman drove south down Highway 29 and pulled off into a residential area. When she turned into a private drive, Karla started seeing prices in her head. *Private drive equals expensive,* she thought. The house was at the end of the drive, surrounded by trees, with brick front, two stories with a two-car garage.

Karla walked into the airy and bright home. Each room looked out on tall oak trees. The backyard made Karla feel faint with joy; a grove of oak trees led down a hill to a creek. The gorgeous summer foliage did not obscure the light streaming in the large windows into the kitchen; a door leading out onto a large deck further entranced her. There was not a single window that did not have a lovely vista. She wanted that house. Al felt positive as well on seeing it. They called the agent.

"Unfortunately, someone has made an offer which has been accepted since we saw the house," she said apologetically.

Karla was despondent. In her heart, she was already living in those spacious rooms with large windows looking out on trees she adored. Al comforted her, telling the agent, "Please let us know if the contract falls through."

Karla turned to the *I Ching*, asking if there were any possibility that the house would be theirs. She was so anxious that she was unable to interpret the hexagrams.

"Don't worry, honey; we'll get the house," Al told her one day in August. How could he say that under the circumstances? But as if on cue, the agent called just at the end of August to tell them the other contract fell through; they could close the third week of September.

Their offer had been accepted amazingly fast, so Karla applied for an equity loan for the down payment, using her Lynchburg house. Getting the loan for the rest of the balance went surprisingly well, given their debt and alimony payments.

Just in time she told their landlord they would be moving out on September 25, almost exactly a year by that time. They had been set to sign for another year had they not found a home, but now they did not have to commit themselves.

Moving entailed emptying the Lynchburg house of all the large furniture and books, then having the movers come to the apartment and pick up the stuff there, plus a third trip to the storage locker to pick up the office charts.

Karla had been very attached to the Lynchburg house and during that first year in Fairfax, she and Al would drive down about once every six weeks, sleep in Thais's bedroom, and spend time boxing items and cleaning. Karla loved those trips, filled with the good memories of times gone by.

Chapter 59

Urged to do so by Al, who was concerned about how bad she often felt and the heavy workload at Kaiser, Karla soon changed her Kaiser job to part-time and took a salaried position for the other two days of the week with Al's practice; they were willing to give her a salary, as child psychiatrists were in demand. She refused to sign up with the insurance as the only means of payment. Soon she was disgruntled for they kept overbooking her, putting two different clients in the same time slot. She felt that it was unethical and she feared that being so pressured, she might make an error, harming the patient, so she resigned.

One of Karla's adult patients at the private clinic had surprised her with a huge potted plant on her first visit. When Karla quit the practice, she received calls from this patient, begging to see her in private practice, but Karla was not in private practice. After thinking about it, she considered the request from this patient as a call to return to private practice. She found a small office in Reston owned by a psychologist who welcomed her into his building. She wanted to practice acupuncture as well and he encouraged her to do that, not interfering in any way and referring patients to her as well.

In October of 1998, after resigning from Al's group but keeping her Kaiser job three days a week, she began her private practice again. Her client was very grateful and came not only for psychiatric care but also took advantage of the acupuncture. Emily, her client had a striking appearance, tall with lots of naturally blonde hair, and an alabaster complexion out of which shone bright blue eyes, full of friendliness. Karla could not help associating the appearance with that of an angel.

The practice built up gradually and really took off after about a year. Karla was thrilled at being able to practice acupuncture as well as psychiatry. She took courses in Chinese herbs and added those to her regimen. She felt magic and excitement and anticipation when she stepped into that dark office with only one window facing west; to her it was her laboratory where she found alternative as well as Western medicine working hand in hand. She had many exciting challenges in both psychiatry and acupuncture patients. She felt fulfilled.

Al asked her one day, "Why don't you quit your Kaiser job? It's such hard work. Just focus on the private practice."

She had not thought about it for she had been happy with Kaiser, but her schedule was always very tight, and there was so much pressure to get the children and adolescents better—it was not easy to convince parents that it would take time and patience. Just at that time she had finally started to feel like a member of the child and adolescent team. They had begun having meetings to discuss cases and going to lunch afterwards. She bonded with the new child psychiatrist just out of residency and another who had moved east from California. Both were a lot younger, but they enjoyed talking together as they ate lunch. She felt really fulfilled, for Kaiser was a hard place to make friends; it was all business.

But the more she thought about Al's suggestion, the more attractive it felt; she would have more time for private patients and maybe even free time. She felt guilty, though. The private practice was not lucrative yet; she was just meeting her business expenses, so she would not be able to add much to the household finances. She didn't accept insurance billing—the patients had to pay cash and bill the insurance themselves, so Karla, always economical and sensitive, charged a very minimal fee.

While she was considering the option, she received a call from a social worker from one of the clinics. The two had a Kaiser patient in common and had been consulting with each other. The social worker told Karla her organization was looking for a child psychiatrists five hours a week, as theirs was leaving. She interviewed and got the job. Two months later, she resigned at Kaiser after eight years.

So now it was just her private practice and the extra income from five hours a week at the community clinic—no comparison to the nice salary at Kaiser. But with some adjustments in their spending, the finances were looking better by this time.

Al had meanwhile also left his private group practice after two years and worked briefly at Kaiser before finding a position at the mental health institute in Falls Church in January of 1998. It was a good salary with very generous benefits. The job itself was hard and demanding, but Al was never afraid of hard work.

Some sense of security began to come into their lives. Once his first wife reached age sixty-five, Al was no longer to pay alimony as she received Social Security checks on his account. That was one major monthly expense less for them. Karla learned an important lesson from the toll the alimony took on their finances: keep putting extra into the house payment and pay off the house. They were getting older and a house payment could be a significant strain should one of them be unable to work, which, with aging, was increasingly possible.

Already there had been some health issues that made them wonder how long they would be able to work. Karla had major backaches that were incredibly painful. The problem had started in Lynchburg, a deep ache in her lower back accompanied by stiffness whenever she changed position. They were always present and excruciatingly painful at times. She quickly found out that anti-inflammatory medicines had no effect so she stopped taking them. Al did acupuncture for her several times and it relieved the pain temporarily. Living in Fairfax, she tried swimming and massage, some walking and yoga, but the pains remained and became spasms so that every time she turned in bed, lightning arrows of pain shot up and down her back. At times she thought it would be better to be dead than this constant unwanted pain haunting her.

Despite this impediment, Karla seldom complained and kept up her busy schedule.

She received Dr. David Williams' alternative medicine newsletter, and in 2003 she read one issue in which he mentioned the Power Plate, a vibratory machine on which one stood while it relaxed and tensed every muscle of the body multiple times over the course of a minute. Karla was intrigued, as the various exercises she had tried for her back had made no difference. She ordered the machine, which had to be delivered from the airport in a special packing crate attended by two men who set it up.

Karla started using the machine and suddenly the backache was completely gone! She could hardly believe it and had to check the daily diary she wrote as to exactly when it left, which turned out to be during the first week of using the machine. This meant that the back pain was due to blocked energy, or *qi*, pathways in her back that had been opened with the vibration.

When the bill came for the machine, Al looked at it. Then he looked again.

"Is this eight hundred or eight thousand?" he asked incredulously staring at the figure owed.

"It is eight thousand," she said hesitantly, feeling guilty.

Karla had not told him the cost of the machine when she ordered it for she was sure he would not agree to buy it, but now she had to confess. He was aghast and chastised her, but on finding out her backache was gone, agreed it was worth it.

Karla felt a tremendous sense of body wellness return and could not believe how easily although costly this complete cure had been achieved. Her backache never returned.

Chapter 60

As Karla and Al aged, they had to face the decline and loss of their own parents as well. Al's parents were long lived, both dying at the age of ninety-two. Toward the end of his life, Al's father became very ill and was hospitalized at Korea University Hospital in the winter of early 2001. Al immediately flew to his father's side, helping to care for him, and the old man recovered. He relapsed the next January, though, and Al returned to Korea to be with him. He returned after ten days when his father's condition improved, only to be recalled a week later when he was died.

His mother then went to stay with Al's sister in Canada because she had health coverage there before, but returned to her home in Korea after a three-year stay. She was very forgetful and needed to be watched constantly, as she left stove burners on. She also easily lost her balance and ell. Her middle son, who lived with her, had to put her in a nursing home where she could be closely observed. Eventually, her memory left her completely, and she did not recognize family members anymore. She died peacefully in 2008.

Karla's parents did not suffer such long declines. Karla's mother was vacuuming the living room when she suddenly collapsed and lost consciousness in October of 2003. Karla rushed to the hospital in Omaha, where Johanna was in the intensive coronary care unit. She had severe heart failure, deemed beyond hope at her advanced age of eighty-three.

Olga, Dimitri, and Michael paid no attention to anything Karla said about letting Johanna die. She was on a respirator and could not breathe on her own during repeated attempts to wean her off. She also kept having repeated seizures when the blood supply to her brain failed with the heart's abnormal rhythm.

On a day when Karla knew she and Al would be the only visitors in the early afternoon, Karla placed acupuncture needles on Johanna to stimulate her lungs into functioning. The needles stayed in place fifteen minutes and were removed.

Johanna's doctors told the family that they should be prepared for her death when they attempted the next removal of the respirator the next day in the morning. That evening they all said their farewells to Johanna.

They were together again the next day when the doctor came and removed the tube from Johanna's larynx. Amazingly, she began breathing spontaneously, even getting some color in her cheeks. The episodic jerks and seizures, however, continued throughout the day. Now the doctor wanted to have her moved to hospice, where she could die in a dignified manner.

Again, Dimitri and Michael refused, instead insisting she was going home with them and they would care for her there. Karla knew this would result in poor care for Johanna, as the visiting nurse only administered medication and then left. Johanna was incontinent and disoriented and had never again achieved consciousness since she collapsed. She had brain damage from the frequent interruption of blood to the brain when she seized.

A couple of days after taking Johanna home, Karla got a call from Michael. Johanna was incoherently insisting she had been kidnapped and perceived all attention to her as negative. Karla felt helpless; her mother needed more care and understanding than could be given at home. She was calling the house daily to check on her mother's condition. On November 1, as she talked to Dimitri, her mother died. Karla and Al returned to Omaha for the funeral. Karla saw her mother being laid to rest and could feel only relief that her mother's aching heart could be at peace at last.

Karla's sadness came later reminiscing about her relationship with her mother: they had never discussed any issues that were emotionally laden for Karla, about her past, about the abuse, about the abandonment, and most of all, how badly she felt about betraying her mother. It was only much later that Karla understood that she never betrayed her mother as it was her mother's responsibility to look responsibly to her daughter's welfare. She had protected her mother out of her own shame and had feared her mother's response had she confided in her.

Her longing for her mother was never satisfied her entire life.

Chapter 61

$\mathcal{K}$arla practiced meditation after taking a walk in the morning, and again at night as she prepared herself for sleep. She found that meditation, in which one becomes aware of the inner self, was healing for her. She wanted to help her patients as well with this knowledge, so she looked for instructors, or rather, they found her. She received a letter in the mail from her first instructor, Joyce Goodrich, informing Karla of meditation seminars held in the Boston area. After writing back about her interest, she was accepted as a member of the seminar. It consisted of a week's training, sharing space in a nunnery house located near the ocean.

Joyce first opened Karla's awareness that thought energy travels faster than light and can reach anywhere in this world or out of this world. She learned that any place, anywhere, can become a focus of meditation, and thus she learned standing, sitting, lying down, and walking meditation. She started by focusing on any object or representation within her visual field, focusing on deep breathing and becoming still inside her mind. It was an amazing discovery, the stillness.

Her second teacher, Lumari, emphasized focusing on one's internal energy source for healing. That energy soon appeared to Karla as a swirling vortex that appeared when she entered inner space, sacred space. Within this vortex she was able to transmit healing matrices to the body. The matrices were mental energy held within sacred geometric figures, one for each *chakra*, seven energy centers along the midline of the body from the base of the spine to the top of the head. These chakras have a profound influence on the organs within their domain and can be accessed through meditation. Balancing the chakra energies is another healing method. Lumari had her focus on the sacred matrices, which she soon memorized and could call up at will, and send them as needed anywhere to anyone. She was taught to ask permission of the receiver before sending the matrices.

Karla also heard the *Om* sound, the sound of the universe referenced in sacred teachings. Becoming aware of it first when she was fourteen years old, sitting at her desk at home and doing math problems, she had no clue as to its origins. She imagined the sound came from a train engine; it was vibratory in nature and changed tones and pitch and speed. This sound was now always present and she could focus in on it in the noisiest surroundings. She let herself lean into the sound, letting it bring calmness and an awareness of dimensions not experienced on Earth. It was interesting to Karla to realize that the sound switched from one ear to the other at various times, and that sometimes it was perceived in the midline of her head. The sound could wake her up in the mornings with its intensity. Karla began to realize the universe is made up of vibrational energy.

Chapter 62

*I*n 2004 Wells Fargo sent Karla a letter saying she could refinance the house and pay only 4.75 % interest for five years; after that it would be that plus the APR. They had been paying 10% with Washington Mutual, so this opportunity was almost too good to believe. She set a goal; in five years they would pay off the house. She achieved her dream earlier than expected: in December 2006 she made her last loan payment.

The same month that Karla paid off the house, Al resigned from his job at the Institute and planned to start a twenty-hour-per-week job at the Alexandria Clinic, where he had been moonlighting since March of 2002. A senior psychiatrist there retired, and the clinical director begged Al to take the job. Al had turned sixty-eight that year so he had already worked three years above the retirement age, but he agreed he would try it for one year. The job was not stressful and his director delighted in Al's ability to do well with substance abuse patients, geriatric patients, and even prisoners at the county jail. So each week he worked in three different locations for those services.

Karla had quit her part-time job at the local charity clinic and was now fully part-time just in the private practice since the summer of 2005. She didn't like the dark room that was her private office; she needed three overhead lights and two lamps just to light it up, and the room was poorly serviced for heating or air conditioning, requiring a space heater in the winter and overhead fan in the summer.

But she loved her patients, feeling joy and satisfaction as they improved and healed. In the last four years of the practice she added meditation healing and therapy, which served her patients wonderfully well as they worked with the energy of the chakras through meditation.

"Honey, you look very tired," Al commented one morning at breakfast. "Why don't you retire? We can make it on my income and Social Security and later on my pension." It was April 2009.

Karla was surprised. She felt her practice was very successful. Yes, she was tired a lot, especially when she did acupuncture—it seemed to drain her qi into the patient. She often needed Thursday as a recovery day after the Tuesday and Wednesday at work. She also found she was so distracted by phone calls from patients on her days off that she really felt she was still concerned with work issues although she was home. And sometimes on Tuesday and Wednesday evening she felt so drained and tired after coming home that she had no appetite and slept poorly.

Al had noticed all of this even though she did not say anything. Just considering closing her practice sent her into a state of anxiety for she had not thought of retiring for a long time, but Al kept reminding her, "You have been working since you were thirteen years old. It's time for you to relax and write full-time."

She gave herself until September to make up her mind and tell her patients. Closing the practice at the end of the year seemed like the best thing to do, so patients had time to find a replacement to start up in January.

It just came out of her mouth one day in September. Talking to a patient, she heard herself say, "I will be retiring at the end of December and we need to think about your continuing care once I close my practice."

The patient was shocked, but so was Karla, and having said that, she had set her course.

She still had a lot of anxiety. Her practice was so diverse she would need to send one patient to several practitioners to fulfill the psychiatry, acupuncture, and herbal medicine needs, as well as the meditation. She knew of no practitioner in her community who did all these modalities. It caused her enough anxiety that she had to take a Chinese herbal so she would not worry so much; at the office she began playing a game on her cell phone in between patients so she would not think too much and scare herself into not retiring.

In the end, though, it went amazingly smoothly. Her clients all had enough time to find replacements on their own or with her recommendation. Although they hated to see her close her practice, they expressed happiness for her upcoming freedom. She had never heard so many "Congratulations!"

The closer she got to December, the happier she felt about her decision. Al was also relieved that she took his advice; he wanted her to have time to follow her other interests.

Chapter 63

$\mathcal{K}$arla often lived in her memories, those in which everyone was well and happy; it helped her because she knew those experiences were real and not diminished by death. Just because Thais's life ended in a horrible death did not alter how happy she had been in life. Karla always felt a response from Thais when her tears and sadness were most intense; a thought would enter her mind to divert her and she would know it was Thais, concerned about her.

Karla had availed herself of Lumari, who had helped her transcend her unbroken grief. She learned techniques of centering herself, focusing on her energetic vibrations and practicing deep, abdominal breathing.

Who can set a limit to grief? Grief takes its own course, the separation from the loved ones never really complete. It just becomes less acute as the years pass and life goes on. Although life pauses for the grieving person, it must give way to the rhythm of time. When her emotions seemed overwhelming, Karla went to her bed, lay down, and closed her eyes. She entered her sacred space, and there she also found Thais. The face was very close to her, beautiful, and then two crystal tears fell from her eyes. Then she disappeared. Adding Thais's tears to her own feeling of sadness and dejection alarmed Karla. What was Thais telling her? She got up from bed, having a sudden urge to find the last pictures she had of Thais taken just a few days before her last hospitalization in July 1991.

The pictures showed Thais in the apartment in Seattle, hooked up to an IV stand, sitting on the couch. Her skin had the bronze color of kidney failure, emphasized by the dark circles around her eyes. Her face was puffy and full of fluid, her eyes a dull blue; she appeared exhausted and very serious, even depressed. A picture of her standing showed how much muscle her legs had lost.

Karla was shocked, recognizing that she had been in denial when those pictures were taken: Thais was clearly moribund.

Telling Al about her emotional distress on seeing visual documentation of how Thais had been reduced to organ failure and was clearly exhausted from her struggle, Karla said, "I think Thais was crying because I am still suffering so much, and she is long past it."

In her meditations she saw Thais mouthing, "I love you." Karla only intuited afterwards that Thais was saddened because Karla still could not let go of all her post-traumatic images of Thais in the hospital before she died. The most nurturing gift was Thais blowing her breath at Karla as if to say, "Look, Mom, I am breathing celestial breath." Karla would open herself up to that breath of heavenly air and feel refreshed.

Karla now knew that our loved ones live on in another plane, and can reach us and are active in our lives. They are touched by our joys and our sorrows. Love cannot be destroyed by death of the body; it is a universal energy that permeates everything. *So,* Karla asked herself, *why am I still holding on to the memories at the hospital when Thais has reached a place where she can breathe and communicate and love?* She concluded that her post-traumatic stress disorder from her experience at the Hutchinson was difficult to heal.

Because Malcolm was a mature person when he died, the grieving for him was softer. As time went on, Karla felt more appreciation and gratitude for his life and what he had taught her. She often appealed in her soul to him when her time with Al was particularly challenging, and it felt as if he responded as things eased up inside her.

Karla relied very much on messages from the universe, God, the Goddess, sages, and invisible friends. She often felt guided, getting help in finding lost objects or receiving a to-do list on days when she felt disorganized. Very often she was reminded to withhold judgment when discouraged, to wait for another day to see more clearly, while at the same time a sudden impulse might prompt her in the right direction with positive results to her day.

Writing, she could not handle the painful resurgence of emotions the descriptions of Thais's suffering at the Hutch brought on until she took a writing class she took in 2009.

The instructor had told the class that when they came to describe an event that evoked overwhelming emotions for them, they should sit down and start to write about it, stop when it became unbearable, but the next day start writing again, continuing piece by piece until they described it fully. Karla kept this as her mantra as she groped with confronting the pain.

On the 13th of June, 2010, Karla and Al had promised to pick up Susie, Al's five-year-old granddaughter, and take her to a picnic. The date coincided with an annual church picnic, which was a nice setting, and if the weather was too hot or rainy, they could eat inside the downstairs hall at the church.

Susie was waiting impatiently for her grandparents to pick her up at eleven. She came out of the house dressed in a flowery sundress and hat, flowery sunglasses, and flip-flops. Karla put her in the booster seat that her mother Louise put in the car and sat next to her in the back seat as Al drove.

At the beginning, they played a game in which Susie hid sunglasses certain places and Grandma Karla seriously questioned whether they were in her shoes, under her dress, behind her back, on her head, and so forth, which brought forth mischievous peals of laughter from Susie. When Karla had given up and decided the sunglasses had disappeared, Susie pulled them out of their hiding place, gleeful over her grandmother's surprise. They played this game in various different ways: Susie was a magician and the sunglasses turned into a rabbit in a hat; the sunglasses grew wings and flew away, into the forest, up into the clouds and then suddenly reappeared.

When they arrived at the picnic ground, Susie was excited and ran ahead to the picnic tables laden with food, but she tripped with her loose shoes and fell on the gravel, skinning her right knee and elbow. Karla rushed to her rescue and picked her up, Susie hiding her face with pain and chagrin, and Karla hugged her. A church member arrived immediately with a Band-Aid and towelettes and they went inside to some chairs. Susie started limping, but Karla whispered in her ear, "You don't have to limp; you're fine. We will just clean it and put a Band-Aid on it." From then on she walked normally and allowed Karla to clean her up and apply the bandages.

She was now very shy. She ate only the cookies and cupcake she had put on her plate and ignored the rice and vegetables and salads. She looked stressed, so Karla smiled widely at her and told her what a good girl she was and she brightened up, focusing on Karla, then smiling and eating.

They returned to the house after the picnic, where Susie began playing with all the throw pillows in the family room and soon engaged Karla in another laughing game throwing pillows at each other. For an hour they played, both totally engrossed in getting the other to laugh.

Back in the car on the way home to Susie's house, they again played a game, drawing on the back seat of the car with their fingers and letting the other person guess the pictures. It was very important to focus. So many memories ran through Karla's head as she played these games with Susie: how she had played similar games with Thais at that age. Talbot had not been into playing games with his mother; he was into boy games. He had a wagon that he steered down the hill in front of their garage on East First Street; he studied insects on the ground for long periods; and he liked to build things and draw. He played much with Thais, usually pretending they were camping out or traveling in a camper.

Susie reminded Karla of Thais with her social poise and her engaging ways. It made her heart ache and at the same time swell with joy that she could experience this happiness again. Her heart felt grateful to Susie; how could a five-year-old give her concentrated joy for four hours that she had not had for decades?

Chapter 64

$\mathcal{K}$arla's family of four that came to the United States as immigrants on November 7, 1951, had sadly shrunk.

Her mother, bereft of two of her children, worked hard to make a new life. But this new life was stained from the start with Dimitri's sexual abuse of Karla, with Karla having to bear the knowledge her mother had married a child abuser. Meanwhile, Johanna saw Karla as a reminder of her pain, and inappropriately expressed her anger to Karla about Anton not supporting her with the children and taking them away from her. She would write cards to Karla in which she would remind Karla that Anton's family treated them badly. One day, Karla wrote back, "You were not alone; we, your children, suffered with you." From then on her mother only wrote cards with well wishes and love.

Many years later, a year before Michael died, he told Karla in a conversation that they had all been angry when Karla left Omaha, blaming Malcolm for stealing her away. When he explained this to Karla, she recognized they were all still resentful of her leaving and they had not wished her well.

Karla often felt guilty for not calling her stepfather more often after her mother's death. Although she acknowledged him on holidays and birthdays, giving him a generous check with a card twice a year, she searched and searched for a card that would not say what a great dad he was, or that she loved him. When she called, he broke into tears of joy, for he received almost no calls that were not from Karla or Olga. Johanna's death left a big hole in the life of the family. Dimitri was alone and emotionally needy, grieving for his wife and son.

She now felt the pangs of guilt. *How will I feel once he is dead? Will I torture myself with guilt feelings for not overcoming my own suffering at his hands and calling him weekly at least, like a good daughter?* If she could just once hear him apologize for what he had done to her, it would help a lot, but he was not a person to apologize. Instead, he would find excuses for what he had done, and after all, wasn't it just fun? For that is what he told her when as a teenager she objected to his advances: "It is just for fun."

Karla could relate to the many stories of sexually-abused children who are not believed by the adults they seek help from, including therapists who have been admonished to take a step back and not probe too deeply into these issues. Karla herself had been a witness how some families will deny or bury their knowledge of abuse of a child in order to keep the family together. She knew from her own history that her abuse was not considered as important as keeping the family together was, even to her.

Karla was not aware, however, until she received more information during her training, that child abusers will abuse any vulnerable child they come in contact with.

It was after her parents told her that Olga got nauseated after eating and was severely depressed that she began to wonder, but it was not something she herself addressed with her sister. Rather, she had her parents send Olga to a psychiatrist, hoping that in that neutral atmosphere she could relate the cause of her distress. Was it her stepfather? Karla never found out, for her sister did not divulge what went on in the therapy, but she recovered from her depression and the nausea stopped.

Then Dimitri told Karla that his daughter-in-law wouldn't allow him to babysit her small daughter anymore, that she suspected him of sexually abusing her. He vehemently denied it, saying, "If you think that, don't bring her anymore." After Johanna died, the daughter-in-law never let Michael leave their daughter alone with Dimitri.

Guilt was a big part of Karla's life. She was sure that when something bad happened to her, that she had somehow drawn it to herself. That, of course, is typical thinking in children who relate everything to themselves.

She was a firm believer in reincarnation, that we live repeated lives for the purpose of cleansing ourselves of our karma and return to the home of our souls. She had learned from her respected Chinese acupuncture teacher that we make a blueprint, a layout of our life that we will fulfill in the next reincarnation, each life helping us learn a lesson. The ultimate lesson is that the greatest ethic of this creation is self-sacrifice.

How different this ethic was from economics, getting the most you can get of anything in your time here on earth and passing it on to your offspring, keeping the wealth growing with each generation.

Karla had a good instinct for self-survival, but she was very much attracted to this universal ethic and by the teaching of Jesus, "It is harder for a rich man to get into heaven than for a camel to go through the eye of a needle." Believing this philosophy, could she afford to forget that forgiveness, doing good to those who hurt her, was the way to reconcile herself with creation? Could she afford to think only of her own comfort and retribution even if only as thoughts in her mind for wrongs incurred by others? It was an ongoing dilemma in her soul, an inner conflict which often stole her peace and serenity. Both teachings affirmed in Karla a deep belief that not only are we masters of our own destiny and create it for our own purification, but also that the self-sacrifice needed is "turning the other cheek" to the aggressor "for they know not what they do."

She struggled to overcome her feelings of resentment and anger and recognize that possibly she created this destiny before she was born. And was it right that she sacrificed herself to her family so that they could continue as an economic unity. She took into consideration how poorly educated her parents were and how unprepared for modern society with its demand for knowledge and finesse. She wanted to help them keep something of a life knowing their fragmented pasts. She did not want to destroy that.

In her spiritual studies, Karla felt a chasm between the economic necessity of her life and the world of the spirit. This duality, she believed, is relieved by death and the return to the spirit world. But she also believed that everything is spirit and that living a spiritual life is more important than any economic considerations. That it is not something that can be put off, but something that has to be actualized in herself.

Karla did have one great relationship from that family of four and that was her half-sister Olga whom she always considered just her sister. Olga was the best aunt Thais and Talbot could ever have, gifting them on birthdays and holidays, calling to speak with them not wanting to miss any part of their lives.

Just as she was wonderful to the children, she was always there for Karla, ever ready to listen, letting her know that she was not only her sister but her best friend.

Karla was amazed at how beautifully Olga prepared their mother's funeral, the coffin embossed with roses, the wonderful Greek Orthodox ceremony and buffet lunch following. Olga could cry at the drop of a hat and her sobbing could be heard through the congregation, such an innocent, love-filled rending of tears that no one had any dry eyes.

And she did the same for her brother Michael after his sudden death, again gathering everyone for the funeral and making it an affair to remember. Although Karla contributed the gravestone and paid for Michael's buffet lunch, she was in the background, quietly grieving but full of appreciation for her younger sister's kindness to their mother and brother.

She was an amazing soul, Olga. Creative in all her endeavors, an excellent writer and poet in her own right, and loving every member of her family without judgment.

It was Karla and Olga's relationship that survived the silent destruction of that immigrant family. It continues to this day.

Chapter 65

She was retired now, so she had more time to do things and stay in contact; her best time was solitude, sitting in bed and meditating or in the soft leather reclining chair in the family room, book in hand. She was reading many books at one time, seldom finishing any of them, merely searching for articles of interest. Even her culinary skills were supported by the many cookbooks she consulted, not relying on any one as she avoided repeating menus.

Al found it hard to believe that Karla actually used the more than one hundred cookbooks in her library, guessing she might just buy them and let them lie around. Even if she did not use a cookbook in over a year, suddenly she would focus on it for a week's menus, compiling them on Monday mornings after Al left for work.

Once, a family member asked Al what Karla cooked. He replied, "Everyday gourmet meals." The description fit; Karla could not resist preparing delicious and attractive meals. She would spend time perfecting a recipe until it fulfilled all her expectations. She mastered Asian as well as continental dishes one at a time until she was satisfied. Al said her love was in the menus she prepared, his lunch sandwiches no exception. It was true; she couldn't cook if she was angry or sad.

Al's diabetes and atherosclerotic heart disease worsened after the stress he experienced in the aftermath of his father's death and his mother's care. He needed extensive stenting to his coronary arteries on two different occasions in 2006 and 2008, beginning several medications to control his blood sugar which had spiraled upwards.

During all this time, he never failed his job responsibilities, going to work every day even when he often felt poorly. Between his and Karla's efforts, they slowly paid down their debts. He insisted that Karla retire once that was completed; she was then almost sixty-nine and he was seventy-two. Both worked well beyond the age when they could collect Social Security.

At last, he could look forward to retiring at age seventy-three. He hoped he could live some years after retiring, for now he cherished his life as never before. He felt at peace.

Chapter 66

*K*arla sat and puzzled over her fate. Never in her life could she have imagined how it had turned out so far; imagining what would happen in the future was probably equally impossible to predict.

Her practice as a psychiatrist, acupuncturist, and alternative physician ended when she retired. Medicine had been a part of her daily life since she was twenty-two years old; she wasn't sure what she would do to fill her time.

She began to think about how every crossroads encountered in life could bring a very different result. Had she taken the scholarship to do a Ph.D., her marriage might have suffered, as she and Malcolm would not have finished their current projects at the same time. What if she hadn't gone with him to Europe? Or what if the trip to Europe had not been as healing as it was? She remembered a female colleague at her medical school who asked Karla one day as they worked in the outpatient clinic, "What are you looking forward to most when you go to Europe?"

"Not getting raped," she blurted. The woman looked shocked and Karla was, too, but it was what had happened to her in Europe. The sudden statement made her realize how that threat permeated her life with fear on every level.

For Karla, every social engagement created anxiety: when invited out by friends, she would raid the icebox to calm her fears. What was she afraid of? Being exposed—not only her private history but also that of her native Austria.

It all went back to her adolescent years, having to keep a secret more awful to some than the sexual abuse she suffered: a Jewish heritage. She didn't know she had a Jewish background, and identified herself as an

Austrian only. Austria was Hitler's birthplace, and thus anything associated with Hitler's atrocities caused pangs of guilt in Karla. Her uncles and father had all served in the German army during World War II; thus, her beloved family members were the enemy as seen from the side of Americans. Her stepfather never let Karla forget the damage done to innocent people by the Germans. But Karla grew up in a community that was scarred by distrust of Jews.

Her stepfather and his friend took Karla to see a documentary about the Holocaust when she was a teenager. Seeing it made her sick and increased her guilt even more. So Karla kept her heritage a secret as well. Having these three secrets, the rapes and ongoing abuse, relatives who fought for Hitler, and later her Jewish heritage, made her clam up in social interactions. She could only let them go so far, because no one should ever know the real Karla, what her life was like or who she was.

Until this identity crisis during her adolescent years, Karla had been outgoing and eagerly participated in social situations. The first rape and the emotional state engendered by her abandonment at the same time were almost repressed, kept deeply buried until her stepfather again resumed the sexual abuse. Then all the anxiety from the original insult came into her conscious mind and altered her social demeanor.

Her healthy, undamaged self was gregarious and outgoing, considering each person she met as holding wonderful potential for friendship. She loved people, and although this quality was submerged by her shame and guilt, it was still there. Interestingly, she could extend her best self to her patients without any problem because they were never going to know the intimate details of her life and history.

Karla had married two men who were socially outgoing and popular. Feeling protected by their love for her, she could interact in social situations to a limited degree. But her spouses had no restrictions as to what they could reveal about themselves; Karla secretly envied that, for she wished she could also be so open and share herself more with people. At the same time that she felt envious, though, she was also proud of her husbands who navigated so easily in social encounters. She enjoyed seeing the interactions and could relax herself to participate as well in their presence.

Although Al could interact socially, talking about his feelings was more difficult for him, although that changed over time. When she would ask him what was going on during his bouts with anger, he often could not say and wound up blaming her for something she had said or done. Only after a few years did he recognize that he had much more anger about his past marriage than the present one. He slowly began to identify the real culprit, his post-traumatic stress disorder, in which any small reminder of what his former wife had done or said would trigger tremendous anger and resentment. Often it was Karla asking him where he had been when he returned late from an outing that set him off; his ex-wife always demanded an exact accounting not only of time spent, but money spent. He finally stopped explaining where he had spent money when Karla reminded him that she never asked. Still, she internalized this guilt, adding to the guilt she felt from her childhood.

For Karla, the hardest test in the relationship with Al was his attempt to solve their disagreements with threats. This happened often during the first ten years. Karla would react by contraction into herself, her body responding as after a major trauma, getting weak and very thirsty, as if she had lost blood. Her fear about being abandoned again seemed to have no end; she could neither eat nor sleep. After he had left, she would call him endlessly on his cell phone, praying he would answer and assuage her fears, but he never did. Then, at least in the early days, she would call Talbot; she just needed a person on the other end of the line to help her anchor herself from the groundless fear. Talbot was helpful and concerned but never took a side, only listening. She realized it was inappropriate to burden her son, so she turned to prayer and meditation to calm her agitated mind. Then, suddenly, there was a wonderful silence in her mind and she knew she wasn't alone—God was always with her no matter what.

In time Al no longer threatened to leave Karla. They learned to give each other time and distance when upset, apologizing once the storm had passed and resuming their loving relationship.

Karla, however, began meditating on a regular basis, a practice that helped her wounds to finally heal over. She also memorized the Prayer of St. Francis of Assisi and would recite it repeatedly to soothe herself. She knew only too well that death is the final separation for everyone. Death of a loved one can also feel like abandonment unless one makes careful reality checks. She could not bear to read stories or see movies that had any semblance to what she experienced with her little family. She could tell people close to her how she felt, later feeling guilty that she had burdened them by touching their lives with her sadness.

Having gone through several such separations, Karla tried to strengthen herself by learning what she could about death and dying. She became *a*ware that connections with loved ones who had passed were not ended, they merely changed in character. Reading Rudolf Steiner's books on the matter was helpful, for he said that dead loved ones continue to care about their living relatives or friends and interact with them through intuition and dreams. He said children who die always are connected with their parents, never leaving them. How true that proved with what Karla saw in her meditations and dreams with Thais.

Slowly Karla recognized that suffering can broaden one's horizons. Sitting pensively at the word processor, the windows in front of her giving a view of the small patch of forest which adjoined the backyard, looking at the trees swaying in the wind, Karla felt a companionship with them, gathering strength from their resilience in the wind, for they swayed from side to side, but did not fall. That was how she needed to react to her fate: bend with it, but not break with it.

She transferred these lessons to her practice. Her focus with her patients was to help them recognize who they were as persons by helping them to pay attention to important cues coming from their intuition, of which they were often unaware. With the acupuncture she was able to address the physical manifestations of stress. She used conventional medicines such as antidepressants and mood stabilizers when necessary, but often with the adjunctive treatments; patients needed less medication and began to take care of themselves better when they had coping mechanisms like meditation. She also offered nutritional advice if patients sought it; she encouraged exercise, good sleeping habits, and dealing with their troubled relationships. Looking back, it amazed Karla that this expansion in her medical knowledge developed as she attempted to cope with her losses.

In her private life, she had to familiarize herself with Korean culture. She attempted to learn the language in hopes of better understanding Al and his family, with whom they were always in contact. Al was a vital member of the Korean community, volunteering to educate them about mental health and helping them to cope with the stresses in adapting to a new home. Karla was very grateful for the opportunity to expand her horizons that her marriage to Al offered her; after all, she already had a deep interest in Chinese culture through the *I Ching*, and in time she found she was at home in these two cultures. Yet she valued Western culture for the freedom and openness it had developed over the centuries. Al on his part began studying German, Karla's mother tongue, coming home from work, asking her what they were going to eat in German. Karla always laughed, appreciating his successful efforts, feeling a great sense of being honored for who she was.

She familiarized herself with the tenets of many of the major religions, reading the Bible, the Koran, the *Baghavad Gita,* and books on Confucianism, Taoism, and Buddhism. She recognized that all of them offered her a deeper knowledge of who she was as a person; they were all rich in material for meditation. Perhaps because of her upbringing, she identified most with the teachings of Jesus Christ. She felt herself going through the Stations of the Cross with her daughter Thais as Thais struggled for life. But Karla also liked how important ideas ran as throughlines between religions. The directive of loving your neighbor as yourself, which was also a Confucian idea, was hard at times of conflict. Turning the other cheek if assailed—also very difficult—dovetailed with Taoism, in which, instead of fighting your fate, you observe what is happening and you let it happen, because there is a plan larger than your own. That we cannot always ascertain the wisdom of our fates increased her empathy and understanding of the suffering of others.

Chapter 67

*A*fter graduating from college in 1997, Talbot had packed his belongings and drove his Saab to move to Brooklyn, New York, renting a studio apartment there. He had found a job working for an internet and television news station as a journalist.

Karla visited him as often as she could and through him became more familiar with Brooklyn and Manhattan and the Bronx. He would also drive home to Fairfax to visit about every three months to ease his homesickness and reconnect with his college friends.

In New York, Talbot resumed contact with a woman friend with whom he had studied at the international school in Vienna. She was completing her studies in her specialty as a speech pathologist. Through her group of friends, Talbot found a partner, Sidney, a wonderful man whose sterling qualities made for a happy relationship.

In 2007, Talbot and Sidney moved to San Francisco. Both found jobs and two years later settled into their own condominium. Talbot told Karla it had always been his secret dream to return to northern California, where he had so many happy memories from his childhood.

Karla, too, could revisit old neighborhoods in Napa when she visited Talbot and Sidney. While visiting, she would cook for them. She felt in some ways she was atoning for the years when she had stopped cooking in Lynchburg.

Karla recognized she would have no biological grandchildren from Talbot. She acknowledged her sadness only to herself. Yes, she would have loved to see kids running around that reminded her of family members, discovering what traits were carried forward and expressed, but over time she accepted her fate. After all, that fate was less cruel than Talbot's, who wanted very much to have his own family.

Karla's brother Franz had fared much better with his three daughters; they all married young and had children right away. Franz was blessed with eight grandchildren, three of whom were already married and expecting babies; he would be a great-grandfather! What a godsend.

Karla's two sisters were not so blessed. Fritzi had one son who never married, living with a divorced woman and her two children. He had no children of his own. Olga, although in partnership with a man, never had children either.

Karla got caught up in reveries from time to time. She had never thought of grandchildren when her kids were little. When Thais was around eleven or twelve, she had said to Karla one day, "When we have children, we will come often to see you." Karla had felt comforted at the time with such a lovely sentiment.

Is there a curse on my family? Karla wondered to herself. But then she realized, they were actually very blessed. Her little family had been so content and looked forward to a bright future for all of them. Malcolm was going to fulfill his dream to be a history professor and teach at one of the universities or work as an archivist at the Library of Congress. Thais went into remission and attended at Oberlin College in Ohio, making it despite all odds and, best of all, making some good friends there. She never lost her spirit; before her health hit bottom the last six weeks of her life, Thais was able to write her donor a letter of appreciation. Now Karla feared for Talbot and his partner, with the occurrence of hate crimes, the lack of acceptance by some members of society, and the discrimination they had to face at places of employment or in the communities where they lived. But out of their honesty about who they were, finding happiness with each other, the two young men were a wonderful example of how to be true to one's inner self. That is who they were and they would make a life with that.

Al's children were all married now and were starting families. Al encouraged Karla to be fully involved in his children's lives and those of his grandchildren.

His children were very supportive of Al and reached out to Karla. They told their children to call her "Grandma," much to her surprise, since they called her by her first name.

After being married over ten years, Karla ventured to Al's children to call her *Omani*, the Korean word for mother. Monica, the eldest responded, "We are so Americanized, we feel more comfortable calling you by your first name."

Felicity, the youngest, was perturbed. "I'm not ready to call you mother, and you should understand that." Felicity let Karla know that the name she was called by was not as important as the feeling shared between them, hugging and kissing Karla with sincerity whenever they got together.

Karla felt guilty; she had asked too much of them. She had wanted them to know she was there when they needed her, that she considered herself more than a friend. However, Alex and his wife started using the Korean word. Alex, too, was demonstrative of his affection for Karla. Karla and Al visited often with the children, although they were scattered over the country, and welcomed them to dinners and celebrations at home. They met seven of the eight grandchildren shortly after their births. What a pleasure it was to hold these infants in their arms. Al's children all welcomed Talbot into their family; his youngest daughter related especially well to him. She was Thais's age. During the main holidays of the year, the family often got together at Felicity's home; her parents-in-law joined as well.

Talbot and Sidney were thrilled to be included. They wanted a child very much and had applied for adoption, but so far had no children.

Karla, marrying Al, finding him a most wonderful man and joining his much larger family, felt she had been given a wonderful new start.

It reminded her of the story of Job.

Chapter 68

*K*arla felt attracted to Jewish people, feeling comfortable in their presence and feeling a kinship she could not explain. Her first hint at her heritage was when Malcolm's mother said, "My God, she's a kike."

That was in 1966; Karla brushed off her mother-in-law's statement but it stayed in the back of her mind. As far as she knew then, she was not Jewish.

She had had Jewish friends starting in high school; the Philips Department Store owners were Jewish. During her internship at St. Joseph Hospital, she met an intern, Irene, a Jewish doctor from Mexico City. They spent much time together over a bottle of wine while Malcolm worked every evening at the Denver University Library. At Napa State Hospital she became friends with Henry, a fellow resident who was also Jewish. She felt she was Jewish because she felt so at home around them socially. In Napa, her violin teacher was Jewish; she also formed a deep friendship with a Jewish woman whose family had been destroyed by the Holocaust. This woman, Hanna, also befriended the children, giving them German lessons on Saturday mornings. She became a grandmother figure for them, especially for Thais, who kept writing to her until she died. Karla was very saddened when Hanna committed suicide upon finding she had yet another cancer, after surviving breast cancer and multiple myeloma.

When Malcolm and Karla first visited Friesach in 1968, he found there was an old Jewish burial ground and pointed it out to Karla. Malcolm hinted at Karla being Jewish in many ways, pointing out to her that Jews had been in Friesach for a long time. In fact, two inns they stayed in while in Friesach were run by old Jewish families. As far as Karla knew, they had been running the inns for three or four generations. But the Jewish *d*enizens of that area in Friesach did not profess their Jewishness openly; there was still much prejudice.

It was in 2000, during her last visit to Tante Mitzi before her death from ovarian cancer, that the old woman whispered in Karla's ear, "Our name Maier used to be spelled with a y in place of the i." They had Germanized the name Hitler annexed Austria.

Then, in 2009, Talbot visited Friesach with Karla and stayed in one of those inns. They were given rooms in a recessed area which the inn owner had prepared for them, as they were the only visitors; most people didn't stay the night in town. Talbot pointed out to Karla that there were numerous stone tablets with Hebrew writing on them. It was apparent that some Jewish people in Austria had not been sent to concentration camps. It could have been due to the remoteness of this mountainous area, but Karla did not know the reason why. It was also apparent that her own father's family had attempted to fit in with Hitler's Germany at a price. It was all about survival in a difficult time. Not until after the end of the war did the ordinary citizen find out about the concentration camps and the death camps. Hitler's propaganda machine, however, did penetrate even to remote areas; they still harbored suspicion about Jews.

Fritzi's husband, drawing up a family tree, left out Gottfried Maier (previously Mayer). Even now, he left him out of the tree; Karla was alert and brought it to her brother's attention when she visited him. The family tree was then redone to include Gottfried Maier as the family scion, but still spelled with the Germanic version.

The valley in which Karla was born was populated by people who had lived there for centuries, Karla's own family's history dating back to working as tax collectors in the fourteenth century. The prejudice she experienced from her peers and the adult who had accused her of being a seductress at the age of eight was deep-seated, based partly on her family of origin and partly on being the child of divorce. Years later, Anton told Karla he deeply regretted his decision, but said had he not divorced Johanna, his family and the community threatened to imprison her and cut off her hair. He insisted to his dying day that he loved Johanna, wanting to get back together with her and run his own farm, but she refused all his offers once she had been divorced and kicked out.

He was a weak man, not able to go after what he really wanted, bending to decisions his brothers and sisters made for him the rest of his life—but he apologized to Karla. "I am so sorry that we adults made you children have such a hard life. I am deeply aggrieved about it," he told her on a walk down the road that led to the two fateful places in Karla's childhood, the family farm and the lumber/dairy farm.

Karla wished she could receive such apologies from her mother and her stepfather.

Only after her father died did Karla acknowledge to herself that Anton's passivity and dependence on his siblings for guidance was what destroyed his marriage and, in essence, their little family. Only belatedly could Karla see that he was never able to take care of himself, neglected his hygiene and accepted the lowest living condition with equanimity. He never grew emotionally. He blamed others for his problems, seeing himself as incapable of managing them himself. Karla asked herself why she always protected him when he was actually an abject figure of a man. She recognized that in her mind, she had made her father much nobler than he was. She was trying to find in him the father he should have been.

Chapter 69

Karla had achieved the most education of all her siblings, but lacked the stability in her life which her siblings enjoyed once they were settled with their prospective substitute parents. By the time she was in eighth grade, she had moved through six schools and would have done seven had her eighth grade teacher not intervened.

Over the course of her life, her address had changed about fifteen times. Her abode in Fairfax represented the longest time she ever lived in one place: fifteen years.

On her trips to Austria, she envied the stability she saw in her siblings' lives. Her sister had never moved more than ten miles from her birthplace. Her brother had moved about two hundred and fifty miles northeast at age ten and had been anchored there since then. Her siblings knew their townspeople and had long-standing friendships. Their children remained close by, with only one venturing even as far as Vienna to become a journalist.

At the same time, Karla was grateful for her freedom from the fetters of community life where you take your place and keep it until the day you die.

When she visited the graves of dead relatives, she could feel the connection while abhorring the thought of one's body buried beneath the earth and people visiting the graves as if the person was still there, for she firmly believed that on death the soul departs the body to decay and return to earth. She had Malcolm's and Thais' bodies cremated and had emptied their ashes into the Pacific Ocean to be immediately reunited with their physical source. She gave firm requests to her husband and son that she was to be similarly cremated and emptied into the ocean.

There were other forms of stability that Karla craved, too. She had harbored a secret wish that on her mother's eightieth birthday, all her children could sit at table with her to enjoy a meal together. In 2000, when her mother's eightieth was approaching and Karla was visiting her sister Fritzi, she mentioned this. Fritzi became vehement, raising her voice and spitting, "I hate that woman! I never want to see her again!"

Karla broke into sobs she could not contain. She left with Al, still tearful. Her sister did not stop her from leaving, and Karla was so upset she forgot her jacket. That night her sleep was broken with sadness and hopelessness, her dream of a reunited family shattered. Al was at a loss, for he had not understood what was being said, and Karla was too upset to explain until later.

They left then to visit Franz and Poldi in Wurflach. Franz took them out to a restaurant called the Schubert Linde, where that famous composer once sat by the tree in front of the restaurant, a huge linden tree. Karla did not tell Franz what she had asked of Fritzi; she knew his answer would also be negative.

Later, when they came back to his house, Franz gave her the jacket which Fritzi had sent by special delivery, a sign to Karla that Fritzi cared about her even if she did not care about their mother. She realized that Fritzi's anger expressed her ongoing disappointment with Johanna. She loved her foster mother and father very much and tended their graves faithfully after their deaths, but that unsatisfied longing for her mother which was never satisfied was still haunting her.

Some years later, after Johanna had died, Franz opened up the subject to Karla. "I would never come visit our mother as long as Dimitri was alive," he said. He was referring to his anger over Dimitri's sexual abuse of Karla. Franz never did visit Karla in Fairfax until two years after their mother's death, and he never went to Omaha to visit Johanna's grave.

Karla recognized that her brother and sister in Austria cared deeply about her and appreciated her many visits and her family loyalty. But that same feeling did not extend to their mother. Although Franz had Johanna's picture, taken when she was sixty, prominently displayed on his dining room wall, he limited his actual contact with his mother to telephone calls he made to her on her birthday and holidays. In that way, he recognized her as the family matron without overextending himself. He always said his Aunt Kunegunde was a wonderful mother to him.

Olga was the only one from Karla's family in Omaha with whom she had a positive and ongoing relationship. Olga had a true Slavic soul; she was sensitive, bursting easily into tears when moved. She had retired as a social security analyst and written a still-unpublished romantic mystery. She had also taken up Karla's suggestion to Michael that he develop his spiritual self. She joined the Catholic church and felt it was a most wonderful comfort when her mother was no longer there.

Michael, unfortunately, did not appreciate Karla's suggestion.

Chapter 70

Talbot had his own set of hurtful memories of family. He had been traumatized by the events leading to his sister's death.

In 2011 he e-mailed Karla that he had felt very upset and fearful the week before Sidney's birthday. He was telling Sidney about his emotional agitation and blurted out, "I wanted to give you your birthday present early because I'm afraid you might not be here to get it on your birthday, just like what happened to my sister Thais."

Once he had found the origin of his pain, he was flooded with the memory of having wrapped several small gifts for his sister Thais days before her twentieth birthday. He was holding them as a surprise for her. She had been home in the apartment from the hospital almost three weeks and they were planning a nice birthday party followed by a plane trip home to Lynchburg. The cardiac tamponade and adult onset respiratory stress syndrome developed three days before her birthday. She spent her birthday with a tube down her larynx attached to a respirator, and she died six weeks later.

"It was so terrible, her suffering and our shock and disappointment, our crushed hope, but most of all her chance of life taken from her in the most cruel way," Talbot wrote to Karla. "I cannot forget it and I cannot get over it. It was so unfair!"

Karla read his message with tears streaming down her face, and wrote back, "Please don't hesitate to call or write when you have these flashbacks and the searing pain they bring with them. We went through it together and I will know exactly what you are talking about." Then she shared with Talbot her ongoing guilt feelings about her absence at the time the nurses woke Thais to ask her whether she wanted continued life support.

How is it that fate always presents us with what we try most to avoid? The fairy tales speak of the forbidden door, the forbidden fruit, the attempts to avoid fate and actually walking right into it.

Karla felt she had somehow let Talbot down. He had been in psychotherapy for three years during college to deal with his losses and now he was taking an antidepressant for these breakthrough memories that he unintentionally fought off with irrational anger. The slightest reminder in his daily life could set off an emotional turmoil. He was spending so much energy not remembering that when the flood of memories burst through, he felt vulnerable and helpless.

Karla mused that psychiatry had lost much of its meaning when it abandoned intrapsychic phenomena for behavioral and chemical brain interpretations. Intrapsychic psychiatry looks deep within the emotional memory, where we protect ourselves from the pain memory would cause. We do so using various defense mechanisms such as denial, compensation, undoing, and projection. Freud, Jung, and other early pioneers in psychology discovered the ways in which we packet emotionally-laden material and put it away so that we can go on with the demands of the present without conscious interference from these conflicting or unresolved emotions. This knowledge is as valid today as then, but the mental health field, now called behavioral health, is distracted by time pressures and pressure from the insurance industry to take care of problems with drugs instead of discovery and understanding—two processes that might result in permanently beneficial life changes once the source of the distress is uncovered and consciously addressed.

Karla realized her struggle with the post-traumatic stress of the rapes and sexual abuse she experienced took years of introspection, identifying how her character had been warped out of its original nature. She often wondered what kind of a person she would have become without these traumas and their aftermath. Would she have been able to accept kudos for accomplishments? Been able to play music without self-reproach for errors, just relishing the sound? Allowed herself to be much more successful in her career? Some of the aftermaths of the traumas were constant self-deprecation and hiding herself instead of affirming herself. Karla had also had years of therapy, but the memories did not fade. Although she had gone on with her life, it was colored by what had gone before. She had integrated her negative life events and maybe even assimilated them, but those events left in her deep questions about the meaning of existence and its purpose.

Chapter 71

*A*fter the health scare and the two hospitalizations for stent placement, Karla grew even more careful in her food preparation. They avoided eating out as much as possible and she planned menus for a week that focused on a healthy balance of proteins, fats, and carbohydrates. Al always took a lunch she prepared for him.

It was fun planning the meals, for she had a wealth of cookbooks to look at and select from for her recipes. All snacks after dinner were discouraged. They also aimed to exercise daily. Karla could walk the mile up and down the hills in their neighborhood; Al stopped midway from work to home to get on the treadmill at the Fairfax Audrey Moore Recreation Center. It was important for him to exercise on an empty stomach, as it challenged the circulation to his heart if he exercised after eating. Karla still used the Power Plate two or three times a week to firm up muscles and lessen tension.

Amazingly, Al's fasting sugar levels began to drop after six months on this regimen. He was also relying on ayurvedic supplements as well as Western medicines. His morning fasting levels had come down one hundred points from the time in August when they were challenged with the double vision.

Karla's weight problem, which resulted from years of stress, was very difficult to normalize. Although she had good resolve, she also had a very good appetite; sometimes she felt she was eating as if to reward herself for a productive day. She still lacked the strong will to transcend her cravings. Walking in the wooded neighborhood kept her in touch with nature as well as improved her health. In the spring the robins would hop alongside, playing a game with her. She watched for the budding of the *t*rees, with their pinks and magentas and white blossoms, soon to unfold into leaves. She felt this budding symbolized purity and virginity. The different birdsongs heralded the spring and new life. Cardinals came to the feeder on the railing of the deck, expressing their joy in the beginning of pleasant weather, grateful that they had survived the strong and bitter winter cold.

In mid-August 2010, Karla was walking and the beautiful Monarch butterflies were out, more numerous than in past years. She broke into tears, remembering that Thais had colored a page on which were drawn a butterfly and some tiger lilies and had presented it to her with the inscription, "To my Mom," while she was convalescing from the host-versus-graft loss of her skin. Karla had the coloring book sheet framed and it hung on the wall facing the bed where she saw it every morning on arising. Now the profusion of butterflies, of which fewer and fewer had been seen each year, overwhelmed her as a personal encouragement and greeting of love from her daughter.

She had also seen Thais in her meditation the night before, blowing her celestial breath toward Karla. The words "I love you" formed on the lips of the fleeting image. Karla inhaled deeply of that celestial breath and felt strengthened. She knew Thais was always with her, hovering there. She was sure the heavenly being had other important things to do, but she was always with Karla, loving and invigorating her.

Karla did not like winter, the cold and wind often preventing her outdoor walk, the stifling air inside the house drying out her skin and hair. Looking out the windows, the gray skies covered everything, making her feel enclosed in a gray bowl. If the sun came out, it meant a happier day. It was during those wintry days that Karla missed California the most: California, where the skies remained blue and sunshine warmed everything. In the summer she missed the maternal, brown, gently rolling hills studded with oak trees sporting small, dark green leaves. She sadly realized that, given their retirements, they would not be able to afford living in California.

Chapter 72

Karla and Al shared a very spiritual love. He constantly reminded Karla that when he first saw her when she came for the job interview in Lynchburg in January of 1986, he intuited, "This is the one; she should be my wife."

Karla heard this many times and when she asked him how he could think that when he was married, he said, "I recognized you as my wife, and now you are."

Karla had a past life regression when she was attending a Transcendental Psychology conference. She felt herself being carried along, seeing only the galloping legs of many horses. Then she was being made love to; she recalled striped pantaloon-like silk covering her legs as she felt them lifted up above her head almost. The lovemaking was very passionate, and she re-experienced every moment of it, never having felt such ecstasy before. Then she was sitting by a well holding an infant, a baby boy. She knew it was Genghis Khan and she was his mother; not only that, she knew Al to be that baby. So Al had been her son in a past life—in the regression there was no doubt: she was there or had been there long ago.

She told Al only that she experienced herself in a past life regression as the mother of Genghis Khan; she left out the part that he was that infant. She was too embarrassed to tell him, especially as she noticed she often did treat him as her child, not her husband. He was well aware, remarking, "There ya go, treating me just like a ten year old boy."

Now when Al had an episode of road rage, she saw again that fury, that unforgiving chasing down of the reprobate driver placing himself and his passenger at risk and the other driver as well. If she tried to interrupt he did not hear her at all; he was in pursuit and only death would satisfy *h*im—it was really frightening. It appeared like some rage out of the deep, distant past: Genghis Khan was remorseless when angered and pursued the enemy until it was vanquished and killed.

Karla wondered sometimes if she was crazy, but since she had experienced the past life, she was no longer haunted by Genghis Khan, a feeling that had pursued her since she studied the Mongol hordes in sixth grade. It always felt as if she knew a lot more than the books described, but at that time she put those feelings aside, not knowing the reason.

It was similar to the haunted feeling she had about her Uncle Albin. Karla had felt a strong presence of her paternal uncle, first recognizing who it was when she was about twelve years old. He was killed by Russians during the advance on Leningrad by the German Army in 1943. She could feel a supportive and protective presence until after Talbot's birth, when she had the following dream. She saw Talbot as a bust in marble, and hovering above him, Uncle Albin as an angel. After that dream, she no longer felt Albin's presence. Exactly what the dream was saying was uncertain, but she knew that there was a connection between Albin and Talbot as well.

Karla had learned from experience that the spiritual world is alive, full of data, recording every moment of everyone's life; nothing is forgotten. When she began to trust her intuitive self, a self above brain and heart, she became aware of how interactive the spiritual world is with our matter based world of existence. Tuning in with an open heart and mind had shown her this time and time again.

Karla relied more and more on spiritual help than on Western medicine. When Al had double vision, reporting some left-sided pressure and low-grade headache, Karla asked for help from the spiritual world. She approached the problem with careful examination, and then focused on the problem area with meditative healing. This was followed by acupuncture addressing the nerves attached to the eye muscles, and also the points for the accompanying sinus problem which was responsible for the dull ache. Both treatments were repeated until the sinus problem resolved and the eye rotator muscle resumed functioning.

"Thank you for normalizing Al's vision," she voiced to the spiritual world.

Karla found she was applying these same principles to any problem of a physical nature, and she got results, either from acupuncture and meditative healing or intuitive sparks she regularly received. She would become very alert to information becoming available once she requested it—put under her nose so to say, addressing the problem she was trying to solve, leaving herself open to invisible guidance from the universe.

Chapter 73

*K*arla saw herself as very blessed: Al and she had a fulfilling and wonderful relationship in which they honored and respected each other. The course had been rough, but each struggle had deepened their tolerance and understanding of each other. Their love ran very deep, their mutual support uplifting. They shared a love of literature, music, psychiatry, medicine, and most of all, family.

Talbot and Karla remained ever faithful and encouraging to each other, nurturing going both ways. Talbot had become a discerning and loving man who wanted to better the world for people in his daily work.

Thais was always there, sharing what was most sacred in the spiritual world with Karla, loving her always and being loved.

It was hard for Karla to accept happiness in her life again—the survivor guilt often dampened it—but slowly she was opening herself up to trust the gifts she had been given in her new life with Al.

Karla felt herself between two worlds, the material and the spiritual, balancing them, learning from both, and transmitting whatever was helpful to those around her.

She had made the journey, starting it badly wounded early in her life. There were many trials along the way, during which she turned inward for guidance and upholding, recognizing in the process that the world, being all spirit, gives many resources in times of trouble, with guides and contact from departed loved ones. In the process she became more compassionate and loving.

Through this arduous process, Karla joyfully found herself. She became aware in the most direct way that love never dies and is the source of all the goodness in life.

She survived childhood and adolescent rape and sexual abuse to tell the story and to relate the effects such traumatic experiences had on a life but also to give hope and encouragement to others who have and are experiencing similar fates. Karla overcame her serious traumas to become a healer in her work with children, adolescents and adults.

Karla's journey has not ended yet. She opens herself to further challenges steeled with the knowledge that she is never alone, for that oneness that we all are is just that: one.

About the Author

The book I have written is a memoir, the story of important events that have shaped my life. It is an introspective piece of work. As I am a psychiatrist, there is a special emphasis on development of character based on early childhood experiences, especially concerning childhood and adolescent rape and sexual abuse as well as parental abandonment.

I have survived childhood and adolescent rape and sexual abuse and deaths of my nuclear family members. My life has encapsulated all the important social concerns of the twentieth century, identity crisis, separation and abandonment, homosexuality, marriage and divorce, and cancer treatment.

The reason I have written this book after I retired from practice is to bring the atrocity of childhood and adolescent sexual abuse and rape to the attention of a wider public. I hope this honest account will bring awareness to the suffering of the many who have experienced these traumas in the past as well as ongoing abuse. Hopefully I have added to the understanding of the psychological and physical damage engendered upon those not able to protect themselves from the perpetrators. Even further I hope that this problem will be addressed with much more seriousness than it has been the case.

I live in Fairfax, Virginia. I am married, the mother of two children, one deceased, and three stepchildren. I just recently retired from a lifetime psychiatry practice. My hobbies are writing, cooking, language study, music, and reading. I am physically active and love walking, swimming and dancing.